Trauma, Drug Misuse and Transforming Identities

A Life Story Approach

Kim Etherington

Jessica Kingsley Publishers
London and Philadelphia

First published in 2008
by Jessica Kingsley Publishers
116 Pentonville Road
London N1 9JB, UK
and
400 Market Street, Suite 400
Philadelphia, PA 19106, USA

www.jkp.com

Library of Congress Cataloging in Publication Data
A CIP catalog record for this book is available from the Library of Congress

British Library Cataloguing in Publication Data
A CIP catalogue record for this book is available from the British Library

ISBN 978 1 84310 493 3

Printed and bound in Great Britain by
Athenaeum Press, Gateshead, Tyne and Wear

This book is dedicated to the men and women who offered me their life stories for this research and to the staff of The Southmead Project, without whose work so many of these stories would remain untold.

All royalties earned will be paid to
The Southmead Project, Bristol, UK.

When we tell or write about our own lives, our stories establish our identities…And we do something even more fundamental – we establish ourselves as persons: I am someone, someone who has lived a valuable life, a value affirmed precisely by any life story's implicit claim that it is worth telling and hearing.

(Eakin 2004, p.5)

Contents

Foreword

I remember 30 years ago going as a student at Cambridge to see the late Juan Mascaro, translator of, amongst other works, *The Upanishads* and *Bhagavad Gita.* I thought that some of his wisdom might rub off on me. However, I only recall one thing that he said, which is the following: 'The great thing with cigarettes is that you should smoke them rather than that they should smoke you.'

This actually encapsulates all the problems of addiction. In my experience of working with heroin and crack cocaine addicts I have learned that drugs take people much more than people take drugs. It is a one-way ticket. I have seen people give away everything – every single last thing – for drugs in the knowledge that what they were doing was hopelessly wrong. But they felt that they had no choice. They were taken.

Some are born with addictive tendencies. But I am not sure that there are many such people. In most cases an addict is looking for a way to escape and drug addiction is initially a blissful release. Almost all of the groups that I have worked with have stories of abuse, loneliness, a sense of alienation or sometimes just crushing bad luck. In some cases drug misuse is the most reasonable response to a set of appalling circumstances. But drug addiction is a great leveller. It is desperately hard to resist the call of an addiction and, once addicted, the person can remain hooked for the rest of their lives. Only daily resistance to that call can keep them clean.

Which is why I set up The Monty Project.[1] It aims to provide a reason to stay clean and a link with the deep and subtle rhythms of life that can sustain the addict through the inevitable ups and downs of life, as well as a sense of belonging. So much of modern life is geared towards the individual that we are forgetting how to live as a community, caring and trusting in each other. In a society where consumption is valued above all else inevitably the mechanics of an integrated community, giving freely and sharing what they have for the greater good, are devalued to the point of atrophy. Ironically the drug addict is probably the most voracious consumer in modern society and yet the most reviled member of it.

The measure of any healthy society is the quality of life of its least favoured members. Any underclass belongs to us. The drug-addicted beggar on our streets is, in a profound sense, a member of our own family, and if we do not care for him or her then we are failing ourselves and our future.

I welcome this study by Professor Kim Etherington because it is part of the process of understanding *our* drug problem and the whole chain of issues that lead to addiction. It tells the stories of real people, and in doing so it holds a mirror not just to other people's lives but to our own.

Monty Don

Note

1 The Monty Project is based upon an absolute belief in the healing properties of the land, of growing good food to share, and of training people to work as an integrated member of a social group – but free from the heavy hand of government bodies and free from all drugs, including alcohol.

Our aims are to:

- provide a safe environment where addicts can work with the land, learning to care for plants, animals and people
- provide specific training with relevant qualifications in as wide a range of skills as possible in horticulture, agriculture and building
- provide social and personal skills to empower addicts to be independent outside of our protected environment and to gain and hold down work
- create a supply of organic food that can be shared with a local community on whatever scale is practical and in the process provide income for the project plus a few full-time jobs
- spread the scheme so that it can be replicated on a local basis wherever it is workable.

Acknowledgements

The creation of this book would not have been possible without the involvement and support of many people. First and foremost I want to acknowledge the commitment and generosity shown by Hannah, Omar, Becky, Steven, Josie, George, John and Levi (pseudonyms), who not only gave their stories to be shared with others but also continued to work with me throughout the construction of the book, answering my ongoing questions, writing sometimes lengthy sections of additional information or fleshing out missing parts of the stories that became essential for the telling of a coherent life story. Their ongoing involvement has been crucial to ensuring that the stories in this book resonate with their lived experience.

However, this book would never have seen the light of day had it not been for the dedication and inspiration of Mike Pierce, Chief Executive of The Southmead Project. Mike's dogged determination to raise awareness of the frequency of childhood trauma in the lives of people using the Southmead Drugs Project and to fund research to explore the links between historic trauma and drug misuse was eventually rewarded by success in securing funding from the European Social Fund, with additional indirect support from the National Lottery Fund. My thanks therefore go to Mike for commissioning the work and to the funders for financing the research.

I have also been helped by others who have read drafts and made suggestions and I would like to thank all of them, especially Shirley Margerison, Sam Chromy, Alison Leftwich, Viv Martin, Nell Bridges and Tim Bond. I am particularly grateful to Emma Barnes who helped with some of the literature searches. Colleagues in the Graduate School of Education and members of the Centre for Narratives and Transformative Learning at the University of Bristol have stimulated me through our conversations and encouraged me to continue when the going seemed tough. I would also like to acknowledge my Doctoral and Masters students whose energy and enthusiasm for learning gives me a very good reason for always trying to extend and expand my own learning about, and experiences of, narrative and life story research.

Once again I have been fortunate to have the support of the staff at Jessica Kingsley Publishers who have always encouraged my ideas.

As usual, Dave, my husband of 44 years, has been alongside me throughout this work, providing me with endless cups of tea and healthy food, quietly nurturing me. I thank him for his willing generosity in giving time and energy to support my work: reading the stories, helping with the technical problems of computing, and creating the indexes. I also acknowledge my sons and daughters-in-law, and my four wonderful grandchildren, who bring so much love and laughter into my life.

Hannah's Story

Hannah's voice on the telephone had been quiet and unassuming, almost timid, when she rang me to offer her story for this book. Her counsellor had told her that I was interested in gathering stories of people who had come to realise how their experiences of childhood trauma had played a part in their subsequent drug misuse and Hannah was quite sure that she wanted to use this opportunity to tell her story, knowing that it would be made public. I sensed that our meeting was as important to her as it was to me.

Hannah lived at some distance from me so I was more than grateful when she agreed to meet me half way at a conference I was attending later in the year. When we met she seemed eager to get started and as we walked along the corridor to the interview room she told me again how glad she was to have this opportunity. Later, as her story unfolded, hesitantly and painfully, I came to understand just how much she needed to have her life experiences witnessed, acknowledged and understood in the light of her family's response to the abuse she suffered, and her traumatic experience of confronting the abuser through the courts.

As I made the tea and handed her the biscuits I explained again the purpose of our meeting and asked, 'Where does your story begin?' Her immediate response captured the heart of her trauma: 'I was abused by my uncle as a child…and it was ignored.' It was not the overt sexual abuse *alone* that had created trauma, but the manner in which her family had responded.

At this point in her life, aged 27, she was bringing together the threads of her story, and focusing for the first time on the links between her misuse of drugs and her childhood experiences. She had told her stories before, in different arenas and for different purposes – in therapy and in court – but this time she was telling her story so that others could learn from her experiences.

Hannah's story is presented below as a prologue to this book in order immediately to engage the reader, and to provide a flavour of what follows.

★　　★　　★　　★

A 'perfect' family

Hannah was born in 1977 two years after her brother James. Her alcoholic mother had divorced her father after he threw Hannah across the room when she was three months old, striking her head against the furniture. Although Hannah continued to have contact with her father after her mother married Pete (when Hannah was four years old), the antagonism between both men prevented any closeness. Hannah's memories of her father are overlaid with images of his anger, his violence towards her brother, and her own fear.

Her father's message, 'if you're female you're not really worth much', shaped her view of herself and made it clear that he considered her 'second class' to her brother: a divisive message that also separated her from James.

When Hannah was four or five, her maternal aunt Jenny married Jimmy – they each had a son by a previous marriage. Jenny's son, Alan, was two years younger than Hannah, and the couple subsequently had a daughter, Sharon, who was ten years younger than Alan. Her new uncle, Jimmy, 'swooped in and said, "I'll be your daddy…I'll always be here for you, trust in me."' She welcomed his attention because 'everywhere else [there was] arguing, and he was always there, to do nice things with me'. Hannah became very close to Alan – 'We were like brother and sister' – and they became like one big happy family. She believed she was part of a 'perfect family'. So when Jimmy, Jenny, Alan and Sharon moved away from the area the families visited each other at every opportunity, staying in each other's homes and sharing bedrooms.

Jimmy began to sexually abuse Hannah before she was six years old and continued to do so until she was 13. She explained how, as a small child, she had tried to avoid the abuse:

> Alan was in the same room as me and Jimmy would abuse me while he was there… I mean, I used to get my cousin to swap beds with me…and my uncle would always find me. Yeah, my cousin had seen him do it… I'd cried to him as a child and he'd seen…the sort of effects that it was having on me…and…you know, he told me to keep quiet 'cos I'd break the family up – which is what my uncle had said to me. He said that they knew what he was doing and that it was all right.

Jimmy was a typical paedophile, grooming his emotionally needy victim with his attention and 'love', leaving her with a longing for him to fill the gap left by her unavailable parents:

> I used to say 'I wish you were my dad' and…that I loved him. Even when he was abusing me I still wanted…him to be my dad, because although…[the abuse] weren't nice…[very quietly] he'd always be extra, extra nice after, and it was the only attention that I ever…ever got, really.

As Hannah spoke I sensed how vulnerable she had been in her need for affection and how easy it had been for Jimmy to confuse her about what it meant to be loved. I also sensed how alone she must have felt as a small child, especially when Jimmy told her that everybody knew what he was doing. Her sense of abandonment, powerlessness and isolation must have been greatly increased by knowing that other people were in the same house, and even the same room, while the abuse was happening, and her mother's encouragement of his contact would have reinforced that.

> Yeah, they always used to make me go and sit on his knee. As I was getting a bit older, I didn't really like...[that] 'cos his hands would be in the wrong place. Even when my mum and stepdad were *there*, he'd still...you know, like...feel me and stuff...and they'd be *there* and I'd be thinking, 'Can they not see what he's doing?' I just...hated it.

> And my mum always used to be [saying] 'Go, go...go and see your uncle Jimmy – Uncle Jimmy loves you', you know, 'Get out of my way, I just wanna have a drink and a fag and you're just like, under my feet.'

> When my uncle used to come in and abuse me...I'd always think that my dad was going to come in on this big white horse and...take me away and...everything would be all right. And it wasn't [my dad], it was always him.

> I spent most of my childhood...waiting...for him to...abuse me and...then go away and be really sad...and that's no childhood really. I mean, I wasn't allowed to play. It was like, 'Hannah, you have to sit there and be a good girl.'

Crossing over from being 'a good girl' to being 'a bad girl'

Hannah's story up to that point had been based on her early traumatic childhood and now she spoke of the turning point at adolescence from being a 'good girl' to being a 'bad girl'.

> I think I was twelve, or just turning thirteen. Um...he tried to have intercourse with me on this particular occasion...and something just snapped within me and I...started to move and say 'No'. Um...and the house was full – he always did it when there were people in the house as well – but this time he left. And then he came back a second time, and I still said 'No', like '*No*' [*emphatically*], and erm...that was the last time he did it. I just woke up like a different person really...cold, and from that day, that was when I started getting into drugs...'cos...something had changed.

I asked Hannah how she now understood that switch in her behaviour and her changed sense of herself:

Well I remember I started big school, comprehensive school, and – as you do at school – people talk about sex and things and...you have sex education, I...already knew...all about...that.

I just knew that my friends weren't having the same relationships that I was having within my family. My mum said, 'You changed overnight to this like...evil person, this evil child.' [She said] that I destroyed all the family...[long pause].

And obviously I knew...my dad...my dad didn't do that to me. I don't know...I'd always been really quiet – always the good girl – you know, 'Don't speak until you're spoken to', and I was so, so good, and all these bad things kept happening, and I was being so good. And it was just like...'I'm not gonna be good any more, I'm gonna be bad.' And, 'This is not gonna happen any more.'

I was hurting. I was really, really hurting. I didn't want him to do it any more... I didn't have anyone to talk to. I was being bullied at school – for being weird 'cos I was quiet – and I didn't want to talk or anything...well, obviously 'cos I was...scared, you know. Then the...school bully...befriended me for some...reason and I hung onto that. I suppose I became a bit of a bully myself, um...and I'd like crossed over. They introduced me to drinking first, and, and then drugs and...

People used to say I was really, really pretty and I always used to try and really hide that. But then I went the other way and I really went into make-up and putting my hair up, and I used to have really...mad hair, and...was like one of the girls that...[people would say]...'better not give her too much eye contact'. People said...I'd just changed. My whole persona and stuff had changed...'cos I thought, 'I'm not gonna be shit on any more'...uh...and if that's the way that it had to be...well, that's the way it was.

At that point Hannah had become aware of her body changing and that she was attractive. Trying to keep herself safe she did everything she could to appear *un*attractive.

I did everything to make myself *not* attractive...I mean, I weighed six stone, I wore all black clothing and...black eye make-up and everybody thought I was...a weird one. And they picked on me for that...but I was just trying to...I used to try and pull my boobs down...

Her weight dropped to six stone and her unhealthy pallor was emphasised by black eye make-up and black clothing with which she tried to flatten her developing breasts. Her family ignored even these dramatic changes:

...and that...that really hurt. I was so...underweight...*deathly* looking...and my mum would just say, you know, 'Are you gonna eat today then, or not?' I didn't have a family meal for two years. I didn't hardly speak to them and...my mum just used to drink all the time. She didn't even care where I was. I'd come in and find her asleep on the stairs 'cos she'd be that pissed that she couldn't even make it to the bedroom.

All I ever wanted was for her just to say…'Why don't you want to eat, Hannah? Why are you so sad?'

From alcohol to drugs

Around the age of 13 Hannah stopped going to school and started hanging around on council estates, drinking heavily with other young people, especially when faced with visits between Jimmy's family and her own.

> They were coming to stay and I said to my mum 'I really don't want to be here', and I said 'When you visit [them], I'm never going there again' and she never wanted to know why. She just said, 'Well they're coming.'

> But you know, when you're telling your parents, 'I don't want to go, I don't want to go', then *why*…why would you force a child and not find out why? They used to leave me at his house and go off and either stay in a hotel or they'd go and stay at her mum's, my nana's. So I'd run away when they were coming to stay.

> This one time I'd gone down into the city centre and drunk a bottle of Thunderbirds… I don't really remember much, but I remember my stepdad coming to get me 'cos the police had been called. This black man had got me in the toilets and I don't remember what happened there…'cos I had drunk…I don't remember…

I asked Hannah how the shift occurred from using alcohol to using drugs and she described how she became involved with older men who gave her pills that helped her to numb her feelings. Although now she looks back and questions why men in their thirties would want to spend time with 'little girls', at that time she saw them as protecting her, perhaps fulfilling her dream of being rescued by her father.

> They'd just pull up in the car and start talking to you and they'd say, 'Do you want to come for a drive?' They'd just start skinning up [rolling cannabis and heroin]. I didn't know I was smoking heroin, just…knew it made me feel really…numb. I didn't really *care*. At the time, when I really started, it was acid – 'trips', they called them – erm…and I just took anything that they gave me.

> They always wanted sexual things in return, erm…but at that point I didn't… My uncle had always said to me, 'You are here for this, for me, for this purpose'…erm, and I did actually believe that.

> I slept with a man – he was twenty-eight and I was thirteen. He took me to this…park…and gave me some acid, and…smoked some…I think it was heroin…and erm, you know, he said, 'Ah, now I want my payment.' He…got on top of me and did his business…and that was that really.

> I remember going home and I was just bleeding…the only thing I thought about really was, 'My God, I could be pregnant.' I mean, I didn't *really* care, 'cos it was just like, 'At least this is better than living in the real world.' I was just so…high all the time. I'd taken that much acid…bringing on the hallucinations and things…
>
> One time it was really, really scary 'cos…I think I'd had…just…so much. I really remember…freaking out and I remember a few of them holding me down, 'cos I was just so angry…and they were like, 'Wow, God, what's going on?' Erm…well I…I was…what they call 'tripping' – going back in time – and I could see my body developing back into a baby, going back into like a little girl. And obviously as a little girl he used to come – that was when it was more frequent, when I was a little girl.

As she remembered this period of her life Hannah seemed particularly young and fragile and I asked if she wanted to stop. She assured me she wanted to continue, so after a short break she went on with her story.

Trying to end it

This life became intolerable for Hannah around the age of 14 to 15. Her drug misuse had escalated and although she did not make a conscious decision to end her life she began to believe she would 'not be here much longer' and she took an overdose:

> I just had like, um…a small mattress on the floor, didn't have anything else in the room. An' I just closed my curtains, laid down there, and after a while my mum came in. She was like, 'What's wrong with you?', and in the end they called the ambulance. I just wasn't coherent at all, just not making any sense. And all I remember is just tears…rolling down my eyes…and like I…I couldn't move my body. I just remember waking up in hospital. My mum said, 'Just don't ever do that again.' And I was waiting for her to say, 'Why have you taken all these?' She didn't, she just said, 'Don't do it again. You know what you've put me through'…and that was it you know, I was back home and…
>
> They sent me to a child psychologist…it was the other side of the city and they took me there the first time and left me. I had to go in on my own after that… I mean…they used to make me go on the *bus*! I used to get two buses to the other side of the city to go and see this guy, and then I had to get two buses back after I'd spent an hour with him. They never asked me how it went.
>
> The child psychologist just said, 'Are you upset because you've got a stepdad?' I just said 'yeah' and that was what we talked about really. He said to my mum, 'She's messed up because her parents have divorced', and…never went beyond that. I just, like, carried on. I thought it was funny…

I asked her if she had wanted to tell him about the abuse and she quickly answered: 'No, because he was a man. They'd sent me to a man.'

Her family's negative judgement of her and their apparent disinterest in her life caused her to believe she was a bad person.

> No-one ever asked me why I started taking drugs. Why? Why did no-one ever ask me why? It was just that you were taking drugs, and you were evil and you were a bad person. No-one ever asked me why I'd got into that…situation…

School – going from 'straight As' to 'ungraded'

The question 'why' hung palpably in the room as she told me about her school days. Hannah had always loved school and dreamed of going to university. She had done well in primary school and was in the top set for maths and English when she went to secondary school. As she remembered this time I sensed the hurt she felt that nobody had questioned the reasons for her changed attendance and academic performance – going from 'straight As' to being 'ungraded':

> The…last time he abused me my learning had switched off. Even now I really, really struggle with maths. And I used to be really, really…good at maths. And it was just like something had switched off in my brain and it was just… 'Why…do I need to learn? I'm here to be used and abused'…that's what I'd honestly thought… 'I don't need to learn…I don't need school.'

> The school weren't bothered. If you wanted to learn then they were prepared to teach you, and if you didn't you could sit at the back of the class and just mess about. It got to the point where they'd send me out of class all the time, and I'd just walk out of school. No-one ever seemed to come looking for me, or…I don't ever remember my parents being brought in to school. It was just like…they let me go, you know? I just stopped…stopped going.

> I hate my family for that 'cos… *Why* did they never want to know? It was just like, 'You're not doing very well. You used to be so intelligent and now look at you.'

However, one teacher did notice her and seemed to realise something was wrong. During the last year she attended school her history teacher would give her detention and tell her to come and sit in his office at lunchtime:

> But he wasn't giving me detention, he was just giving me the opportunity to stay away from all the bad people…an' I did sometimes just go in his office and he'd share his lunch with me…and I didn't feel, like, threatened by him being a…man or anything, and I thought I would. But he was genuinely…I knew he knew. And I knew that he wouldn't say anything unless *I* wanted to.

Trying to ask for help from her mother

When Hannah was 16 she told her mother about the abuse. By then she had become aware that her uncle was abusing others, including his own daughter. As the older person, Hannah felt it was her responsibility to disclose the abuse and thereby protect her cousin but, having been told repeatedly by him that she would be held responsible and break the family up, she was in a no-win situation, and afraid. But eventually she gave way to the overwhelming need to unburden herself to an adult who would know what to do to stop him. She was unprepared for her mother's response:

> My mum said he did it to me because I was 'special'…which…didn't really help me at all. I said, 'I don't believe I'm the first and I don't believe I'm the last person', and she said, 'No, you're the *only* one because you're special. He's chosen you.'

> I said to her, 'Please don't tell anybody, because it's my fault, and I'm…going to be responsible for breaking up all the family'…and she didn't tell anyone. She didn't tell me it *wasn't* my fault. She said, 'I'll keep it quiet until you feel ready to tell Jenny' – her sister [Jimmy's wife]. And my mum went down and sat round the table with my uncle and drank beer with him and she knew what he'd done to me. I'd already told her, but all she says about that now is that 'you must understand how hard that was for me to sit at a table with…that man'.

> I wanted her to be the adult and say to me 'well, I *am* going to tell people, Hannah. *You're* the child, I'm the adult'… And no…she just kept quiet…

Breaking free

Around the age of 16, Hannah started going out with drug dealers who had money and plenty of drugs. By then she was 'tooting the dragon' (inhaling heroin), and people around her were beginning to inject. She knew she didn't want to 'go down that road' because at this stage she still wanted to go to university and make a success of her life so she sold her belongings and used the money she had been given for 'doing favours for people' to buy a ticket to Majorca.

I asked her what she meant by 'doing favours' and she mumbled, 'Anything they wanted really; doing drug runs or sexual favours':

> I didn't really know any better. I thought that it was their right to do that. I thought, 'God, well, I'll get some money from you if you're going to do that anyway.' And then I went to live in Majorca, for…I think it was two years…and I cleaned myself up, I didn't take *anything*. I was keeping fit, on the beach all the time, working, doing really, really well.

> I did bar work, waitressing, I sold time-shares, PR work. Everybody was just so nice. It was all like…a ho-…a family, you know, that was just the happiest time I'd ever experienced in my life up to that point.

> People…kind of say, 'God, that must be a really big thing' [to do at 16] but it…it wasn't. Just felt…it was right. It was better than where I was at the time, 'cos I knew that I was gonna die. I knew that I was either gonna do it deliberately or…the drugs were gonna do it to me anyway, so I left…

As soon as I walked off the plane it was like…this was like – a life. I could have a life here. I've always wanted to be healthy. I enjoy going to the gym, I enjoy eating well, I enjoy looking after myself, I enjoy looking good…and…I did, I just stopped. Even out there you could get drugs just like that… I didn't need it because I felt…less pressure. Being in a different country I felt free from…Jimmy, and…I didn't need it.

As I listened I marvelled at her courage and ability to step out alone into the outside world in a brave attempt to escape the life she knew she didn't want. I asked her how she had managed that. She told me that, in spite of all the negative messages about herself she'd received from her family, she knew somewhere deep inside that she was worth more. 'I just have this strength. I want to change things 'cos it was all so horrible for me.'

But having indeed changed her life, two years later her uncle came to Majorca with his family for a holiday. Although she didn't see them she was all too aware that they were there and her safe haven felt 'contaminated'.

…that was the end to that really, for me, and…I wanted to come back and to prove to myself that I could come back to *this* country and be drugs-free, and…do all right.

The abuse was haunting me – all I could think about the whole time I was away was his daughter, Sharon. I knew what he'd done to me so I need to tell…my auntie, erm…

Relapse

Hannah moved back in with her mother while she prepared herself to tell her aunt about the abuse, but it wasn't long before she came into contact with the drug-using people she had known before she left:

And then I fell in love with this bouncer. I thought he just looked so much like my dad, and he was so strong and…you know, he said he'd look after me – protect me. I'd not done any drugs the whole time I'd been away – and I just felt really off my head one night. I knew I was on something but I knew I'd not actually taken anything.

He'd spiked my drink which I didn't know [*sighs*]. I stayed with him for a while and he…he was giving me drugs… He was a dealer and he'd have bags of pills and stuff and…I knew he was spiking me, but I didn't say anything, I don't know why…

I was using ecstasy, mainly. There was just so much about at that time. Different…tablets. I used to get diazepam [valium] and temazepam. He was dealing in ecstasy, and used to have a lot of cocaine…and really…I had a…bit of an addiction with that.

He'd come round whenever he wanted sex…and my mum… You know, I would never have let my child ('cos I still think I was a child at that age) be with a man like that. I mean, he had a different car every night, money, wheeling and dealings and

> drugs. He used to bring her crates of wine and stuff to sort of keep her…happy…and I fell pregnant [*quiet*], that was quite…was quite hard, 'cos I wanted the baby.
>
> My mum said…'We'll get rid of it.' That was that – decision made – off to the hospital. And I was never allowed to tell him. Just…kind of said, you know, 'Can't see you any more.' But I…I knew what he was doing was really bad and that I was getting into drugs and stuff. And then…the baby and having the abortion and then…I was just about focusing on telling Jenny, and the court case all came and…it all…
>
> But I'll never forgive my mum…for taking my baby away. 'Cos she just said to me, 'There's no way you can cope. You can't even look after yourself, let alone another life'…

Her mother's judgement that she could not look after herself stung Hannah because she knew she had been stronger than that, having taken good care of herself for two years whilst living abroad. Once again she resolved to prove that she could give up using drugs and, having ended the relationship with her drug-dealing boyfriend, she moved into a council flat with her brother:

> So we lived in the council flat. But the guys that I'd hung around with in primary and secondary school were living upstairs. They were all smoking, injecting and there were needles on the stairs. It was a horrible place.

However, Hannah's brother introduced her to his friend Joseph, who became her new boyfriend. Joseph realised that Hannah needed to disclose the abuse if she was to be able to give up using drugs and he became the 'solid rock' who supported her in spite of her family telling her she should keep quiet.

In desperation, worrying about how she could tell her aunt about Jimmy, having nightmares and experiencing flashbacks in which she relived the abuse, Hannah took a second overdose:

> This time I'd really, really done it properly. I didn't think anyone would find me. I'd drunk a bottle of beer, or cider or…something…and I'd been on anti-depressants and I'd saved a lot of them up and I'd gone and bought a load of pills – I didn't really ask what they were, I just used to say, 'Yeah, I'll have them.'
>
> One morning after Joseph had gone to work I'd got myself into bed…and I took all the pills and stuff, and drunk… Then I just remember being slapped across the face, someone calling my name, the ambulance people trying to get me to…to…to walk. My partner had sensed something wasn't quite right and he'd come back.

She was terrified that when she disclosed the abuse to her aunt she would not be believed – as Jimmy had said – and that they would all think it was her fault. However, she knew that she could no longer allow people to ignore her reality:

'Cos it was like, they'd look at me, but they'd see right through me 'cos if they looked at me too long then they're going to see my pain and then...they can't bear that. That's why I took drugs because...*I* have to bear it.

My cousin said to me: 'Don't tell my mum (Jenny). 'My brother said: 'Don't tell mum.' Everyone was always telling me to keep quiet, and I remember saying to my cousin and my best friend at the time: 'I'm going to do this again and I'm gonna die. I want to die. I either tell Jenny or I want to die', and they said: 'She won't believe you. Keep quiet.' And I knew at that point then I was really on my own.

Telling Jenny

Following the second suicide attempt Hannah was referred into the mental health system where she was offered counselling from a community psychiatric nurse to prepare her for the possibility of her aunt's denial. Finally Hannah told Jenny about the abuse.

When she turned round and said she *did* believe me I was quite shocked. She said, 'He's a bastard; I want that bastard locking up. I hate him. I believe you 110 per cent, Hannah' [*vehemently*]. Um, and then she said to me, 'Can you phone the social services and get him away from *my* daughter' – 'cos she said it was too upsetting for her [to do that].

Although all Hannah had wanted was to tell her aunt in the hope that she would then do something about it, Hannah was left to inform social services and the police in Jenny's local area. The Crown Prosecution Service decided to prosecute.

The psychiatric nurse said: 'I've been working in this for ten years and you're the first client I've ever had that's taken them to court.' And I was like...shocked. I was really frightened.

The policewoman said to me: 'There's a one in ten chance it'll go to court.' She said, 'There's no DNA evidence, it's your word against his, and the likelihood is it's not going to go anywhere.' I just said: 'I'm not even doing it for me; I'm doing it because my auntie wanted me to.' I didn't even think I had a right to make...a statement, 'cos I didn't even think...I had any legal...rights.

The court case

The belief that she had no rights was reinforced when she finally attempted to tell her father about the abuse. Feeling unable to disclose directly to him she asked her brother to tell him.

And he phoned me up and said, 'Well, did he fuck you?' and I said, 'No, he didn't do *that*.' He said, 'Well then, it's not that bad.' So I spent quite a while thinking it didn't really count. So...then I asked my dad to come to the court case and he said he couldn't get time off work. So I was very much on my own with that as well.

When finally the case came to court, Hannah was once again betrayed by her family. Her cousin Alan, who had originally made a statement supporting everything Hannah had said, changed his evidence and supported his stepfather on the day.

My barrister had been taken ill so I had a new barrister who'd only read the file the night before. I turned up at court and…and they said, 'He's got a witness', and I was like, 'I don't understand, what do you mean?' And it was Alan. He stood up in court and said what a good man Jimmy was. The jury said that [this] doesn't match the statement he [Alan] had made against him as…my…witness…and now he's his witness. They wanted to re-try him and to put Alan on trial for perjury as well. I didn't want to go through with it. [Pause]

There was no way I could have possibly gone back into the courtroom. All I had was my word against his and for me it was all about showing the jury my honesty…the pain. You know, [them] seeing me an'…I didn't want to go through with that 'cos it had taken (I think) three years to get to court.

I was in court six or seven hours – we had a break – but I was on the stand for that length of time. They used everything – all the drugs that I'd ever taken, every situation I'd ever got in was used against me in court. They said that I was a prostitute, that I was just a drug-taking…whore, and…I just kept saying 'but it's because of what he did…because I wanted to forget'.

I was devastated because it wasn't until the actual day of the court case that I understood what Alan had meant when he'd said to me a few weeks before: 'No matter what happens I will always stand by my mum.' Obviously she'd made a decision to stay with her husband an'…

I felt really…sad, but I also knew that I'd done the right thing and I also knew that the only reason he'd walked free was because they'd lied. The policewoman even said to me: 'Unfortunately people can be manipulated and…bought.' He [Jimmy] has got a lot of money. Straight after [the court case] Alan got married, a big white wedding. They went to Barbados, and had a new car, new house – all bought by him [Jimmy] and…I was just very…

It was a hung jury, which they said proves that I'm a liar. Obviously it doesn't. He went back [with Jenny] – they stayed together for a couple of years – but my auntie let other girls come over, to stay. He's abused quite a few. An'…my cousin, his daughter, she's come out about it now…and about these other girls too.

I've not spoken to [my aunt] for years and years and years. And she kept saying she wanted to speak to me. So I went to see her a couple of months ago…and she asked me if I could take it back to court.

She said, 'I don't want to put Sharon through that. Can you do it?' And I just said, 'I can never do that now. The decision that was made on that day can never be reversed. He can't be prosecuted for that again.' And it's like…he's kind of laughing in a way, because he knows that. His daughter can never do anything 'cos his wife…and stepson have already lied. It's just destroying more and more lives really. He's hooked up with another woman with two kids now…and she sat there, my auntie, saying 'I'm so sorry' and 'I believe you' and…I said to her: 'Jenny, I've heard all that before. You told me that all those years ago.' I said: 'I can live with my conscience. I can walk, day to day and know I did the right thing, 'cos the reason he isn't locked up is because…you lied.'

Recovery and renewal

The court case happened six years ago and nowadays Hannah has a different life, a good husband and a small son. Although she had given up using 'hard' drugs she continued to use cannabis until she became pregnant. In spite of that final betrayal by her family Hannah is now happy with her life. She had a miscarriage three years ago and became very depressed. Her GP referred her for counselling within the surgery and she was later referred on to a specialist abuse counselling service where she saw a counsellor for a year. Hannah has taken every chance to help herself and used every opportunity offered to build up her confidence and self-esteem.

I *am* happy, I'm happy…and I know I can be happier. I've got my one-year-old son now, and my husband. We've been going through a difficult time. We're…separated…only because I can't deal with the physical side of the rela-tionship at the moment. He's…he's fine with that.

He's brilliant. I think a lot of it is…*I* don't let him in. I wasn't aware until a couple of months ago of how much I've put the shutters up. I didn't realise how much the drugs had…numbed me to everything as well, and how alone I actually *was*… Then I met my husband and I thought: 'God, this is the first time I've ever laughed, in my life, and…felt love.' And it's…learning to accept the love that I find hard. 'Cos when you don't have that from your own family…and you're shown love in such an inappropriate way…

I felt I needed to be on my own. He is there whenever I need him, and he comes round nearly every night. I've enjoyed being on my own. I've enjoyed looking after myself and my son – on my own. Before I've always had the drugs, or drink. These last couple of months have really been…about me being capable of living a normal life.

Yeah, it's been…it's been really good…'cos I look back on my life and I think, 'God, there were days that I didn't even want to get out of bed.' I just used to wish…you know, or pray to the Lord, I used to pray to Him, 'Please don't let me wake up', and I'd wake up with a feeling of…just, pain and sadness and it's like… 'Oh, I'm here again.'

'Cos I always thought I was like, the devil. I used to devil worship and do ouija board…and was really into all the…dark…things and…then when I miscarried, only recently…in the last couple of years, I've gone…I've gone to church and lit candles and prayed. Well, people laugh, but it does help me.

I want to use everything that I've experienced to help other people. Well, I accept what's happened…to me, and…the only thing that really, *really* hurts me is that my…my family don't accept me. They don't…they don't *know* me.

Since I had my son, and I look at him growing now and…you know, there's just something in me, whether it's…good or bad, I think: as long as you face it together, then you'll get through it. But I haven't ever had that, and I don't know if that's what's made me stronger.

But I am proud of myself now, very proud of myself. I'm proud of whatever it is, the energy in me that keeps me going. I feel…I feel like burning my bra [*laughs*] and wanting to help change things.

I do speak to my mum now, and she loves my son and you know, she said, 'I'll never let anything happen to him', and I truly believe that she has…changed in that way now. There's just something…I'm not able to [have]…the love that I want, with her. If I listen to my true self I'm not able to have that. The thought of her touching me, or becoming too intimate, is just like, gosh, no. It's too late now – too late.

No-one's ever acknowledged that my trust *has* been betrayed and that really, really hurts.

[*Long pause*] I'm a strong person, and I know I've always been on my own…and there's just something that's different in me. I won't ever lay down and take it. I feel an energy [*rise in voice*]…an energy in me to say, 'No, you know, this is not going to happen any more. It's going to stop.'

★   ★   ★   ★

For two hours Hannah and I had shut out the outside world as she told her story. It seemed as if we had been on a roller-coaster of emotions and as our time together drew to a close I wanted to check that she was ready to face the outside world again. We chatted about practical matters such as how I hoped to go about using her story and the time scale that might be involved. I wanted to ensure that she was capable of driving herself home. However, she was way ahead of me: expecting that she might feel disturbed after our meeting Hannah had made arrangements to spend the night at a hotel on her own, after treating herself to a good meal. Her husband was caring for their child and she knew she could return home the following day when she was ready.

As we parted I felt as if I had known her a lifetime and I knew that our relationship would continue as we worked together to co-construct her story for this book. At each step of the way I would consult her about what I'd written and ask her permission for each new use of her material.

As I waved goodbye my heart was full of admiration for a young woman who had made certain that she would no longer allow herself to be ignored or unseen.

Part 1

Setting the Scene

Traumatic events call into question basic human relationships. They breach attachments of family, friendship, love, and community. They shatter the construction of the self that is formed and sustained in relation to others. They undermine the belief systems that give meaning to human experience. They violate the victim's faith in a natural or divine order and cast the victim into a state of existential crisis.

(Herman 1992, p.51)

Chapter 1

Introduction

No-one ever asked me why I started taking drugs. Why? Why did no-one ever ask me why? It was just that you were taking drugs, and you were evil and you were a bad person.

(Hannah's story: Prologue)

All too often societal narratives tend to judge negatively the personal and psychological characteristics of drug misusers rather than asking 'Why?' or taking into account the life experiences and conditions that surround that person's life. Research in the drugs field often focuses on 'addiction', treatment approaches, or the complexities of different substances and their effects. Much of that research is based on medical and scientific interests: less often do we find research that focuses on what a person has to tell us, in their own words, about how they retrospectively make sense of their drug misuse, and/or its relationship with trauma in their lives – although a few notable exceptions can be found in Plumridge and Chetwynd (1999), Ainscough and Toon (2000), McIntosh and McKeganey (2001) and a rich and informative biography of a man called Stuart (Masters 2005).

Having read Hannah's story I imagine you, the reader, can well understand how her drug misuse caused her family to make negative judgements about her behaviour, but you will *also* have some very clear ideas about *why* she turned to drugs, and how they helped her to survive a life that many people might want to end prematurely, as indeed she did. Her story shows in graphic detail how her sense of self and identity were affected by the negative attitudes and abusive behaviour of the very people she needed to protect her from harm and to encourage her development as a self-confident human being. Alongside that, her story also shows the pathways she followed towards transforming her identity from 'druggie' to 'non-drug user'. The richness and complexity of her story, and the other stories in this book, thereby create a new basis for understanding how people are drawn into misusing drugs, what life is like for a person once they are addicted, and what helps them to leave that lifestyle behind and to find ways to construct new and preferred identities that will enable them to pursue a more fulfilling life.

Background

It is not a new idea that people sometimes turn to drugs (and other substances) to 'self-medicate' against the pain and distress created by unresolved and unprocessed loss and trauma in their lives (Griffiths 1998; Lubit *et al.* 2003; Marcenko, Kemp and Larson 2000). Workers in the field of drug treatment and rehabilitation have long heard such stories from their clients without necessarily understanding *how* the early trauma or abuse might have led to drug misuse. It was this gap in understanding that provided the impetus for me to undertake the research for this book, commissioned by The Southmead Project, a community drugs project in Bristol, UK, which provides free counselling for abuse/trauma survivors in recognition of the frequency of trauma histories among the clients using the methadone, outreach and other services they provide.

So this book is built upon the life stories of eight people who responded to an advertisement asking for 'stories from people who have linked their history of problematic drug use with their experiences of childhood trauma/abuse'. This kind of research is ethically complicated (Josselson 1996) because personal stories, whilst 'most instructive', are also likely to make their tellers 'most vulnerable' (Elbaz-Luwisch 1997, p.82: cited in McCormack 2004, p.233). Advertisements were placed in several university departments where students of counselling and psychotherapy would see them, staff rooms of drugs agencies, and in a counselling journal. My decision to advertise for participants in those places was based upon moral and ethical principles to 'do no harm', and on my belief that participants would need to have acquired enough reflective grasp on their life to tell their stories without becoming re-traumatised. I assumed that students in the psychological therapies, staff members at drugs agencies, and readers of a counselling and psychotherapy journal would have/be engaged upon their own therapeutic journey, as expected by their professional bodies, and that they might also be able to assess (and pass the message on to) clients who could gain something from telling their stories of drug misuse in a research context.

The stories in this book were therefore offered by five people who were trained as psychological therapists – three males and two females – and by two men and one woman who were not therapists. All of them were drug-free: three having undergone detoxification and rehabilitation, two of those being counsellors now. The others had found a variety of ways out of their drug misuse and transformed their lives and identities. All have received some form of therapeutic help at different stages in their journeys. Although this sample may be seen as atypical of the general population of ex-drug misusers it is not altogether unusual for people who misuse drugs to follow the pathway from 'drug misuser', to 'counselling client', to 'counsellor' – the concept of 'the wounded healer' being very familiar to those in the field of drug treatment. Indeed, as at least two of the stories will show, meeting a drug worker who has been addicted to substances in the past can become a turning point for some drug misusers: meeting someone who has managed to transform their identity from drug addict to helper creates a sense of hope for themselves and the possibility of a better future.

So this book, rather than focusing exclusively on stories of drug misuse, explores the individual's understanding of their drug misuse within the context of their life story, their social environment and the wider social/cultural resources they relied on to help them make sense and meaning of their lives.

Life story research

By using established life story research methodologies (Holstein and Gubrium 1999; Josselson and Lieblich 1999; Ochberg 1994; Roberts 2002) this book provides an account across the length of lives whilst focusing on particular aspects of lived experience; that is, drug misuse and the transformation of identities.

In life story research we can hear the subjective meanings and sense of self and identity being negotiated as the stories unfold, whilst bearing in mind that stories are *reconstructions* of the person's experiences, *remembered* and told at a particular point in their lives, to a particular researcher/audience and for a particular purpose – all of which will have a bearing on *how* the stories are told, *which* stories are told and how they are presented/interpreted. The stories I present are not 'life as lived' but my own re-presentations of those lives as told to me.

This approach to research draws on what Bruner described as 'narrative knowing' as opposed to a 'paradigmatic mode of thought' (Bruner 1986). The latter draws on reasoned analysis, logical proof and empirical observation and is used to explain events in terms of 'cause and effect', to predict and control reality, and to create unambiguous objective 'truth' that can be proven or disproved. However, those methods do not help us to make sense of the ambiguity and complexity that is often attached to human lives. On the other hand, narrative knowledge is created and constructed through the stories people tell about their lived experiences, and the meanings they give to those experiences that might change and develop as their stories unfold over time.

Even within narrative paradigms there is an ongoing debate between those who approach stories as a 'window' onto a knowable reality, which can be interpreted by 'experts', and those who view stories as knowledge constructions in their own right (see Atkinson 1997; Frank 1995). My own approach takes the latter position: so in this book I invite the reader into a relationship with eight people's stories, acknowledging that I do not offer the stories as causal explanations or to make generalisations other than from the standpoint that the 'personal is the political...and the reverse is true – the political is personal' (Ellis 2002, p.399). These stories tell of 'a kind of life' (Scott-Hoy 2002, p.276) so they will reach readers on many different levels. I believe that this kind of in-depth, small-scale study can result in 'intimate knowledge' that is 'likely to teach us more than distant knowledge' (Mair 1989, p.2) by allowing the reader to respond emotionally *and* intellectually. My intention is that you will be informed, moved, challenged and perhaps stimulated to action by these stories and that you will feel engaged and interested as you learn.

Knowledge embedded in 'good' stories is memorable, interesting and sometimes transforming. Stories allow us to bring together many layers of understandings about a person, about their culture and about how they have created change in their lives. We hear people struggle to make sense of the past and create meanings as they tell or 'show' us what happened to them. The shape and form of a story helps the teller (and the listener) to organise information about the storyteller's personal and social lives, how they have interpreted past events, the values, beliefs and experiences that guide those interpretations, and their hopes, intentions and plans for the future. As researchers try to analyse or re-tell those stories we find complex patterns and descriptions of identity construction and reconstruction and evidence of social discourses that impact on a person's knowledge creation from specific cultural points of view (Daiute and Lightfoot 2004; Harber and Pennebaker 1992). Knowledge gained in this way 'is situated, transient, partial and provisional; characterized by multiple voices, perspectives, truths and meanings. It values transformation at a personal level, individual subjectivity and the researcher's voice' (McCormack 2004, p.220).

Telling life stories can also have a 'recuperative role' (Frank 2000), for individuals, relationships and societies, and therefore becomes a moral act (Frank 1995). For Hannah, whose family had attempted to silence her, this book has become a means by which she has met a long-standing need to have her life story witnessed and accepted by an empathic audience, and to have it used in ways that are worthwhile. Others in this book have also been silenced, not necessarily by oppression as in Hannah's case, but rather by family or cultural loyalties, by their own or other people's denial, minimisation or normalisation of painful events, losses and bereavements, or because they had no frame of reference or language for describing their traumatic life events. As an academic and researcher, as well as bearing witness to the lives of my participants as I gather and work with these stories, I can provide a platform from which those stories can reach the wider community, and thereby potentially contribute to a field of study concerning many thousands of people who are currently misusing a variety of substances.

Stories have meaning beyond the local and personal context; stories resonate and outlast their telling or reading, and sometimes have unintended consequences. They change us in ways we may not always anticipate because they can move us emotionally, change our attitudes and opinions, and sometimes influence our future behaviour. Stories are powerful because they touch all our lives. Bruner tells us: 'The stories we create influence the stories of other people, those stories give rise to still others, and soon we find meaning and connection within a web of story making and story living' (Bruner 1990, p.37).

Theories are constructed and exist within societal contexts that represent socially and interpersonally defined stocks of knowledge available at any given time. These theories provide us with systems of meaning, which help us define our experiences and to make judgements about the behaviour of others. Michael White captures this idea neatly when he writes: 'People's lives are shaped by the meanings they ascribe to their experience, by their situation in social structures, and by the language practices and cultural practices of self and of relationship that these lives are recruited into' (White 1992, p.122).

However, as members of a society, we sometimes limit the kind of stories available by privileging some and denying others, or by foreclosing on new learning because some information is too painful to take on board, even when we know how important it is. This phenomenon was described by Judith Herman who commented that knowledge of childhood trauma has been limited by 'a will to deny horrible events and the will to proclaim them aloud' (Herman 1995, p.7).

How we respond as readers will depend upon what we bring to these stories from our personal and professional lives and experiences (Etherington 2004). As my father (who died when I was 15 years old) was a heavy drinker, my own experiences will almost certainly shape the work that I present, as will the stories I have listened to as a therapist, trainer, supervisor, researcher and consultant to a drugs agency.

Selves, identities and narratives

My view of self (ves) and/or identity (ies) is in line with Bruner (1994, p.41) who says that: 'Self is not an entity that one can simply remember, but is, rather, a complex mental edifice that one constructs by use of a variety of mental processes, one of which must surely be remembering.'

Autobiographical recollections such as those told by participants for this book create a 'remembered self' (Neisser and Fivush 1994). Research has shown that certain kinds of self-narratives may originate from scripts found in interactions between parents and children early in life which are internalised by children as they develop speech and language (Barclay 1994). The internalised stories contribute to how the person perceives themselves to be, and the identities they construct.

Concepts of identity have been explored by a variety of researchers using narrative approaches over more than a decade, with a recognition that the stories are a means by which both the researcher and the storyteller are richly informed, and identities formed (McAdams 1993; Mishler 1999):

> If you want to know me, then you must know my story, for my story defines who I am. And if I want to know *myself*, to gain insight into the meaning of my own life, then I, too, must come to know my own story. (McAdams 1993, p.11)

By examining life stories through a research lens we can open up spaces between fixed and often negative ideas of identity, and invite instead more hopeful life-enhancing self-stories to emerge.

When I set out on this research journey I was interested in learning about how a person moves from one particular identity to another, for example 'recreational drug user' to 'addict' or 'druggie', and then again to 'non-drug user'. I also wanted to understand how people resist falling back into previous and familiar identities, and about the behaviours attached to different identities.

Critical incidents, epiphanies or turning points (Bruner 1994) are sources of knowledge about how people redefine themselves (Denzin 1989). Participants in this book gave up misusing drugs once they realised drugs were controlling their lives. However, the changes these people have undergone are much more than a change in their drug misusing behaviour; they have transformed their identities, their sense of who they are, and who they want to be. This requires not only a new understanding of the world, but a new understanding of themselves and their lives, and a re-interpretation of their past.

About the book

The stories re-presented in this book have been offered by people who are all at different stages on unique journeys that will probably continue as long as life itself. They are not offered as a 'right way' to give up misusing drugs but rather as an acceptance that there are many ways, and that each person can find their own.

During my meetings with each of the storytellers I had invited them to focus on what seemed most important to *them* rather than having a set of questions that arose from my agenda, asking each of them, 'Where does your story begin?' As they told me their stories I asked questions arising from my curiosity, whilst trying to locate their experiences against the backdrop of the era in which those lives were happening, asking questions like 'What year was that?' or 'How old were you then?' People do not tell stories in a linear fashion, moving from one point in time to another, so for me to rewrite their stories coherently I needed to order their experiences by asking such questions as 'Was that before or after you left home?' or 'Was that before you quit using drugs?' I also invited them to reflect upon how they made sense of their experiences, both at the time they were happening, and now, thereby encouraging them to become theorists on their own lives and to recognise how their beliefs, values and self-interpretations might have been shaped by the cultural stories and myths available to them at different stages of their lives. Their explanations/theories, like mine, were influenced by societal and cultural discourses, literature and media information, sometimes helpfully, sometimes not.

Sometimes I picked up on *how* the story was being told: perhaps the storyteller appeared to be puzzled, hesitant, angry, or experiencing a bodily response as they remembered past events. Sometimes I drew attention to what seemed like a celebratory statement or high point in their narratives, or when I noticed that they seemed distressed. At those times I would ask if they wished to take a break or change the focus, not wishing to lead them into areas that may be better supported in a therapeutic arena. At some such points I asked 'How did you cope with all that?' or 'How did you manage to survive in those circumstances?', questions to help them reconnect with their strengths and resources, often related to spiritual moments in their lives. In this way I invited them to think about their lives and drug misuse in ways that did not reinforce internalised negative and stigmatising stereotypes, but rather to restore(y) 'the valued sense of who they are, the preferred sense of identity or personhood' that Michael White refers to as 'a sense of myself', which can then become 'the foundation for a rich story development of the person's life' (White 2004, p.47). At other times I noticed how some stories were repeated or emphasised, believing this might indicate the importance of that particular aspect of their experience (Etherington 2007).

By immersing myself in interview transcripts whilst re-listening to the taped conversations, and reflecting on my own responses to them, participants' stories became catalysts for my deeper understanding. With this understanding I used participants' words to construct *my* stories of their stories. Once written down, my stories were sent to the storytellers who were asked to comment upon them, make any corrections where I might have misunderstood something, change any identifying details to protect their anonymity and choose a name by which they would be called, and return the script to me. At this point several storytellers offered further information or wrote additional sections that were incorporated into the finished manuscript, along with their responses to their experience of being involved. Our relationships have developed over time and are still ongoing as I write.

Because I want this book to be read by people struggling to overcome the influence of drug misuse in their own lives, drugs workers, policy makers, health professionals and educators, I use a range of different styles of writing throughout the book. For example, in some chapters I have presented the stories in stanza form, and focused on metaphor and imagery, to capture the rhythm and poetic quality of the spoken word that allows the reader to appreciate their narrative structure, meaning and emotional impact (Gee 1991; Mishler 1991; Richardson 2000). I locate the stanzas within my re-telling of other parts of their stories and make links with some of the theoretical 'stories' evoked in me. Whilst I have deliberately excluded the use of academic references in chapters that contain the stories, in Part 1 references are included to draw attention to theories that form part of my background understanding as I approached this task: theories of research practices and the philosophies that underpin them, as well as theories related to the topic of this book – trauma, drug misuse and identity transformation. Part 3 also includes references to theories as I draw attention to some of the patterns that emerged across and within the individual stories and which provide a sense of both the uniqueness *and* commonality of experience, and to attend to practice issues.

In the prologue I presented Hannah's stories to engage the reader and to provide a flavour of what follows. Hannah's stories show how her experiences of childhood sexual abuse and neglect were precursors to her misuse of alcohol and drugs. Her story also shows how those experiences impacted on her education and her physical and mental health, and how her very life and existence was threatened by suicide attempts. Hers is also a painful story of abortion, loss and betrayal. Alongside all of that we hear of her attempts to find help and care for herself, even when others did not seem to care; about the courage she demonstrated by leaving her familiar environment and going out into the world alone, at the tender age of 16 – leaving her country to find a safe enough place in which she could become healthy; about how she tried to protect others by putting herself through the distress of a court case; the resilience she showed by taking back her power and standing up for herself when others refused to support her; and her loving attempts to make a safe home for her child and establish a good relationship with her current partner.

Part 1, 'Setting the Scene', consists of this introduction and a chapter that introduces the concepts and theories that underpin the focus of the whole book. My intention in writing this chapter is to provide a backdrop against which the personal stories that follow can be read and understood. As I wrote it I was aware that I had set myself a difficult task: trying to build conceptual links between existing understandings of trauma, drug misuse and identity transformation, knowing that each of these concepts is separately informed by a vast literature of its own. I have therefore needed to be selective in the literature I have drawn upon, knowing that I do not, and cannot, claim to have done justice to all that has gone before. So I simply present my current understanding, accumulated over several years of reading research and other literature, and experiences of learning through my work as a counsellor, supervisor and consultant in the field of drug misuse, as well as the learning I have gained from the storytellers in this book who have opened my eyes to worlds I have not personally experienced. In this respect I am very aware that I am an outsider, but the stories I re-present are those of insiders: people who know the terrifying landscape of drug misuse, drug dealing and, in some cases, the criminal and violent world inhabited by gangsters.

Part 2, 'The Stories', runs from Chapter 3 to Chapter 10 with some of my personal and theoretical responses added, beginning with two chapters in which I re-present Omar's story, gathered over two separate meetings. Omar's story shows us what it was like for a Pakistani Muslim child brought up in the UK to experience racism and bullying outside the home and physical and emotional abuse within the family. It vividly shows the strains and stresses of growing up in a racist society, and within a family that upholds cultural and religious loyalties that contrast starkly with practices outside the home. A child whose racial identity is being attacked and reviled, whilst his body and mind is being violated at home, will need to find ways to build up self-esteem and a sense of self-worth, and Omar did this by adopting the lifestyle of a drug dealer, seeking respect in the only ways he knew at the time. His portrayal of his life as a homeless person, living on the streets as a heroin addict, and his life in the shelters provided for people in those circumstances, graphically demonstrates the depths to which a person can be brought by drug misuse. However, Omar's story also shows how, in spite of his painful reality, he was able to use the help that was eventually offered, and the spiritual message of Alcoholics Anonymous, to risk the intimacy of helping relationships, which offered him the hope of a new beginning and new life in which he has used his experience to help others.

Becky's story in Chapter 5 clearly shows how children can be impacted by their parents' unprocessed trauma. Becky's father, who had been brought up by *his* alcoholic father since the age of three when his mother died, also became an alcoholic, and was physically and emotionally abusive to Becky's mother and brother. In an effort to protect her little girl from her husband's violence, Becky's mother sent her to live with her own mother, Nan, an event which led Becky to believe she was 'defective' and unwanted. As a child Becky had experienced her mother as distant and unaffectionate – something she now understands as the impact on her mother of having been sexually abused as a child. The intergenerational patterns are vividly demonstrated in Becky's story of how she sought affection through connection with a violent and addicted man like her father, who re-traumatised her over and over again, and led her to self-medicate constantly against the pain and distress of feeling stuck and powerless to change her life. The story includes her experience of abortion at 14 years of age, and an insight into the role of shoplifting, fraud and prison in a drug misuser's life. All of this led to a meeting with a positive role model, who enabled her to access a mother and baby unit that encouraged her to develop her inherent and learned resourcefulness, creativity and intelligence and turn her life around, become a good mother to her child, and eventually take on a new identity as a counsellor.

Intergenerational trauma is also a theme in Steven's story, Chapter 6. Both of Steven's parents had been sexually abused as children. In Steven's view this had led his mother to become overly protective and controlling in her attempt to keep him safe. Her extreme anxiety over sexual matters and masculinity had also impacted negatively on her son's self-confidence in constructing his identity as a man. In his efforts to relax socially and become accepted by his peers Steven became involved in using drugs to a degree that eventually led to an extreme and terrifying psychotic breakdown which became the turning point that guided him towards a spiritual journey. After taking several 'wrong turnings' Steven was eventually led to a 'therapeutic faith community' where he began to make connections between his childhood experiences and his adult problems. The strength he has gained from that community has enabled him to develop as a person, form an intimate, committed, loving relationship and enjoy a satisfying working life as a productive member of a research community.

Josie's story, Chapter 7, deals with two very common issues: cannabis misuse and the impact on a child of her parents' divorce. Josie shows us, by recounting her powerful memories of the traumatic loss of her father, how her constant search for attention and affection from men led to her involvement with a male drug-misusing subculture where she was exposed to pornography, sexual exploitation and led into inappropriate and abusive relationships. Her story illustrates how disturbance to her general and sexual development impacted on her sense of identity and self-worth, and how all of that shaped the kinds of intimate relationships she fell into as a sexually maturing young adult. Her story, like Becky's, also draws attention to the importance of becoming a mother, a role that became a turning point for Josie, whose values about parenting helped her challenge some of the choices she was making and transform the way she lived her life. Once again her story hints at the intergenerational issues that shaped her parents' relationship, which in turn shaped her own.

In Chapter 8 we have George's story, which also begins with his parents splitting up. George's description of the impact of his mother leaving home seems to parallel Josie's experience when her father left home. During the period George's mother was absent from the family he was sexually and physically abused by one of his brothers, and on her return a few months later she took George with her, travelling from one place to another to seek work and establish a secure base for her youngest son. George was attracted to the music scene during adolescence and his story graphically shows the importance of ideological influences on an adolescent's identity construction and subsequent drugs misuse. Once again we see how childhood trauma has impacted on a person's ability to create a sense of self and to form satisfying relationships during adulthood. This story also indicates how a person's sense of themselves can become 'split' between two or more aspects of self, sometimes each at war with one another. George shows how he creatively used that split to integrate aspects of himself and how that led to a sense of wholeness from which he was able to construct a preferred identity.

John's story, in Chapter 9, shows how, as a neglected child of a drug-using single parent, he was exposed to the risk of emotional and sexual abuse. As a little boy of seven John was raped by a stranger and, without a frame of reference or the language to describe his experiences, he was left alone to deal with fluctuating rage and fear created by the rape and childhood neglect. His early trauma and disrupted childhood led him to seek out a 'family' of his own within the culture of a biker's club, where he felt accepted and understood, and drugs were a major part of the scene. His attitude of indifference, which had helped him to survive, was stripped away by his experience of fatherhood and the loss of his first baby. His experience of losing his second child to adoption because of his inability to care for her became a turning point in his life, when he finally acknowledged that drugs would never fill the aching void inside him. At this point John went into treatment, and after several lapses he is now on firmer ground.

Traumatic loss of identity is at the heart of Levi's story in Chapter 10. Having reached the age of 13 in the belief that he was the youngest child with three older sisters, Levi discovered that the basis upon which his life story had been built up until then was untrue: his 'parents' were really his grandparents, and his 'oldest sister' was actually his mother. From that moment Levi's recreational use of drugs changed to being a way to escape the painful reality that his family had lied to him and that he could no longer trust them. His story shows how a young person's sense of self, his education and his plans for the future can be disrupted as he tries to deal with such losses. His experience of racism in the army and his use of alcohol created a violence within him that led to him being punished with an extended term of front-line duties which further exposed him to trauma. The drugs world became his chosen 'family' where he was able to earn money and respect, and to feel at home as a mixed-race young man, able to move between both worlds. Levi's involvement within the drugs world led him into seriously dangerous company, where weapons and violence were commonplace, and caused him the loss of the only woman he had ever truly loved. His additional loss of close friends eventually helped Levi to see the real cost of being part of that world and to acknowledge that he was indeed addicted. Without the drugs Levi became aware of fear of the dangerous world he had grown accustomed to and that awareness helped him to find another way to live.

Part 3, 'Thinking across the Stories', consists of three chapters (11, 12, 13) in which I try to make sense of what I have heard across the stories and to organise my own responses and understandings. The connections between adult behaviours and traumatic childhood experiences are often so clear that very little interpretation is required (Sorlosi 2004, p.95) but in Part 3 I make some further interpretations of the stories, using the storytellers' own words alongside my own theoretical and personal responses. Each person's narrative needed analysis on its own terms (Harvey and Chavis 2006), so by paying attention to each one separately in Part 2, before analysing them alongside the others in Part 3, I have tried to make meaning within and across the narratives.

In doing so, I do not claim that my way of making sense has any more validity than ways in which the storytellers themselves make sense of their lives, but rather that what I bring to the exercise of sense-making will be different from what each of them brings. Indeed, as 'an outsider' – that is, someone who has not used illegal drugs as a way of coping with childhood trauma – my views cannot be considered as more 'expert' than the views of those who have lived those lives and told those stories.

Chapter 11 examines the stories to discover what storytellers told me about how they came to define themselves as young children through their interactions with other people and the discourses that informed those interactions. Additionally, it examines how their self-definitions were impacted upon by the traumatic events in their lives and influenced their construction of a 'drug-user' identity.

In Chapter 12 I focus on the interrelationships between drugs and alcohol in the lives of the storytellers, noticing how discourses shape attitudes towards, and away from, different substances. This chapter also continues to weave the thread of identity construction and the events and experiences that shape a person's view of drug use as problematic and supports them to change.

Chapter 13 explores the different ways storytellers find to transform themselves and to shift to a non-drug user identity. By noticing their personal resilience and strengths and what their stories show about the positive growth potentially available to those who are able to overcome and integrate trauma, this chapter creates a different discourse from which to offer support to people trying to quit using drugs. It raises our awareness of the impact of intergenerational trauma when traumatised parents pass on to their children the effects of their own unprocessed trauma, and how people who *are* able to integrate their woundedness reach out to help others once they have paid attention to their own wounds. It also addresses how helpers who value life stories as opportunities for 'creative re-engagements with their own histories' (White 2002, p.66) – once they become aware of them – offer cause for hope and an antidote to stigma and despair (ibid, p.67).

These final chapters of the book have brought into focus recurrent themes across the stories and recurrent experiences within interviews in ways that systematically connect the past with the present. By differentiating trauma stories into separate narrative threads, I was able to examine closely the behavioural and emotional impact, the storytellers' reflective understandings of their experiences, and to observe the nuances among these different threads of experience.

In this way the reader can see many examples of 'resistance' to the dominant and potentially stigmatising discourses of 'drug addiction' – not to encourage us to view the storytellers as representatives of a group with essential and intrinsic qualities or characteristics, but rather to highlight differences and experiences that invite us to think with the stories (Frank 1995) in terms of how a person's sense of self and identity has been shaped within the contexts, discourses and relationships they have inhabited, and the potential for a person's idea of who they are to shift and continuously evolve in relationships.

These stories place importance on ideas of:

> emancipation or empathy – either exploring narratives in order to generate alternatives to the status quo, or for generating a first-hand understanding of the other. In both cases the research interests are tied more closely to the concerns of the society as opposed to intellectual issues. (Gergen 1999, p.96)

In this way I hope to make a difference.

Chapter 2

Trauma, Drug Misuse and Transforming Identity

In this chapter I will bring together concepts that have separately accumulated an extensive body of theoretical knowledge. By positioning myself at the 'cross-roads' where trauma, drug misuse and transforming identity meet, I attempt to create a multilayered and flexible story of how each concept might contribute to, or be dependent upon, the others (Erbes 2004). The theories I present below are neither 'truths' nor 'untruths', they are simply offered as ways of thinking as you read the stories in this book.

For the purposes of this book I use the term 'trauma' to mean a stress response that has gone awry. When most people are exposed to extreme or prolonged stress they suffer for a time, then find ways to deal with it, avoid or escape from it, and gradually find ways to calm themselves until the effects and memories of the events fade away. For people who are traumatised this does not happen: they remain trapped in their initial response to the stressful experience(s), storing unprocessed sensory images and feelings out of awareness. These are sometimes triggered by areas of their current lives that carry fragments of past events. The feelings and sensations stored within the person are re-experienced as if happening 'now', leaving the individual with a terrifying sense of being out of control of their thoughts, feelings and behaviours. In this way a person is repeatedly re-traumatised, as the 'mental wall between "now" and "then" is too thin and horror seeps through every fabric of mental defence to interfere with their day-to-day thinking' (Batmanghelidjh 2006, p.96).

Living with that kind of horror can be unbearable and people find different ways to escape or regain control or dull the pain. Drugs, whether prescribed or illegal, are known and effective ways to deal with pain, and they are widely available in our society. Initially drugs might prove effective in helping people cope with lives that might otherwise be unmanageable. Drugs can create a distraction, a sense of relief, even pleasure and peace, but eventually the very means by which a person escapes their distress can itself become an unbearable burden in their lives.

When drugs affect the way people feel about themselves to the degree that once again they feel out of control and despairing, or they wake up each day not wanting to face the day ahead, or when the shame they feel about their drug-centred behaviour means they cannot face their children or other family members, or when they have become the kind of person they would want to avoid, then they begin to look for ways to reconstruct their sense of self and identity. The task of reconstruction not only requires a change in their behaviours, but also a fundamental shift in their beliefs about the world, themselves and others – a transformation and reconstruction of identity. That was the journey travelled by the people who gave their stories for this book.

The kind of self-defined trauma experienced by participants in this study included chronic parental neglect, sexual abuse within the family, childhood rape by a stranger, racial abuse and harassment, physical and emotional abuse by parents and the witnessing of violence being perpetrated on other family members, loss of parents through divorce and separation, and in one case the loss of genetic and social identity on discovering his true parentage. These experiences rarely occurred in isolation; more often they overlapped and were concurrently experienced.

So none of these traumatic experiences was caused by catastrophic natural events such as earthquakes, tsunamis and calamities that are outside our human control. Rather these traumas were imposed on children by other human beings, many of whom were the very people upon whom they should have been able to depend for their well-being and survival. Betrayal of this kind can shatter a child's trust in humanity.

Catastrophic events and natural disasters are easily defined as traumatic, and society recognises the need to treat and heal a child's physical injuries, and to attend to their other needs for food, shelter and clothing, but less often do we recognise and provide for the emotional needs of a child, who may then be left with unprocessed trauma that can disrupt their future well-being, health, and their ability to participate fully in society in a fulfilling way (Lubit *et al.* 2003).

Childhood abuse as trauma

Over the past three decades researchers have identified a range of negative outcomes associated with a child's experience of sexual and physical abuse (Bailey and McCloskey 2005; Gold 2000; van der Kolk 1996). However, emotional abuse and neglect can seem at first sight less serious, and are often more difficult to recognise for what they are, and may therefore be more difficult to acknowledge and heal, seeming to be less dramatic or obviously traumatic. When seemingly 'minor occurrences' accumulate over a prolonged period this can lead to the creation of 'a passively traumatic environment' (Meares 2000, p.122), where a child's needs are ignored or dismissed, or where they are trained to meet adults' needs and ignore their own, or where adults are overly controlling and critical, constantly overriding the child's opinions. This kind of experience will have a long-term and profound impact on the child's sense of self and identity. As a child struggles alone to make sense of their negative experiences they begin to question why these events are happening to them, and form beliefs about themselves, other people, and the world in which they live: 'I am a bad person', 'They don't like me', or 'The world is an unsafe place' (McCann and Pearlman 1990). These beliefs can lead to social withdrawal, isolation, and a lonely, fear-based life. Others respond to such negative self-beliefs by raging against the world, adopting antisocial behaviour or by turning anger inwards against themselves, either physically or emotionally, perhaps through self-harm, suicide or depression.

Additionally, children who are exposed to chronic emotional abuse or neglect often become prey to those who inflict further harm as they seek out someone to give them comfort and attention. These children can be targeted by abusive adults who, recognising their need and vulnerability, give them the attention they long for whilst grooming them to satisfy their own desires (Etherington 1995, 2000). Hannah's story shows how, as a five-year-old child whose father had left home, and whose mother was emotionally unavailable, she needed (and deserved) the attention of a kind and loving adult, and how that neediness made her vulnerable to her uncle's sexual abuse.

Impact on development of trust

When those who inflict injury are people upon whom the child depends, the impact on the child's development of trust is severely damaged. The closer the relationship between the child and those who betray them, the greater the rupture in their ability to bond with others and form secure attachments (Cameron 2000, p.4), which for us, as social beings, is important for our very survival and the development of meaningful, trusting relationships (Bowlby 1969, 1973; Etherington 2000, 2003).

One-off traumatic events that occur within an otherwise secure environment may have little impact on a child's *overall* development, although their immediate impact may be huge. However, even those events can create long-term and devastating effects if the environment surrounding the one-off traumatic incident creates additional trauma. For example, the trauma response created in John (see Chapter 9) who experienced a single incident of rape by a stranger was also impacted by the conditions of neglect in which he lived with his mother, by the absence of his father since infancy, and by his inability to communicate to anybody what had happened to him. Without any way of making sense of such events the child's subjective experience is of uncontrollable and existential threat.

Children whose parents are inconsistent in their behaviour towards their child, sometimes loving and sometimes neglectful or abusive, leave the child confused and afraid, not knowing upon whom they can depend.

Children who have caring, loving attachment figures in their lives can demonstrate resilience (Cloitre, Morin and Linares 2004; Masten 2001; Scheering and

Zeanah 2001; Terrr *et al.* 1999) and overcome the effects of trauma, not only by reaching out to the adults around them for support and care, but also by being able to soothe themselves, having learned how to do so through the model of good parenting they have received. Without that, children are doubly compromised and at risk.

Impact of trauma on self and identity

Children need to depend on others for their existence and survival so when they are ill-treated by the adults around them they are likely to tell themselves that they deserved the ill-treatment for being 'bad', or that bad things happen because of who they are, or that ill-treatment is the norm, for example '*all* the kids in our street are beaten' (Herman 1992; Meares 2000). This view of themselves and the world, whilst helping children to survive, also hinders the development of a positive sense of identity. Children who blame themselves (if only I'd been good...), or are blamed by others (you'll be the death of your mother), for parents splitting up, or for a parent's illness, or drinking, etc. develop feelings of guilt and lack self-worth. In other cases, children who are unable to prevent bad things happening to themselves or others often take on the shame of being powerless. Children who have placed their bodies between parents when one parent is assaulting the other sometimes feel ashamed and humiliated by their inability to protect the victim. Children who are unable to deal with a crisis might develop an image of themselves as helpless, ineffective and therefore shameful. Without an internalised positive sense of self, traumatised children have to find other ways to soothe themselves – ways that may turn out to be detrimental to their health and well-being.

In 'normal' circumstances children will gradually come to terms with their parents' limited abilities but premature or traumatic collapse of the image of their parents as 'all-powerful' and 'all good' can weaken a child's attachment to a parent figure and cause them to seek out others with whom they can identify (Lubit *et al.* 2003). Having lost the image of an omnipotent, protective parent the child may become anxious and withdraw from social or school activities that are essential for their development. Alternatively, in the face of what they perceive as an uncontrollable threat, the child may respond with rage, hatred or aggression against the object or person they see as causing their distress.

Without an experience of being cared for to mediate their experiences of trauma, children who are exposed to violence and abuse may identify either with the role of 'aggressor' or the role of 'victim', or may fluctuate between the two (Etherington 1995). In their attempts to overcome their sense of vulnerability and fear, a traumatised child may also identify themselves as the 'rescuer', wanting to save others from the kind of harm they have experienced themselves.

All of this indicates how important is the need for adults to recognise and define childhood trauma. Support that is offered early can prevent the development of negative self-identities and ensure that children are helped to achieve the developmental tasks needed to become healthy adults.

Surviving trauma – coping mechanisms

Trauma can overwhelm a child and leave them feeling powerless, but most children find ways of surviving by adapting to the environment or by accommodating to the needs of others. Hannah had to accommodate to, and find her own ways of dealing with, her uncle's abuse, believing that her parents had abandoned her. Family members told her that any attempt to disclose the abuse would threaten the entire family structure. This represented a threat to her very existence. The absence of a secure base, which is normally provided by the parents, is viewed by van der Kolk (1987) as 'the earliest and possibly most damaging psychological trauma' (p.32). In order mentally to preserve her image of 'a good family' upon which she could depend, and thereby allay her existential threat, Hannah adapted her view of herself to accommodate her mother's view of her as 'evil'. In that way she was able to survive psychologically by avoiding the distress of knowing that she had indeed been emotionally abandoned by her parents.

Each separate experience of betrayal is traumatic and yet another blow to the child's experience of self. A child can come to believe that being dependent on an adult usually results in pain, disappointment and betrayal, and then create a situation where they avoid depending upon others and become overly self-reliant. Winnicott (1960) describes this as the child developing a 'caretaker self', adopting an appearance of independence and an ability to look after others, notably their parents – a means by which they can vicariously experience nurture. A child in these circumstances might believe that if they take enough care of their parent then the parent might love them in return.

In their efforts to hold onto the belief that they can depend upon their carer, children may ignore what is happening or forget about the unbearable experiences. This way of coping has been called repression. The child learns to 'get on with it', and because nobody speaks about what is happening no cognitive memory is laid down.

A child may also cope by splitting off aspects of their experience through 'dissociation' (Levine 1997; Rothschild 2000), a mechanism that creates a split in conscious awareness. This allows the traumatised person to disconnect from sensory, emotional or cognitive aspects (and sometimes more than one) in order to reduce the impact and thereby survive (Whitfield 1995).

They may dissociate their sensory experience by 'leaving the body', 'floating', 'feeling dead', automatically and habitually dissociating in response to anything that reminds them of the original trauma. For some, these 'absences' may become frequent or prolonged and thus cause disruption of memory that creates a disconti-nuity and fragmentation of existence and an inability to tell a coherent life story (Meares 2000). Dissociation therefore can impact severely on a child's ability to learn or concenrate at school, which, in turn, might create problems in behaviour when the child falls behind in their education.

Trauma survivors may dissociate emotionally by remembering traumatic expe-riences factually and in detail, relating horrific events in a flat, unemotional voice, and without having any means of making sense of what happened, but then become greatly disturbed by what seem like unrelated events, becoming enraged or fearful, or experiencing bodily sensations such as shivering, hair standing on end or a racing heart, in circumstances that seem unconnected to the trauma. Others may seem numb, lack vitality and present as passive, 'dull' or 'heavy'.

They may dissociate cognitively by appearing to forget the traumatic events whilst at the same time using behaviours that symbolically re-enact them, perhaps playing over and over the same game of murder, violence or mayhem, or developing obsessive behaviours, or becoming violent, abusive or aggressive as they try to make sense of their disconnected experiences of victimisation (Etherington 1995).

Disconnected anxiety and distressing ruminations may threaten to overwhelm a young person who has no means of controlling their unconscious reactions. All they can do is deal with their symptoms of distress, and in many cases they do so by using drugs to escape from the pain.

Post-traumatic stress disorder

In 1980 the medical world officially recognised post-traumatic stress disorder (PTSD) for the first time by including it in the third edition of the *Diagnostic and Statistical Manual of Mental Disorders* (American Psychiatric Association 1980). Twelve symptoms were listed, providing diagnostic criteria for acute, chronic and delayed manifestations of what by then had become a recognisable response to extreme stress. A revised version in 1987 included the idea that the impact of trauma depended on a person's individual perception of their experience, and recognised that this is shaped by their personal and historical context. A later, updated version (American Psychiatric Association 1994) reflected an increasingly complex understanding, particularly in relation to the idea that PTSD was a more common occurrence than previously believed, and particularly as a response to childhood trauma and abuse.

More recently, neurophysiological research has increased our understanding of *how* trauma affects the physiology of the body and creates PTSD. To understand this we need to know something of how the brain normally functions. Detailed explanations can be found in Rothschild (2000) so here I will offer a simple (and maybe simplistic) overview of what happens to brain function in people who develop PTSD as a result of trauma.

The limbic system, situated in the centre of the brain, regulates survival behaviours such as eating, sexual reproduction and the instinctive defences of 'flight or fight'. It also influences emotional expression and memory processing. The limbic system is intimately connected with the autonomic nervous system (ANS) which regulates muscles, and internal organs, such as lungs, heart, bladder, etc. The ANS has two branches – the sympathetic branch (SNS) and the parasympathetic branch (PNS) – which usually function in balance with each other, one being at rest when the other is activated. The SNS is aroused when effort or stress is activated, and the PNS is aroused in states of rest or relaxation.

In the face of perceived threat the limbic system responds in two ways: by releasing hormones to prepare the body for fight or flight, which increases breathing and heart rate to provide more oxygen to muscles used in those activities, and by releasing cortisol which halts the 'alarm' reaction and the production of fight/flight hormones once the threat has passed. It is this system that goes wrong in PTSD.

Individuals with PTSD have been shown to have lower cortisol levels, leaving them permanently in a state of heightened 'alarm' when threat is perceived, even when current events may not actually hold a threat. So a woman who was sexually abused as a child might feel threatened whenever a man approaches her intimately. The current situation, which may not in itself pose a threat, might unconsciously trigger a response from the past. Without adequate cortisol, she can remain trapped in the aroused state required for fight/flight, unable to modulate emotional reactions aroused by current events which are responded to as though they were emergencies requiring action. She may withdraw (flight) or lash out (fight), or behave in other ways that appear to be inappropriate to the demands of the current situation.

A study of pregnant women who developed PTSD after witnessing the attack on the World Trade Center in New York on 9/11 found that the mothers *and* the babies subsequently born to them had abnormally low levels of cortisol, a situation which heightens the risk of both mothers and babies developing stress-related conditions and health problems associated with regulation of the immune system (Yehuda *et al.* 2005). This was most apparent in mothers who were exposed to PTSD during the last three months of pregnancy. Those mothers were *indirectly* involved through witnessing extreme violence and yet their bodies, and the bodies of their babies, were *directly* affected.

As well as raising awareness of how PTSD can be transmitted between generations, this research helps us understand how PTSD can develop, not only in response to extreme stress that is experienced directly, but also in response to non-direct violence such as incidents that are, or are perceived to be, life-threatening to oneself or others. All of this helps us realise how children may be affected when observing or listening (perhaps whilst lying upstairs in bed) to a parent being assaulted, watching or hearing their siblings being beaten or sexually abused, and knowing they are powerless to intervene.

Although the label or diagnosis of PTSD can be a useful means of validating a person's experience and providing them with a framework for understanding their experiences, it might also be limiting if applied rigidly (Erbes 2004). The danger is that PTSD does not fully capture the range of possible reactions to, and consequences of, trauma and may lead to the invalidation of the suffering of people who do not meet the diagnostic criteria.

Post-traumatic stress exists along a continuum, and people who have shared the same traumatic experiences do not necessarily develop the same severity of response (Terr 1991). It is important to remember that trauma does not *invariably* leave people with long-term damage, and to recognise and acknowledge the strengths and resiliencies demonstrated by many survivors. It is therefore important to acknowledge both strengths *and* difficulties, and that traumatic experiences, and outcomes, depend upon the context in which they are experienced (Erbes 2004).

As stated previously, children who can explore the world from a secure base, who receive care when they are hurt or traumatised, and who know how to soothe themselves, can recover from their traumatic experiences. However, prolonged, repeated trauma, where children have little or no support, can lead to a range of physical, emotional and behavioural problems (Bernstein, Stein and Handelsmans 1998; Dembo *et al.* 1992; Felitti 1998; Smith *et al.* 1995), not least substance misuse (Bailey and McCloskey 2005; McCloskey and Bailey 2000; Ravndal *et al.* 2001).

Trauma and drug misuse

The association between substance misuse and post-traumatic stress has been addressed in a range of studies that recognise how sexual, physical and emotional abuse and neglect in childhood can lead a person to turn to drugs and alcohol (Najavits, Weiss and Shaw 1997; Porter 1994; Ravndal *et al.* 2001). Post-traumatic stress has also been implicated in higher rates of relapse (Brown and Stout 1996; Rohsenow, Corbett and Devine 1988; Wallen 1992).

Associations between substance abuse and the trauma of childhood sexual abuse have long been recognised by workers in the field of drugs who have increasingly noticed that clients in that setting disclose histories of sexual abuse more frequently than the general population (Wilson 1998). This recognition has only become possible since feminism raised our awareness of abuse in the 1960s and 1970s by encouraging women to speak out about experiences that had been hidden until then. Without a language or frame of reference to help name abuse and without an understanding of the long-term damage it can cause, sexual abuse had, until then, largely remained unreported and, therefore, unexamined.

A study of in-patient substance misusers published in 1988 by Rohsenow *et al.* found that two in three substance-abusing women, and around two in five men, said they had been molested as children. These figures are extraordinarily high for an era in which male sexual abuse (in particular) was severely under-reported because of problems defining what constituted sexual abuse for males (Etherington 1995).

The family, social and cultural context also plays an important part for those who have been traumatised. In areas where poverty and other psychosocial problems feature in the family, drug misuse might be the norm. In a study conducted in a Dublin suburb, 73 per cent of injecting drug users came from families where substance misuse was an existing problem and where 39 per cent of participants were living with other drug misusers. A range of traumatic experiences was also reported in the lives of participants, including childhood injuries sustained through road accidents, falls or fires, deliberate self-harm, suicide, homicide, and sexual assault within the family (Quigley 2003).

Substance misuse might be related to 'culturally sanctioned' ways of dealing with distress created by trauma (Waitzkin and Magenta 1997, p.818), and patterns of behaviour might be passed down from one generation to the next as a child observes drug or alcohol-misusing parents dealing with what might be their own unprocessed trauma (Hoffman and Su 1998). A mother or father who displaces emotional distress onto substances teaches their child an important lesson in coping.

The inter-relationship between substance misuse and trauma goes both ways. Children of parents who misuse substances are more likely to be exposed to traumatic experiences than others (O'Donoghue and Elliot 1992; Rounsaville *et al.* 1982). Some young people, by trying to escape from homes in which they are exposed to the trauma of sexual or physical abuse, end up vulnerable to drug dealers and pimps, thus increasing their risk of further trauma.

Physical problems

When a young person's mind becomes overwhelmed as a result of trauma the 'physical self' can split from the 'mental self'; the mind has little or no awareness of the body as a physical reality, and emotions are not expressed directly. However, the body responds to the emotions, even while the mind denies or ignores them (Miliora 1998). When a person cannot speak of their trauma, either because they have no language to explain it, or because they are silenced as a result of repression, threats or their carer's refusal or inability to hear, no verbal link can exist between dissociated parts. Without any way of verbally representing their traumatic experience, a child or young person needs to find other ways of communicating the separate experiences of these split-off parts in order for all parts to survive. So the body may speak a language of its own, perhaps through illness, pain, compulsion or addiction (Felitti 1998). These patterns of coping, necessary for survival during childhood or adolescence, may be carried into adulthood, and the very mechanisms by which the child has survived become problems in their own right (Etherington 2003).

In some people, the body might react to the unexpressed emotions connected to unprocessed trauma by developing stress-related behaviours such as drug or alcohol misuse or by developing psychosomatic disorders such as asthma, skin disorders, duodenal ulcers, neck and back pain, premenstrual tension and miscarriage; a range of diseases that are known to have an autoimmune component, such as arthritis and heart disease; and certain endocrine problems such as thyroid dysfunction (Cameron 2000; Gold 2000; Levine 1997; Northrup 1998; Williams 1984). This is not to say that all such conditions are related to unprocessed trauma, but that studies of traumatised people have shown the prevalence of such conditions in their lives.

A study of 9000 people in the USA found that those who had been exposed to four or more episodes of childhood trauma had a four- to twelve-fold increased health risk for alcoholism, drug abuse, depression and suicide attempts. They were also between twice and four times more likely to smoke, to be generally ill, to have more than 50 sex partners and thus to have sexually transmitted diseases, and up to 1.6 times more likely to be obese (Felitti 1998). Further research shows that both men and women who were physically or sexually abused in childhood had more severe problems with drugs or alcohol and were at greater risk for sexual transmission of HIV or other sexually transmitted diseases (Morrill *et al.* 2001). Yet other studies linked chronic pelvic pain with severe childhood sexual abuse (Walker *et al.* 1992) and with sexual, physical and emotional abuse before the age of 15 (Lampe *et al.* 2000). A report from the Department of Health in the UK (Itzin 2006) showed clear evidence that child physical, emotional or sexual abuse and neglect and domestic violence affect the physical and mental health of children, adolescents and adults, sometimes throughout their lives.

Identity construction

As shown earlier in this chapter, identity construction in young people who have been traumatised can be severely and detrimentally affected.

The concept of 'identity' has been variously defined and understood over time. My current position, whilst still informed by traditional psychological and sociocultural notions (Erikson 1968; Mead 1934; Vygotsky 1978), views selves and identities as multiple, socially constructed and constantly re-constructed through the stories that we tell, the stories that others tell of us, and the situations and relationships in which we find ourselves (Burr 1995; Gergen 1999). Rather than viewing identity as part of 'an essential self' I believe identity construction is shaped and guided by our past experiences and memories (Bruner 2002, p.64) and by the discourses that we draw upon to make sense of our lives.

Identity has been described as a new way of thinking about oneself that emerges during adolescence, when a person begins to notice differences between who they are now and who they believed themselves to be, and the difference between good and evil (Bruner 1990):

> In order to know who I am, I must first decide what I believe to be true and good, and false and evil, about the world in which I live. To understand myself fully, I must come to believe that the universe works in a certain way, and that certain things about the world, society, about God, about ultimate reality of life, are true. Identity is built upon ideology. (p.79)

During adolescence a young person begins to ask profound existential and ideological questions such as: Who am I? What does my life mean? What do I believe in? In the safety of a secure and loving family, questions like these are expected and supported.

Bruner (1990) also acknowledges that early childhood years contribute to identity construction during adolescence:

> Although we generally begin to think about our sense of identity during adolescence, our early childhood years provide us with a great deal of the raw material for the identities we then create; some of it laid down before we are capable of conscious memory or thought, leaving us with 'a legacy of hope and trust and about how the world works and how stories are supposed to turn out'. During later childhood, as we listen to the stories people tell about who we are, we collect 'a wealth of imagery that we will later make use of to embody the narrative pattern' of our stories of identity. (p.40)

Children whose identity construction has been shaped by unresolved traumatic experiences are not left 'a legacy of hope', but rather a legacy of potential despair and mistrust, and imagery coloured by experiences of trauma.

For these young people adolescence can be a time of particular pain, especially when making sense of past experiences through the lenses of new information and understanding. At that time, sex education threw Hannah into the turmoil of understanding that what she had previously thought was 'love' was instead sexual abuse. This was a time of painful and profound realisation about the degree of betrayal she had been exposed to, not only by her uncle but also by her parents and other members of her family. Her already negative sense of self and identity was reinforced by her mother's judgement of her as 'evil' and by her uncle telling her 'this [abuse] is what you are here for'.

This is often a crucial stage for young people, who turn to drugs to escape from their sometimes unbearable reality (Downs and Harison 1998; Jarvis, Copeland and Walton 1998; Rohsenow *et al.* 1988).

Developing a 'recreational drug user' identity

Although it has been frequently acknowledged that poor family functioning influences a young person's development of drug misuse, research has also shown a surprisingly high level of drug use in 'seemingly unremarkable families', and despite this 'it is possible that these findings are actually an under-statement of the true level of addiction' (Forsyth and Barnard 2003, p.468). This finding indicates that, as stated in many other studies reported in Harris (2005), it is nowadays the 'norm' for young people to experiment with drugs. However, not all of those young people go on to become problematic drug users. So what creates the shift from being a 'recreational drug user' to a 'problematic drug misuser' or 'addict'? Clearly, from what has gone before, young people who have been abused and traumatised enter adolescence through a 'different door' from those whose lives have been relatively unproblematic.

The adolescent's search for identity is initiated and played out in a social context. We come to know who we are through relationships and in social settings.

To depart from the past is not to leave the world behind, it is rather to move from one world to another (Bruner 1990).

The experiences of early trauma and abuse may lead young people to feel 'different' and unable to identify with others whose lives seem unproblematic. Whereas young people from stable backgrounds may seek identities through conventional activities (such as sports, the arts or membership of a church), marginalised young people may find their identities in drug subcultures, where they can be with people they perceive to be like themselves, among whom they can develop new shared identities and lifestyles, and a sense of being understood and belonging (Anderson 1994). The need for acceptance and membership of peer groups during adolescence makes it likely that marginalised young people will join in with drug use as a way of conforming to certain groups and relationships (Miller and Plant 2003), as shown by all of the stories in this book.

The illicit nature of recreational drug use further bonds the group, having shared secrets that are hidden from parents (Aldridge, Parker and Measham 1998). Secret activities are shared through telling of their experiences, strengthening a sense of group membership and reinforcing a sense of distance and difference from other friendship and/or family groups (Etherington and Barnes 2006). These friendships provide a new social identity and membership of a subculture with its own language, lifestyle and out-groups (Anderson 1995) that further isolate the individual from non-users and 'normal' life.

The practicalities of maintaining the drug-user lifestyle and identity, such as truanting and shoplifting to fund the drug habit, can lead to expulsion from school, thus reducing the young person's affiliation or identification with any form of mainstream group, and throwing them back entirely on the company of other drug misusers.

Moral judgements about drug misusers made by others also shape a person's sense of self and identity. When young people judge themselves negatively, and are judged negatively by others, they may seek out even more the company of 'deviant' people and reject 'normality' as a means of lessening the discomfort of being reminded of the distance between their own lifestyle and that of 'normal' society (Kaplan, Martin and Robbins 1984, 1986).

Moving from 'recreational drug user' to 'druggie' or 'addict' identity

All the time a person sees themselves as a 'recreational drug user' there is no real reason to change. Indeed, as shown above, this identity provides affiliation with social groups that ease the person's sense of isolation and alienation and provides a sense of pleasure and relief from pain.

Drug use becomes problematic when the motives for using change, rather than when the amount used increases, when 'addiction' is seen to take hold, leading to a physical or psychological state that requires constant 'medication' to avoid unpleasant withdrawal symptoms. The person accepts they are no longer the person they were and that they have indeed become a 'druggie' or 'addict', with changed beliefs and moralities, and sometimes an altered physical appearance. By resisting an 'addict' identity, believing they were 'not like other addicts' (because there were still things they believed to be morally wrong), they may have managed to hold on to a shred of self-respect and self-esteem.

In accepting that their behaviour *has* become like other addicts – such as Levi's realisation after a 'dirty hit' that he still wanted another one – denial of an addict identity is no longer possible. Once the person understands, internalises and becomes emotionally connected to an 'addict' identity, the full shame attached to the stigma hits home, and the adoption of an 'addict' identity can lead to a renegotiation of their life narrative, possibly starting from the need to cope with the past and current traumatic events in their life. In Hannah's case, she came to a point in her life when she recognised she was indeed 'an addict', and that the drugs would kill her, or she would kill herself in order to escape from her unbearable reality. She knew she needed to deal with the impact of her childhood sexual abuse.

Transforming identity

Having experienced life as a 'druggie' or 'addict', without having fully identified themselves with the lifestyle, some people stop using drugs without making a firm decision to do so, simply drifting away from their addiction and getting involved in other aspects of life, having maintained links with situations and self-identities that were still available to them. If a drug misuser does accept the label of 'addict', and acts upon their identity of an addict, the transformation from 'druggie' or 'addict' to 'non-drug user' will require a radical transformation of who they are, and a re-interpretation and re-construction of their life narratives (Cain 1991).

Many users reach a point in their life beyond which they are not willing to go (Stall and Biernacki 1986; Stimson and Oppenheimer 1982; Waldorf and Biernacki 1981). This group makes an explicit and rational decision to abstain from drugs, having experienced events that shatter their complacent attitudes to addiction and 'awaken perspectives that are rooted in identities that are not related to the use of opiates' (Biernacki 1986, p.50). Observing their own lives as 'addict', as well as seeing what happens to addicts they know, can heighten fears of what addiction will do to them (McIntosh and McKeganey 2001). The lifestyle becomes unacceptable to themselves and significant others, and they become concerned with repairing their 'spoiled' or stigmatised identity (Goffman 1963). The cumulative effects of their addiction become wearisome, especially as people mature.

Yet others, especially those who have become immersed in the illicit world of addiction to the exclusion of participation in a more conventional world, make the decision to stop using drugs after experiencing a sense of being at 'rock bottom' or an 'existential crisis'. Rock bottom is defined by Biernacki (1986, p.57) as 'the point at which people reach the nadir of their lives and decide, with some emotion, that they must change'. He distinguishes 'experiential crisis' from a 'rock bottom' phenomenon as being a more profound emotional and psychological state when people come to question their whole life pattern, and their 'core' identities as drug addicts, whilst believing they have no place left to turn to salvage a sense of self-worth. This may lead to suicidal thoughts or attempts as the only way to escape their suffering and humiliation. Suicide is preferable to the pain of being alive in such an undesirable state.

Adjusting to life without drugs may be very difficult. Overcoming addictive behaviours may involve profound changes in a person's self-concept and values, and a re-orientation of life, social status and relationships with other people (Koski-Jannes 2002). These changes may be difficult to manage in the face of opposing forces in their social world (McIntosh and McKeganey 2000b). For example, while supportive relationships, stable environments and rewarding employment may help change addictive behaviours (Stall and Biernacki 1986), factors such as bad housing, poverty, limited occupational opportunities, poor relationships and dissatisfaction with one's own life may hinder any attempt at change (Saunders and Allsop 1991). This suggests that the need for support of some sort is vital at all stages and not only during initial detoxification.

For this group the potential to relapse is high: a void is created when they remove themselves from the company of other addicts who are often the only people with whom they have contact within their 'world'. However, if the person's decision to stop corresponds with their involvement in a new group and the establishment of a new identity (perhaps as a 'Christian', as Steven describes in Chapter 6), then the activities required of membership will support them on their journey. The person may become focused on their new identity as a means of dealing with any uncertainty or anxiety about their ability to remain true to their resolve. By surrounding themselves with others who share their identity, other church members for example, the person develops social relationships, outside the drugs world, that provide new perspectives, behaviours and vocabularies which help them manage and overcome their cravings.

Transforming underlying trauma

When a person uses drugs as a way of dealing with trauma they may try to ignore thoughts about, or memories of, earlier experiences, preferring to avoid connection with the pain of repressed or dissociated emotions. The drug misuse can take over and develop a life of its own that consumes the person's attention and distracts from underlying material that feels too unsafe (Sansone, Wiederman and Sansone 2001). At this stage transformation is not possible. Transformation becomes possible when there is a strong enough desire to heal, and the person finds a safe enough environment in which to begin to pay attention to the messages carried by the body that tell of their past hurts. Transformation is a word that implies more than recovery or healing; it implies a fundamental shift at the core of our being (Etherington 2003).

As stated earlier in this chapter, trauma can lead to repression and dissociation which impact upon memory and a sense of continuous existence. Memory is not necessarily a factual, coherent or linear record of something that actually happened. Rather it is a process of bringing together parts of experience to create a coherent and organised whole (Whitfield 1995). Transformation does not depend upon memories, even if remembering were possible, because this is not necessarily what will transform trauma. On the contrary, by attempting to chase memories as if they were concrete 'truths', the person can become sucked back into the 'trauma vortex', causing further distress and reinforcing their sense of powerlessness and inability to take control (Levine 1997, p.204). In these circumstances recovering drug users who carry within them unprocessed trauma might relapse (Brown and Stout 1996; Rohsenow *et al.* 1988; Wallen 1992).

When a person accepts that memory of trauma is *not* necessarily something concrete that needs to be 'unearthed', but rather a 'gathering together' of different kinds of information – images, metaphors and somatic responses – they can explore creatively, flexibly and spontaneously, beginning from a place of 'tacit knowing' (Polanyi 1974) or 'felt sense' (Gendlin 1978). In this way a person can begin to reconnect with their capacity to reorganise information and create new meanings. Connecting sensation, feeling and thinking allows the brain to re-learn that traumatic events can be remembered without the extreme fear response that has held the person captive in the past.

Herman (1992) suggests that memories can be transformed, both in emotional meaning and in the effects in the emotional brain, if we can: (a) create a safe environment in the present, (b) gain some control over life, (c) tell our stories in the harbour of a safe relationship, and (d) mourn the losses created by the trauma.

When we acknowledge inner and bodily wisdom we can recognise the body's inherent capacity for healing. When a person is encouraged to pay attention to the messages carried by their body – messages about just how bad they feel – and accept those feelings without judgement, they can free up energy that may be trapped in denial or in endlessly searching for 'cures', and move towards what they really want (Northrup 1998). By deconstructing or re-interpreting 'addiction', it may be possible to name the emotional distress that drives drug misuse and begin to explore that distress and its meaning: 'What did drug misuse give me that my body knows I need?'

Transforming trauma involves recognising that identity is not fixed but constantly reconstructed as a person gathers together aspects of past and present that will help them meet the future head-on. As they begin to tell their stories they find out things about themselves they did not know before; they discover strengths and resources they did not know existed; they enjoy feelings that they no longer need to medicate against or feel controlled by; they acknowledge and welcome thoughts that might previously have been feared.

A person can experience new strength through their connections with body, mind and spirit and find a 'voice' to tell their stories, sharing experiences and newly discovered self-knowledge. When a person gives testimony to experience through telling their stories, they bear witness to the past and challenge the idea that terrible experiences are too awful to be told (Frank 1995). They also create a possibility for change and a better future as demonstrated through the stories that follow.

Part 2

The Stories

These stories are taken to reflect not only the individual experience of the teller but also to place him or her within a cultural time and place. We tell our own tales but do so by drawing on a cultural stock of narrative forms (Rapport and Overing 2000). We are born into the story of our family and community and the story of who we are (e.g. the birth story, the story behind our name), and as we grow up we adopt narrative templates provided by myths, films, novels, and other cultural resources to give shape and meaning (Sarbin 1986) to our individual live narrative.

(Lieblich, McAdams and Josselson 2004, p.22)

Chapter 3

Omar's Story, Part 1

Omar had seen my advertisement for participants on the notice board at the university where he was studying. He telephoned me to express his interest in being involved in the study which was two-fold: first, he was interested in the links between early trauma and subsequent drug misuse from his own experience and also from working with clients in a drug rehabilitation context; and second, he wanted to learn by being involved in narrative enquiry as a participant. Having been trained in quantitative and traditional research methods he was curious about how I would use his stories for research.

Between the ages of 15 and 24 Omar had used alcohol, cannabis, cocaine, ecstasy, crack, LSD, benzodiazepines and heroin. At the time we met he had been abstinent from all substances for eight years.

He chose to meet with me at my home a few days before Christmas after we had been communicating by email. I had sent him the information sheet and consent form, suggesting that he might want to leave the signing of the consent form until after our first meeting when he would be more fully informed about what he was consenting to. I explained also that obtaining consent would not be a one-off event, but rather a continuous process throughout the life of the project.

★   ★   ★   ★

The 'heydays'

Omar was 32 when we met. He had been born in Pakistan in 1973 and came to live in England with his parents, an older sister and two older brothers when he was three years old. Another brother and sister were born after the family arrived in England. They lived in an 'all white' area on the South coast of England where they 'stuck out like a sore thumb'. Their father was an extremely hard-working man who was rarely at home. Although they were a Muslim family the children attended a Catholic primary school which had a reputation for providing a 'good education' and a 'strict' regime, in line with his parents' values. He enjoyed his primary school and described himself as 'leader of the pack'.

Me and my brothers were captain of the football team, we were stars of the school play, we were in our heyday really, really fond memories. Yes, so looking back at those times, I really enjoy those memories.

Secondary school…the bloody 11 plus, it's got a lot to answer for. My parents wanted me to go to grammar school, so they put quite a lot of pressure on me to take the exam and I failed. I distinctly remember that as something really powerfully embarrassing. And then they got me into a comprehensive school, which was well away from where my brothers and sister were, in a completely different area than where we lived.

Internalising racial abuse

Omar was bullied from the moment he set foot in the secondary school, being called 'dirty Paki' and similar racist names. He was at an age where he was particularly self-conscious about his appearance and he became 'embarrassed' about having a different skin colour and religion from others in his school.

I've had this really powerful memory of my mum coming to the school gates when I started that school. I was standing with two kids and they were going, 'Ooh, look at that Paki', taking the piss out of my mum…and me not defending her and thinking, 'Oh I wish she'd just go away.' I think I said at the end, 'That's my mum', but I was crying, and went to the toilets.

His memory seemed to capture not only the shame he felt about being Pakistani, but also the humiliation and shame of not defending his mother. I asked him how his mother dressed and he answered with a faint smile, as though the memory of his mother's appearance now gave him pleasure…

Yes, she wears her shalwar kameez, and she used to wear this white furry coat and all her gold jewellery.

It's funny, I feel a bit tearful at the moment anyway, but I'm proud of my parents today. I really respect what they have. I have a different relationship with them now from my adolescent years when I really didn't want anything to do with Pakistani culture. I just wanted to be one of the lads. I just wanted to fit in with those people.

Apart from his skin colour and his mother's dress, religion also set him apart from other children:

Also I think religion was forced onto us as children. A God of fear: if you don't do that God's going to punish you and on the day of judgement you will burn. I've got so much of that belief system instilled in me right to this day. I mean, I'm not a practising Muslim but I don't eat pork.

I'd read the Koran in Arabic by the time I was eight years old. I don't understand a word of Arabic but I was taught to recite and memorise the Koran. That's the really peculiar thing about Asian families, they seem to think you've just got to read it in Arabic and go on your parents' word of what it's actually saying. A lot of Asian families *do* learn Arabic and understand the Koran, but I never understood what I was praying, or saying.

Impact of culture on a developing sense of identity

During the first two years at secondary school Omar was constantly involved in playground fights, defending himself but also instigating fights. I asked him how he had coped with the bullying and the assault on his identity during adolescence. He told me he coped by steeping himself in his religion and by being the 'good boy' of the family:

> The emphasis is on boys anyway in those families, and my two older brothers weren't doing well at school – they got into the wrong crowd, so all of a sudden I had this focus on me. So I used to pray quite a lot. I used to stick with my mum quite a lot.

He was seen as his mother's favourite, something he views now as a way he kept himself safe:

> I've always been sort of teased about being the one who…Mum extra cared for. I've definitely got a sense of being my mum's favourite. I always stayed with her and, like I say, the obedient conforming sort of safety.

Omar also coped by spending time at a friend's house:

> I used to have a friend named James, quite a middle class family they were, and I spent a lot of time round there – beautiful house they had. He had this play room, his own bedroom. I wanted that kind of life.

> Around the age of twelve James and I started shoplifting. I suppose I was the instigator. We were both caught and charged at the police station and I wasn't allowed to see him ever again. I used to steal toys – and actually I think that came from being around my brother, and seeing him stealing. My brother had already been to prison by then for breaking somebody's jaw. I remember visiting him in prison. And my other brother was getting arrested as well.

> My oldest brother fought to a different level, trying to get that 'fear' type of respect – got in with a gang – went down a criminal route. My other brother was the same, not much of a fighter, but he was very mischievous and getting caught stealing and getting arrested, and running away from home. There was a lot of that going on.

It seemed clear that Omar's life during those first two years of secondary school was severely impacted by being bullied at school and on top of that his family seemed to be falling apart:

> My older sister tried to kill herself on a number of occasions. She was sectioned. Horrible! I don't really know what was going on.

She must have been at an all-girls secondary school. It's really much more difficult for girls in Asian families. She wanted to go out, she wanted to have fun with her friends or go to a disco and she wasn't allowed out ever. I was against her going out too, without realising what she was going through. My parents sent my sisters to Pakistan for a year and enrolled them into an Islamic school so I didn't see them for about a year. And they sent my older brother to Pakistan to be with my grandparents, to sort him out. I suppose there was a bit of fear of me being sent to Pakistan too.

A new story of childhood fear

As he was remembering the fear of being sent away from home Omar was thrown back into remembering the fear he felt at a much earlier stage of his life:

I can remember being really, really anxious as a child, and I always used to think 'there's something wrong with me'. I used to get my mum to take me to the hospital and the doctor used to say it was anxiety.

I used to be really, really scared. I have memories of having nightmares and being really, really anxious and therefore I'd want to be with the family and then I'd start praying. That would give me a bit of safety. Being religious protected me. I think that was to do with things that were going on around me.

As he spoke about his extreme anxiety as a child I wondered what it was about his life during his primary school years that had caused him to be so fearful. When he had first begun to tell his story his memories of those years had been of 'heydays' with 'fond memories'. It seemed clear that fear could have been caused by being racially abused in the secondary school but at this point he was talking about a much earlier stage in his life.

I asked if he meant that he was anxious *inside* the family or out in the world. He responded that he was anxious both inside the family *and* outside in the world. He then remarked that, as he was speaking to me, he was having memories about his life and finding it difficult to keep on a 'constant track'. He began to sound slightly confused and I noticed that his language had begun to move in and out of the present tense. I was concerned that talking about his childhood may have been triggering him back into trauma.

I reassured him that we could stop, or take a break, and that the story did not have to be coherent at this stage: that we could co-construct the meaning afterwards. And when he said he wanted to continue I asked him if he could say more about asking his mother to take him to the doctor's because he thought there was something wrong with him.

Yes, I have a memory of my mum taking me to the hospital and they'd given me the all clear. I remember coming out crying, because I knew there *must* be something wrong with me.

Having something to prove

At this point he returned to the period of his life around the age of 14 when his family moved to inner London. The move had allowed him to distance himself from an episode at his previous school where he had been badly beaten in a fight he had initiated with a boy who had previously called him racist names. However, Omar identified *himself* as the 'troublemaker', and stated that he might have lashed out with no provocation:

> I did have something to prove. There was something inside me that…I wanted to beat people up, almost…I don't *really* want to beat someone up. It was more like…dignity and respect…trying to gain some respect with my peers. The only way I can see that happening was through violence. There wasn't any other way.

I found myself wondering where he had learned that being violent was the only way to gain respect, imagining he may have learned this from his oldest brother whose prison sentence had earned him a reputation as a 'tough guy'. Omar had used his brother's reputation to scare off the racists at school:

> A lot of people were scared of him and after my brother came into the school and threatened one of the lads I started getting respect from the kids in the top years who were saying, 'Do you know whose brother that is?'

Who do I hang around with?

The school he went to in London, unlike his first comprehensive school, was a mixed race environment.

> …and that really threw me because you'd get a couple of Asian kids, you had black kids, white kids, and it was quite confusing actually. Who do I hang around with?

> I started hanging around with the Asian kids who were very much more into their studies. It was the start of the GCSE years. My parents wanted me to take sciences, they wanted me to be a doctor basically [*laughing*] – every Asian kid has this – their parents wanting them to be doctors. So these Asian kids were doing GCSE chemistry, physics and biology, maths. I liked some of the sciences actually, but not all of them, but I got into this competitive thing with some of them. They were really bright and it was going okay until I started noticing that they were getting really bullied because they were the 'nerds', studying all the time. They used to get bullied by the white kids *and* the black kids. I was quite confused. I didn't like the idea of getting bullied again, and then it was that whole 'embarrassed to be an Asian thing'…not wanting to be Asian.

> In London the kids were a lot bigger – they looked a lot different. I think by then my whole confidence was shattered really. I remember being really scared of taking on these groups of big black guys. I was pretty much lost really. I was fascinated by the whole network – trying to work out who's the toughest in the school and wondering, 'Where do I get in here in order to be safe?'

Earning respect through sport

Omar was aware that he needed to work out who held the power in this network so that he could align himself on the right side. Having escaped from the bullying in his previous school he wanted to make sure he did not end up being bullied again. He explained how he managed to find a safe niche through sport:

> I used to *love* playing cricket when I was younger. I was quite an obsessive child, and in primary school I was very good at sport. When I first moved to London I tied a cricket ball to a rope attached to the washing line in the back garden and started practising a straight bat. So I got to be quite a good cricket player and met up with the local kids. I remember that summer was really nice actually. I got into the school cricket team.

> At this time I'd been getting bullied and nobody liked me. I was a new kid – nobody knew where I was coming from. I entered for the school cricket team, so they put me in as number nine batsman and we went to play against this public school where there were full-on cricket players and they were absolutely annihilating us. But they couldn't get me out. It was one of those great days…I stayed in, and I think that's where I gained a bit of respect…from the white kids *and* the black kids and they were saying: 'OK, you're number one batsman next week.' And from there I started making friends with one of the white kids. He used to go out and have a fag. I definitely wasn't into education any longer – I was into sports, and having a fag.

Discovering drugs

Drugs are commonly obtained from older siblings who arouse curiosity or competitiveness in their younger siblings, and legitimise their use.

> When I first went to London I remember it being really boring, didn't have any friends, being indoors a lot of the time, so I used to go back to where we lived before…to see my brother and stay with him. My brother had got into drugs by then and I remember having a chunk of puff, cannabis, chipping it up, having a smoke, and James, that guy I got caught shoplifting with, I managed to meet him again.

> There's this one incident where I remember needing a suit and going to borrow one from my brother. I remember finding about four or five ecstasy tablets in the pocket and taking them.

> Like I say, when I first moved to London I was very much with Asian kids. Mum was protective, wouldn't let me out, plus she didn't like me going around with Indian kids, she'd be saying, 'Are they Muslim? Oh, they are Hindu?' The whole religion side came into it, found myself having to defend that. I don't think she wanted me to go out with anybody really.

During these two years – when I was supposed to be studying for GCSEs – quite a lot happened. I stopped doing PE classes, and in the end I started hanging about with this white kid who was the toughest in the school. So I got in with that crowd, and they were smoking cigarettes, cannabis. I do remember taking amphetamines. The guy who I was hanging about with was selling drugs, eighths of puff, cannabis, small amounts really, and he got these tablets and gave them to all of us.

I asked him when he got into more serious drug taking and he replied:

Around fifteen. I used to smoke cannabis heavily – and alcohol. [*long pause*] I think I was a heroin addict by the time I was eighteen.

This sudden jump – from smoking cannabis at the age of 15 to being addicted to heroin at 18 – took me by surprise. Omar noticed this jump too and was curious about how he had leaped in those intervening years. I asked about the years from 15 to 18:

I'd failed my GCSEs and gone back to take them again and I got expelled from school in the sixth form for selling cannabis. And then they put me in a college down the road. I was expelled from there for being drunk and disorderly.

And at that time I had contact with my brother who was a drug dealer. It's a way in, isn't it – cannabis? It's almost like it gives you some sort of identity and you fit in. You're a drug dealer, and it was cool, get a bit of hash and sort out your friends or...

A new story of physical abuse within the home

I asked how his parents dealt with his drug using and dealing, and suddenly he began to talk about his early years again:

I remember my parents being disappointed and I remember kind of...I'm not...my dad was quite violent when we were younger – really violent – to me, but a lot more to my older brothers. He just used to pick up anything and whack you with it. I mean literally anything, like a cricket bat, anything, because he just had this temper – which was really scary.

I was very surprised by this sudden revelation. We had been talking for over an hour on the links between early childhood trauma and subsequent drug misuse and this was the first time Omar had mentioned his father's violence. I pointed this out to him:

I know. I know, I know. Yes, we were all very scared. He was a big man.

I asked if this had been why he had been very anxious as a child. Was he frightened of his father?

Don't know if that was to do with it, still can't...I was scared of his temper. I was scared of my mum as well. She...was violent, not as violent as my dad. And both

> my parents were very critical, and very abusive with that, 'Oh you're failures', or 'You're bad kids', or 'Why do we have to have the worst kids in the world?' There was a lot going on. My sister taking her overdoses…

So Omar, whilst being physically and verbally abused as a young child, also watched his siblings being abused. He began to speak of his father's religious hypocrisy:

> D'you know what? He was a Muslim man but it's only come to light recently that he drank a lot. I used to sit in a treatment centre and listen to people saying, 'My dad sexually abused me, my dad was violent because he was a drunk.' And I used to sit there thinking, 'Well, *my* dad never drank, but he was quite capable of violence.'

> But then recently I have memories of him having a drink, little flashes of it. So I'm not too sure really how to excuse his behaviour. It's almost like I want the alcohol to excuse his behaviour.

> Nowadays he's an old man and he's become very religious. He's at Mecca at the moment – both my parents are. And back then, he was a big guy, really healthy, and he just used to lash out. We didn't see a lot of him, but when we did, he would lose it – because he used to hit Mum as well. And those kind of arguments…I've forgotten about all that – and trying to separate them…all of us trying to protect my mum from my dad. He used to have this fuse, just go ballistic. You would be in fear of your life actually – my mum as well. But my mum's violence wasn't on his level, but we were scared of my mum, she used to hit us as well.

I felt myself shiver as he spoke of being in fear of his life, imagining what it might have been like for those children, and his mother, and I was making theoretical sense of his dreadful anxiety as a child. I was understanding the additional distress of being told by the doctor that there was nothing wrong when he had been trying to tell people there *was* something *really* wrong – but without a frame of reference through which to understand his experiences, or language with which to communicate what was wrong, he was left to suffer alone.

We know now that living in such an environment can leave a child with chronic post-traumatic stress (PTS) and the links between early PTS and drug misuse in adulthood have been made over and over again (see Chapter 2). I made those points to Omar, knowing that as a psychologist he would understand the language. I also acknowledged the cultural/family norms that lead children to believe that this is 'normal'. He responded:

> We've actually got a family video from when I was at primary school. I was one of the extroverts then, and Dad took us to Chessington Zoo and we're like six brats, taking the piss out of each other – such a fun day. And we bring the family camera back home and we're still doing some shots because we wanted to send a video to my grandparents in Pakistan. And there's a bit on the video…one of my brothers is upstairs watching a film, but we're meant to be downstairs acting in front of the camera. Dad just loses it.

You can see it on the film. You're hearing us screaming, getting battered upstairs – me and my brother. Then the camera cuts to me. I'm on my mum's lap in bits, crying. I don't know where my other brother is [*he laughs as he speaks*].

This is something I don't really talk about, because it's upsetting for me. It's funny how I can just dismiss it.

As I picture him seeking protection from his mother I began to wonder how he had coped with her being sometimes protective and sometimes abusive. Like him and his siblings, she was also a victim of their father's abuse – as well as being an unsafe person to be around sometimes. Maybe his positive memories of primary school are because it was the *only* safe place for him, growing up without a secure base at home.

I observed to Omar that he seemed to have been triggered into remembering his experience of physical abuse as a child when I asked how he became a heroin addict. I was interested in how he understood that. Up to then, as with many young people, his story of substance misuse had been part of a social and recreational activity, following a fairly slow and steady progress from first using tobacco, to smoking cannabis, to dealing cannabis, to using alcohol. But suddenly, he had introduced heroin into the conversation. This led him back into his story of the years between 15 and 18.

Humiliation and alcohol

When I was still at school I started hanging around with a lot of black kids from one of the estates near us, and I got into this whole black culture – wanting to be part of them, dressing like them, sounding like them, and getting involved with a lot of crime with them. I thought it was cool, and I felt safe. Some of the older black kids used to rob us and force us to rob handbags and bring them to them. I think I got more into drug dealing and I was drinking a lot, just found alcohol was a real release from everything and I'm selling cannabis – £10, £15 bags.

There were women involved…to be honest I used to like women when I was younger. My first girlfriend was an Asian girl at college. I remember it being a hard chase, trying to chat her up, and then when I finally got there it was really nice. I enjoyed it.

Mm, so I'm still having problems with these older black kids who are robbing me and she couldn't really handle me drinking. I was also using LSD with one of my brothers.

I remember her finishing with me, and then going out with her again. After that she finished with me again. It was a really embarrassing kind of ending, because it wasn't dignified on my part, more like me pleading with her and she got her ex-boyfriend involved and was *really*, really horrible.

> I remember *really* drinking heavily after that – a lot of spirits – a young lad drinking a lot of spirits, vodkas, heavy, heavy drinking. And I think, that's what shifted it – that experience of loving somebody so much, and them leaving you and the whole embarrassment…of getting robbed by these black kids in front of her.

Children who have coped with physical abuse may become very sensitive to humiliation in later life. If they coped with the early abuse by detaching from their experience, they may have become a 'witness' to their own humiliation, as they plead for it to stop. Current experiences of humiliation trigger past experiences and become unbearable.

I sensed the power of Omar's humiliation but missed the chance to ask him what the 'it' was that shifted, assuming that he meant his drug misuse. Did the loss of his girlfriend under such humiliating circumstances change the purpose of his substance use from a social and recreational activity to a means by which he avoided being overwhelmed by feelings of humiliation related to his early trauma?

I commented that in spite of enjoying the feeling of giving and receiving love he still needed to use substances. It seemed as if her love was not enough to make up for the negative parts of his life.

> She wasn't enough, yes, exactly! That's what she used to say in fact. She wasn't nourishing me enough; she wasn't filling me enough.

Living a drug dealer lifestyle

Alcohol had given him the confidence he had lost through being bullied again by the black guys who stole from him and forced him to steal from others and also helped him to deal with his girlfriend's rejection. At this point, feeling lost and alone, he met an older Asian man who took him under his wing, fed him large amounts of drugs and set him up to deal large quantities. His new friend introduced him to a different kind of world and, because he was respected by the older black men, Omar felt safe around him.

> Eventually I got into selling ounces. I was making more connections and making money, getting fancy stuff and nice cars, meeting nice people. That was a different world really, pubs and bars, nice areas. I think that became my mission, to become like this drug dealer – and like my brother. I remember wanting to be this kind of, almost like a gangster. I wanted what he had – respect.

> I wanted to be like these guys. Cocaine, ecstasy, lots of ecstasy. I started to sell ecstasy tablets, cocaine, yes. Little bit muffled around this…

He noticed that his memory seemed 'muffled' around this period of his life. This seemed to parallel what he might have felt like when using so many different types of drugs at that time.

> It's all part of the adrenalin buzz, to go out, and being flash around it. Your leather jacket, the designer clothes, enjoying it with other people – still not having much

luck with women but I think I was more interested in the alcohol and the drugs really, and the cocaine came hand in hand with that.

Becoming a heroin user

Up until then, Omar had maintained a degree of self-respect by seeing himself as doing better than the 'smackheads', living a drug dealer's high-living lifestyle. He did not see himself as an 'addict' because drug misuse had not yet come to dominate his life, and in other areas he was doing better than before. Although Omar was at that time selling heroin, he was not yet using it. I asked him about becoming a heroin user:

> I was in a pub in London and I got chatting to a guy who'd been in prison in Spain for trafficking cannabis, so we got talking and went back to his flat. We did a lot of cocaine, drinking. He said, 'Have you got any coke left?' I said, 'No, but I've got some of this' – which was a wrap of heroin. He goes, 'What's that?' I said, 'Heroin.'

> I'd never seen anybody use it before. So he just put it on some foil and smoked the whole lot. So that was it, he'd call me up and I'd sell him heroin, and then one day we were really drunk and coked up to our eyeballs and I said, 'I want some.' It went from there really.

> I remember not liking it at first, but getting used to that kind of escapism basically, because it was all really about going to a different world, and it was perfect for coming down off of cocaine.

Experiencing 'cold turkey'

Up to then, his experiences of drug using all sounded fairly positive, in that his life seemed to have improved in the ways he wanted: it gave him a chance to escape the pain of the loss of his girlfriend, and it improved his level of confidence – so I asked him when it had all started to go wrong.

> I was going out drinking and spending quite a lot. I remember getting into debt with some people and I had a heroin habit by then. My dad was in Pakistan, and I thought, 'I'll go to Pakistan to come off it.'

> I'd been on it probably for near enough a year and I'd never experienced a cold turkey until I got to Pakistan. I actually thought I had the flu for a week: it was boiling hot over there but I had cold shivers, and then it really clicked.

> I'd always had money, so I didn't have to go without [heroin] and it was only in Pakistan that it first hit me. Strange experience, Pakistan – because I didn't know what was happening to me. I started praying again. I was really lost over there. I was there for about six weeks, staying with my dad.

★   ★   ★   ★

The tape clicked off and outside darkness had fallen. I realised we had reached the point in his story where he was beginning to realise he was 'addicted' to heroin. I knew that by accepting his addiction there was a possibility of transformation. I wanted to hear how and when that happened but I also knew we had to postpone hearing the rest of the story until another day.

I felt very connected with the young man sitting before me whom I had known such a short time. He had allowed me to know the circumstances of his life that had conspired to shape his identity. So much pain in one short life is hard to hear and hard to tell.

We talked for a while longer, of this and that, of how Omar felt now that our time today had ended, and if he would like to tell me the rest of his story at some time in the future. We talked about what might happen next: about me sending him the transcript to read and check out, and to alter anything he needed in order to protect his identity.

I was aware that he might feel churned up after talking about so many difficult areas of his life and wished we could have ended on a more positive note. But Omar seemed energised by the telling of his story, and enthusiastic about meeting again in the New Year that lay ahead.

I waved him goodbye from the front door, turned back into the hallway where the Christmas tree lights were twinkling on and off, and began to prepare for the arrival of my grandchildren later that evening.

Chapter 4

Omar's Story, Part 2

It had taken almost a month for us to arrange our second meeting and, having done so, Omar had cancelled because of flu. When we eventually met up again the weather was harsh but inside the conservatory we were warm and cosy. I had sent Omar the transcript of our first meeting and suggested that we both read it prior to meeting again so we could pick up where he had left off. I enquired how he had been feeling about our previous conversation and he answered:

Omar: Actually since the last time we met – which seems like quite a while ago now – I've been talking to my therapist about my anxiety as a child. *Now* it fits into place with my dad's violent behaviour, and I had never made the connection before. It's really odd – I've never looked at it that way. It was really interesting to make that connection and to be aware of what was going on for me at the time.

Kim: So you hadn't made that connection in previous therapy?

Omar: No, no…

Kim: It seemed to come up quite late in the conversation, didn't it? I was quite surprised.

Omar: Yes, it's almost like I'd blocked it out really. It's like it's there, but isn't there – but now it's very visible to me that that *was* going on and it was very scary for me as a child. That definitely *must* have had an impact. And my mum and her part – there was quite a lot going on for me over the years. I was a very quiet child. It must have led to some sort of anxieties.

I was curious about how our conversation had helped him to make those connections even when therapy had not. I am aware of a growing literature about how the boundaries between therapy and research are often blurred when using qualitative methods. Indeed, in some cases participants have found research conversations *more* therapeutic than therapy itself. So I asked him how he saw the differences and/or similarities between our conversation and counselling/ therapy.

Omar: Yes, I don't see it as counselling. It has its similarities, but no, I think it's really *me* restructuring or mapping. It's almost like mapping my whole life, and…yes, putting it together, because it is pretty much all over the place. And I don't think in therapy you get that opportunity – well I haven't really – unless you're given some sort of homework or a timeline or something.

Kim: Ordering it?

Omar: Yeah.

Kim: So the telling of the story meant that you needed to order it? And I've helped you with that a bit in saying, 'What happened then?', or, 'How old were you when that happened?' That's kind of kept you a bit on track?

Omar: Yes definitely, because it has been all over the place and I think once I finally read the whole…I think I'll get a good…it's almost like a jigsaw puzzle, that's the way I look at it: it's almost like missing pieces making more connections. It's been a very useful experience. Like I say, I keep keying in on that part about the connection with the anxiety as a child – that has baffled me for years. I've always wondered what was going on for me that I was so anxious…and it sounds so simple after hearing what was going on in my life with the violence. It was just like, 'Of course – *that* was what was going on in my life!' I feel relieved.

I was reading the transcript just now actually, catching up on where we'd left off and I was talking about being in Pakistan and experiencing cold turkey and coming back again to this country. I was quite contented in Pakistan actually: it was quite nice because I was drug-free for a while – probably going through a lot of physical change [*small laugh*]. Coming back here I just fell into the same kind of patterns of behaviour, going back to the pubs, drinking.

The next few years were pretty much like that. I was becoming more of a heroin addict, injecting myself and using different drugs like crack. I became 'a drug addict' – I needed to get a fix before I had a cold turkey.

Becoming homeless and sleeping rough

Omar explained that this was when he defined himself as an addict. He had woken up to the fact that he was 'completely and utterly taken over by the drug'. He knew he needed heroin to keep well.

I was actually homeless. Once I ran out of drugs money I started burgling my families' houses. They pretty much kicked me out and cut off all ties with me. That was really a strange experience. My mum was completely in denial that I had a drug problem.

So for just over two years, from twenty-two to twenty-four, I was always short of money and trying to beg – robbing people, shoplifting. I was sleeping rough: hanging about in central London in cold weather shelters, mixing with other heroin addicts. You learn so much from hardened heroin addicts who've been at it a lot longer than you. About different ways of getting rid of the pain, different *types* of drugs, different ways of injecting, what you can inject and what you can't inject. I was pretty much injecting anything – pharmaceutical drugs, pills…so it's a whole new arena really, for understanding drugs. At that stage I was in a very bad state. I just completely lost respect for myself.

It was hard to imagine that he was talking about the same young man who was sitting in front of me. I thought about how often I had seen people such as he was describing sitting in doorways or tramping the streets of Bristol, and wondered about what had brought them to this. I felt a huge sadness as I imagined his suffering, his loneliness and despair.

I was on the streets right up to going into treatment really. But those last two years were very hard work. I felt a lot of fear on the streets. It was just about waking up, feeling sick, going out and doing some crazy things to get money – back and forth, back and forth, a daily process…just wanting to die really. Waking up, heroin fix and just really not wanting to face reality at all.

I asked him what had kept him going, what had kept him alive? He paused before answering:

I don't know. I do remember praying at one stage and just asking God to get me out of this. It was almost like there was *something* there keeping me going, this little glimmer of something. I just didn't know what to do. I was stuck in this rut. I just couldn't get out of it.

I asked him if he had *wanted* help and if there were people around who offered help:

I definitely wanted a way out but I couldn't see a way out. No, there was absolutely no-one. I did try to get help. I had been into drug services to get a methadone script just to maintain me but I kept failing the tests. You have to test clean to get a methadone script. That's basically what I needed – more methadone. It would hold you so you don't feel sick for two days till you get some heroin or crack.

That shelter I lived in was horrible – eight men sharing a room. You'd get robbed in there. There was a lot of partying, people dying: it was like a living hell. You'd get breakfast in the morning, go out robbing and come back and there'd be all sorts of shady characters. There was a guy I met there called John who looked after me – not really looking after me but if he had a bit of gear… There were four of us actually, and there were older lads that'd been using drugs for a lot longer, but yes they kind of looked after us. They used to get me to rob and do stuff which they didn't really want to do, so it was that sort of relationship, not like a loving caring relationship. I still thought of it as…it's good to have friends rather than not have friends out there. I've done the same as well to other lads. A lot of madness going on. I've done a lot of crazy things under the influence of drugs.

Turning point

At his lowest ebb, Omar met an outreach worker who approached him on the street and asked if he wanted to come off drugs. At this time he was unable to inject himself because he had an abscess on his arm. With his arm out of action he was also unable to shoplift, so he knew he needed help, and although he'd never been in a detox unit he had heard that it initially involved being prescribed high doses of methadone which were reduced over time. He knew he had nothing to lose so he was admitted to a residential detox unit for three weeks. Few drug misusers are successful the first time they attempt to detox and, like others in the group, Omar left before the three weeks were up.

> Coming off drugs with a lot of other people who were all in the same boat is hard – we were all equally fucked up. That was my first experience of being in a group and talking about feelings. There were so many feelings going on. There were some nice women there, some nice caring people looking after us. But I left there because I had a bit of a fight with a guy.

A condition of admission to the detox unit was that residents had to book a place in a rehabilitation centre to follow on from their period of detoxification.

> I rang up my oldest brother and said, 'Right, I've cracked it. I'm off the drugs. Come and pick me up in London.' So he came to pick me up and took me back home. Then I had to go by train to the rehab, so they gave me money for the train fare, and that was it. I was gone again for another few weeks, just using and going back into the shelters – because that's what I was used to.

> I just couldn't handle myself when I came out of detox. I wasn't on anything for about a week, first time in years.

Relapse

Omar described how his detox left him without any means to deal with the feelings that had driven him to drug misuse. Being with his family, even briefly, whilst also being newly connected with his previously buried feelings, had aroused his rage and sadness:

> I just kept crying. I was very angry: my feelings were all over the place. I was in pain. I'd always been angry with the family. I couldn't handle being cared for, or being overly protected by them, like a baby. It was more like seeing reality again I suppose. There was a lot of anger in me about what I'd done, a lot of stuff coming up from treatment. But I do remember actually being in the kitchen at one point, and my sister's purse was there and I took some money and went to phone a dealer, and then I put the money back. I really didn't want to do it but I had to do it in the end.

So for that few weeks I just went off again and then, once I ran out of money, I got back on the phone saying, 'I need some help.' This time round they basically said, 'We're going to take you to the rehab.'

The night before rehab I went out for some drinks and in the end I was just doing loads of cocaine. I just couldn't face reality. I really fought it that day. They pretty much stuck me in the car and dragged me down to the rehab and pushed me into it.

Later I put a complaint in the about the guy at the rehab because when I phoned up I'd said, 'Well there's been a delay.' He didn't believe me so it was quite comical, because I went back to see my social worker. She said, 'We could put you into another type of programme, but this one is a really good one. If I ring him up and maybe patch things up...?'

Meeting positive role models

She was the first heroin addict in recovery that I've ever met and she was a social worker. Amazing, really amazing, she kind of stopped my brother telling her what I needed and that was really cool. She just said, '*He* needs to tell me what he wants without you speaking for him.' And then she put him to the side and actually explained to me about her being a heroin addict. She said how she was from Thailand – born into a family where her father smoked opium for eighty years and died an addict. It was fairly normal in her country – so it was an amazing story.

I asked Omar what it meant to have a social worker who was herself 'in recovery':

It meant somebody understood! It was really nice to talk to somebody who actually understood. And I trusted what she was saying to me. I'm not sure I'd have trusted the person or their judgement if I hadn't known she'd been an addict.

She really emphasised the fact that this would be beneficial to my life. I didn't know much about rehabs. I really thought it was a place where they teach you to shave and wash, cook, didn't know it was anything about therapy intervention so I trusted her judgement.

I'd forgotten about getting into rehab. It was really tough...you have to get into rehab clean: you're not allowed to be using. So I got in the door and they challenged me immediately. This woman counsellor just said, 'Look at the state of you, you're unshaven, you're unwashed', blah blah. I thought, 'God, what have I got myself into here?' And then this big Scottish guy called Mac came in to do an assessment – the one I put a complaint against. He was very challenging at the assessment. He asked me, 'Why do you want to get sober?' I said, 'I want to be normal.' He said, 'D'you know what normal is like?'

I really didn't take to him – but he was really gentle, saying, 'You've had a hard time getting here. Are you still using?' It's funny how you still hide things at that stage, but I said yes. He said, 'Okay, best thing to do is get yourself washed up, and we'll give you some drugs to get you to sleep – just something to take the edge off and relax .

you.' He didn't have to do that, which was really nice of him. My brother gave him a tenner for me to get some fags and then that was it – they went.

That was pretty much my journey to here. Treatment was really hard work, but what an amazing experience. I stayed in treatment for seven months.

Being in treatment

The programme offered by the rehab Omar attended was a challenging self-empowerment programme where residents were taught to admit to and examine their behaviours and acknowledge their responsibility for the harm they had done to themselves and others whilst misusing drugs.

It almost took me three months to realise what I'd done with my life, to get grounded, about hurting my family and robbing people and what I'd done to myself. I had an emotional breakdown whilst I was in treatment. For about two weeks I just couldn't stop crying. I had a lot of realisations, but *that* was a turning point for me.

I asked him how he managed to stay with such a tough regime:

I think the relationship I had with Mac was a really powerful one. A lot of people in the centre would say that about him. Maybe fear – it might have been a fear relationship – because he was quite a presence, but he was coming from a caring place, you just knew this. He'd challenge you – he'd annihilate you by taking you to one side – he did it to me many times, called me a fraud.

He always used to say, 'I'm only treating you the way you've treated people in your entire life.' I must admit, it was quite a harsh programme. I needed a kick up the backside and a good shaking up. I think I would have just abused a gently, gently approach.

It took many talks with him to keep me there when I wanted to leave. I'd have my stuff packed and he'd say, 'OK, what do you want to do?' And I'd say, 'I want to go and have a drink. I think I deserve a drink after all this time.' And he'd help me to weigh it up. He'd just say, 'Well, why don't you just stick it out for six months? Make a decision after that.' He'd say a lot of things like that, practical things, very helpful. Many, many times I went through that.

Leaving treatment

Omar was 'terrified' when he left the treatment centre and moved into a flat on his own. Mac had persuaded him not to return to London but to stay in the locality where he had the option to attend courses at the local college. He was in a fragile state and still processing the traumatic experiences of his life hitherto.

I was scared of people. I used to have a lot of panic attacks. I wouldn't go out. I was very anxious. It was all the same feelings from back when I was a child really. But by now I started getting to know a few people who'd also been in treatment who were living in the same area, and that was really helpful. I remember crying a lot, walking down the beach, being alone a lot. It was really like processing my feelings and my past again and again…

I asked him if he had spoken about the physical abuse he had experienced as a child while he was in treatment and he explained that although he had mentioned it, and his counsellor had helped him understand cognitively how that may have affected him, he had not really grasped the full import, or connected with those experiences emotionally. He was still avoiding the pain by excusing his father's behaviour in terms of them being 'bad kids' who deserved that kind of treatment, still trying to preserve the image of his parents as 'all good'.

> They used to say to me, 'You've got a lot of misplaced loyalties. You never talk about your family because you feel so guilty.' I still do in a sense. I always talk about how good they are now. I've got a relationship with them now and I've never brought these things to their attention.

As he spoke about this Omar explained that he was beginning to realise that he did not have to give up on the 'goodness' of his parents by acknowledging that their behaviour was not *always* good, or that sometimes 'good' people do 'bad' things, and that he can still love his parents even whilst acknowledging the harm they did to him and his siblings.

Standing on his own two feet

Omar had coped with his family during and after treatment by putting up rigid boundaries, afraid that if he let them near him, or accepted any help from them, they would resume their old patterns of trying to control his life.

> In treatment it's all about boundaries and preparing yourself to change and not relying on other people. You do it yourself. I saw that my family enabled my flaws in the past. So I *had* to do this myself, because it's really important, and there was a lot of stuff in my family about arranged marriages and 'You be a doctor, do this or that…'

> Mac said to me, 'Just lead your own life. Part of this is that you're trying to live your life for your parents.' And I think that was really helpful – but I almost took it to an extreme. I wouldn't let them give me anything, even on my birthday.

After leaving the treatment centre Omar was offered an office job back at the treatment centre, recognising that nowadays this would not happen until after being 'clean' for two years. In some ways this was a kind of sheltered employment for Omar because if he had a 'bad day' the counsellors who had known him in treatment gave him support. Later, he was employed as a drugs worker alongside the counsellors. This was when he became fascinated by therapy, a fascination that probably led him into his current professional life. By this time Mac had become like a 'father figure' and they grew very close.

Whilst working at the centre Omar starting taking courses at the college: first, a diploma in computing, which he didn't take to, and then a counselling skills course, followed by an in-house addiction diploma. Then he went to university to do a psychology degree.

> I didn't have any qualifications, absolutely nothing. So I kind of talked my way into that course. I told them I'd had a lot of problems in the past, and they accepted me, but I didn't know what to expect. It was hard work, being at that level of education and having no idea of how to write an essay properly.

Going out into the world alone

After some time Omar began to realise that he was becoming complacent and that there was still something missing in his life. He was living alone, going to work and university but he was without friends and still keeping his family at arm's length.

> But like I say, I was working hard but something was always missing. I wasn't completely happy and I was very confrontational. I think I got that from Mac. I was very angry, taking a lot of that anger into the centre and I'd use that – almost displacing anger onto clients. I'd be saying, 'You're not doing it right, do it this way otherwise you're out.' It was almost like telling myself that, through other people. And so, in hindsight, I was quite abusive – which wouldn't be the way I'd work today.

Discovering AA and spirituality

A major shift came when Omar visited his sister in the USA and went off travelling on his own for three months. He described having a 'mad type of breakdown' while he was there, wanting to drink and use drugs again. Feeling terrified that he might relapse, having gone through so much to become drug-free, he rang Alcoholics Anonymous and was taken to a meeting:

> It was the first time I'd been to a meeting of my own accord and I went for nearly three months while I was abroad. I had a fantastic connection with the American fellowship. That's what I needed. I was scared of people but I *needed* to be with people, to overcome that fear. That's one thing that was missing in my recovery.

I was making sense of Omar's fear of people by understanding that physical violence perpetrated by the very people upon whom a child depends leaves them fearful of being close to anybody. He had frequently mentioned how he had always been hyper-alert to the possibility of being bullied again and how, by working out who was the toughest person and making friends with them, he gave himself the best chance of being safe. He had become independent and self-reliant, not necessarily out of choice but as a response to his disconnected fear of being close to people. I found myself wondering if the close relationship he had developed with Mac was also partly out of his need to be safe around a frightening person, who in some ways might have reminded him of his father.

> I've always been pretty independent, and what I feared was being co-dependent, and I needed to be with people to get that kind of balance really. I wouldn't ask for help. And with Mac – there was a lot of pleasing there – I wouldn't tell him everything because I knew what he'd say – like a father type of thing. So I wasn't completely honest, but AA was a perfect outlet.

When Omar returned to the UK he found an AA sponsor and started going to meetings – much against Mac's advice. Mac had himself fallen out with AA and talked negatively about the organisation. Omar's decision to continue with AA seemed almost like a young person making a stand against his parent in an effort to claim a separate and adult identity. Omar went on to explain how AA meetings help him, even today:

> AA really knocks my arrogance out of me, my cockiness and know-it-allness: it really grounds me. Another part of AA that's been good for me is that I lack a lot of spirituality in my life and it gives me that connection…it's a spiritual type of programme: twelve-step orientated. It made a lot of sense to me, without me knowing what it was really all about.

> During the next few years I started a counselling business with Mac. He was diagnosed with liver cancer, and basically within about two weeks he passed away. To see a big guy like that die in two weeks was absolutely horrible and I think it's taken me these next three years to come out of that. I'm living without Mac or anybody really. I mean I've got a good relationship with my sponsor which I've been building up over four or five years, but I'm still missing some sort of guide you know, the sort of relationship I had with Mac. He wasn't just a guide on a spiritual programme, he was in every area of my life. I always put Mac down as the father I didn't have.

After Mac's death Omar sold the counselling organisation they were setting up together and went into the business of providing supported housing for people after they leave drugs treatment centres. He is now providing for others what he most needed for himself. By using the learning he has gained through his negative life experiences Omar has turned them into something positive that he can now offer other people to support them on their journey towards health.

★ ★ ★ ★

Bearing in mind that Omar offered his story for this research in part because he wanted to learn something about narrative enquiry, I was curious to know if he felt he had achieved that goal. In response to my query he responded:

Yes. I am learning definitely from being a participant in a piece of research. Do you know what? It's been a really cool experience, and when I was reading my transcript today, I was thinking, 'Wow, it's all being formulated for me, it's almost like my whole story is there.' I'm sure there's probably going to be bits that come up but…I've always thought about getting my story together. I keep thinking about emailing it to my sponsor, just so he can get a real good insight into what's been going on.

I think it's been really useful, very insightful, especially when I was talking about the younger years, because I've been having problems opening up with my therapist, in the sense of thinking, 'There's no use in going back into the past again, is there?!'

Chapter 5

Becky's Story

Becky volunteered for this study when she heard about it from another counsellor whose work I supervised. We met first to discuss the pragmatics, purposes, processes and ethical implications of the research, so that she could make an informed decision about her involvement. This kind of research is ethically complicated because telling personal stories can make people feel vulnerable, as well as being in some ways therapeutic, even when that is not the primary intention.

Becky's story draws attention to the discourses that influence how we construct our sense of self and identity. It also shows how, in the act of narration, she presents a range of self-representations that enables us to see how the stories she told me were influenced by societal, personal and professional stories, and how this changed over time. It reveals the gendered discourses women in general are exposed to in a patriarchal society that often lead to a sense of powerlessness and responsibility for the care and well-being of others (especially males). It also reveals how challenges to the discourses of religion and culture were made available to Becky through undergoing drug treatment and her subsequent training as a counsellor.

I have represented below parts of Becky's story, using her own words in a stanza format to encapsulate powerful images and self-defining memories. Stanzas capture the rhythm and poetic quality of the spoken word, allowing the reader to appreciate their narrative structure, meaning and emotional impact.

★   ★   ★   ★

Becky was born in 1974 into a Catholic Maltese family who arrived in the UK shortly after World War II. Becky's mother was one of eleven children born in the UK who remained closely connected to their mother, Nan, whom Becky described as 'the matriarch'. When I asked Becky if she thought of herself as Maltese she told me: 'Being Maltese meant the same as being Catholic – but it was being a Catholic that was uppermost in the family.'

Becky spent her earliest years living with her parents and her brother, who was seven years older than her. Her alcoholic father was verbally and physically abusive to her mother and brother, and she was often awoken at night by violent rows. Around the age of four and a half Becky was sent to live with Nan during the week but Nan's household had its own problems, eight of her eleven adult children having been sectioned under the Mental Health Act.

Becky began her story with a memory of violence from when she was four years old.

> I can remember this one time
> my mum was screaming 'Get the police...'
> and I picked up my toy phone
> and started to try and ring the police...uhm...
> I don't kind of like, remember...what happened next...
> and then my Nan kind of took over a lot of the parenting,
> which I didn't understand.
> It was just like 'plonk'
> and I would just be in this situation.
> I took that as abandonment.
> I just took it that there's something defective with me.

So from a very early age Becky had begun to construct her identity as 'defective', which has been linked with feeling 'different'. During her first year at school Becky began to steal from the other children and, later, she would 'mysteriously' find the missing items, 'hoping for a reward from the teacher'.

Living in Nan's house with an 'alcoholic schizophrenic uncle' meant Becky had to 'carry a lot of secrets' – secrets about him taking her begging rather than taking her to nursery school as instructed, and being sworn to secrecy by her aunt whom she discovered overdosing with pills in the kitchen one day. She 'carried a lot of shame' about her family, particularly about her uncle who was 'overfriendly' when she invited her friends to Nan's house. Becky spent most of her time playing outside, hiding when her uncle approached because she never knew if he would be elated, aggressive, or shouting and swearing. She was 'fine-tuned' to the atmosphere surrounding her family and described herself as being 'taught to be co-dependent', adjusting her own behaviour to the needs of those around her.

In spite of the lack of safety in her home, Becky used her imagination to create a sense of safety:

> Where I lived next to the dockyard,
> they used to sound this siren.
> I used to imagine it was the end of the world.

> So I used to cut armchairs
> and store all my erm...like prize possessions [stolen items]
> in the chair, and under my bed...
> and [I thought] I'd be OK because I had these things.

> I used to go round stealing ornaments...
> and then Nan would say 'Where's that ornament gone?'

I used to imagine
that I could build my own little house
in the outside toilet…
and that I wouldn't have to deal with other people.

By the time she was nine years old Becky had stopped going to her parents' home at the weekends, staying full time at Nan's instead. As she grew into adolescence she was unhappy about herself, her appearance and her life generally. She was self-conscious about 'a really noticeable scar right on my eye' caused by a stone thrown by her brother, and after smashing her milk teeth in a fall her adult teeth came through 'completely fucked up'.

Appearance becomes central to identity during adolescence, and like many young females Becky was 'starting to become aware that bits were growing'. She saw herself as 'an ugly duckling' when she compared herself to her pretty friend.

During the 'big transition' of going to secondary school Becky began to use solvents and became…'a bit of a joker':

I was really popular in school…
I was always a bit of a joker,
but I was also quite violent.

I did have loads of fucking anger, you know…
I think my schooling started to fail round that time
and, as well, Nan got cancer.

Around this time Becky's parents' relationship worsened and her mother wanted a divorce but Becky had always felt more emotionally connected with her father in spite of his violence and drinking, and she felt angry with her mother.

Then it wasn't long after that
that my brother went to Australia…
I was 13 when he left…

Well again, I didn't understand it.
I was told he was going for a year…
[and he never came back].

Again I was being re-abandoned.
I was using gas, solvents…
I don't know how that happened…
I mean it wasn't a major problem…
it would be something [to do]
with a certain group of people…
we'd use to kind of 'gel' with each other,
have a laugh…

Becky rarely saw her parents, and her brother was going to the other side of the world. Alongside that, Nan's illness threatened the loss of the only stable presence in her life. She began to move from group to group, seeking attachment and affection from boys, identifying with a drug-using subculture where she knew she would be accepted and which offered her a new social identity during a period when she lacked a more satisfying one.

> Around…13, my movements changed.
> I would see myself as a bit of a nomad,
> going to different areas and groups of people…
>
> We'd go to these house parties
> where I'd just get pissed, being sick…
> that's where I met Jamie's dad…
> yeah puffing.
>
> So that was quite normal,
> to be drinking and smoking cannabis…uhm.
> I suppose it was just escapism…
> to feel out of my body…
> out of my own head…
> out of reality…

Becky described what she saw as 'normal' substance-using behaviour among peers – a theme I was to hear repeatedly from other participants. However, not all substance-using adolescents become problematic drug users. Becky connected her own shift with a traumatic experience of abortion at the age of 14, which was made worse by feeling out of control of the decision-making process, the conflicting attitudes and values of her mother and her Catholic school, and the punitive attitude of hospital staff. It seems little attention was paid to her wishes or her distress.

> I said to my biology teacher:
> 'I'm pregnant.'
> I just didn't want to believe it was happening.
> I wanted to keep it,
> which *is* a normal reaction,
> but I kind of knew it was not a good idea.
>
> So the school called my mum in…
> She was saying:
> 'There's no way she's having this kid.'
>
> The school were saying:
> 'Abortion's wrong,
> we could put her in with a good Catholic family
> where she could have this baby…'
>
> I didn't want to go and live with a Catholic family.
> I was 14 [*she yawns*].

I can remember
going down for the abortion,
I was really upset,
really, really upset
and the nurse's attitude was:
'Come on pull your socks up,
this is your fault' [*sternly*].

That's when I started drinking more.

Her alcohol consumption increased, as did her truanting and stealing. In turn, these activities led to her meeting the '*really* wrong people'.

I was always a magpie anyway
so I would just go in after school stealing...
and that was when I met up with the *really* wrong people,
who were into acid, ecstasy, drink, doing crime...
But I'd always been a thief anyway.

At 15 Becky was expelled from school, thereby losing her last remaining connection with a mainstream institution, and at 16 she moved into her boyfriend's flat. Michael began to beat her when he discovered that she had had a one-night stand with his friend, attacking her in the street in front of his probation worker, who did not intervene.

Becky became pregnant again, hoping that Michael would treat her better, but instead he wanted her to have another abortion. She became increasingly terrified of him.

Being with him was so *traumatic*...you know,
he'd battered me (*very quietly*)
and then it started getting into his head...
He'd start interrogating me
and I knew at the end he was going to hit me.
So no matter what I said
I couldn't pacify him.

He was physically abusive while I was pregnant...
stamped on my stomach
you know...
he'd do it in front of other people too.
And you know, I'd try and leave
and he'd come chasing me.

Michael had begun dealing ecstasy and using drugs more heavily, and eventually she plucked up the courage to leave him. While she was pregnant Becky stopped drinking but continued to smoke cannabis. In a vulnerable state after the birth of her child she allowed Michael to persuade her to move back in with him.

Our cannabis use was really heavy…
we got involved a little bit in the rave scene,
taking 'Es',
then someone introduced heroin into our group.

I didn't think I'd get addicted because…
I'd see…someone who was addicted to heroin
was someone who…had needles hanging out of their arms…
who didn't have nice clothes…
like *Big Issue* sellers.

So I didn't see myself like that.
None of my circle of peers was like that.

The social stereotype of 'an addict' didn't fit with Becky's view of herself or her friends. Up to this point she had seen her drug use as 'normal' – a way of escaping from reality, but finally she had to face the fact that it had become more than that.

After a month…
I can remember crying and thinking:
'I'm addicted to this',
and Michael saying,
'Don't be stupid.'

I just took it as my responsibility…
that I earned the money.
So the more I tried to keep up my responsibilities,
the more I needed heroin
to alleviate the feeling of being stuck and in pain.

I had to put the heroin on the table
in order to pacify him
so that I didn't get physically abused
or ashamed or shamed.

I didn't love this person [Michael]…erm…
I just couldn't see a way out
other than…heroin really.

Becky seems to have followed the pattern described by many abused women: defining herself only in relation to her partner, feeling worthless, having been treated as worthless, and, gradually, becoming more and more isolated.

But as she began to acknowledge her 'addict' identity a sense of conflict emerged with her preferred identity as 'mother', causing her to review her behaviour and sense of self dramatically.

I'd take Jamie with me to the dealer's…
all these like…dirty dealers, you know…
ugh…not on my wavelength…

and a couple of months later you're licking her ass
because you know you've got to score...
and you've got to keep her on your side...

Mostly it was really lonely...
just feeling the guilt and shame around Jamie...
I just felt bad because I had a child,
I was a woman, a mother, a drug addict...um

Even as Becky began to realise the depths to which she had sunk, her feelings of shame and guilt about her child led her to think how she might want his life (and her own) to be different.

...as soon as I started smoking heroin, erm...
it wasn't that long
before I started getting involved
in the criminal justice system.

I went to prison for cheque fraud...
come out –
just coming back into the same situation,
the same flat,
him being on the gear...

I really fucking hated him...
despised him...
Then he went to prison for a driving offence.

During the month Michael was in prison Becky began to mix with cannabis-using friends who tried to help her give up heroin. She slept with someone who treated her well and made her feel attractive and she knew that if Michael found out he would end up 'fucking killing me'. As she told this part of her story her language became stronger and she raised her voice. She knew she had to leave the relationship to break her heroin habit and by this time she had 'really had enough'. The break from Michael changed both of them, as often happens in 'co-dependent' relationships. So she moved in with her friends.

...the power had shifted
and I'd started to say:
'Fuck you, leave me alone.
Don't fucking come near me.'

And he'd become needier,
whereas I'd always thought I needed him.
I started to find a voice and say:
'I'm not taking this any more', er...
So I got up the courage...and left him.

But Michael continued to stalk and threaten her, and in response to fear and anger Becky started 'drinking heavily, taking pills, going out raving' and ended up back in prison for shoplifting. As an alternative to prison she was offered a referral to a probation officer on a 'bail support scheme'. This man – the first person to ask Becky 'Do you want help?' rather than saying, 'Why can't you stop?' – disclosed that he was 'a recovering alcoholic' himself. Becky told me: 'He was the first person who empathised with me, who believed…that I could do it.' This was a major turning point for Becky.

Becky went into a treatment centre for 12 weeks whilst her aunt took care of Jamie. When she was offered 'secondary care' her aunt refused to go on caring for her son. Becky believes that was probably the best thing that could have happened, because then she went to one of only two mother and baby units in Britain where she was helped to prioritise her identity as 'mother'.

Mixing with other mothers who were also addicted to heroin helped reduce her sense of stigma and shame. Jamie had his own development worker whilst she had access to parenting and life skills training, and individual and group counselling.

At this point Becky's story changed, focusing more on her dreams, values, beliefs and strengths.

> From when I first started seeing that guy
> I'd say, 'I want to be a probation officer.'
> I had that dream.
> I'd done cleaning people's houses and waitressing,
> because I didn't want to be working
> before Jamie went to school.
> And I got to the point where I thought:
> 'You know what? I'm worth more than this…'

Before meeting the probation worker Becky had never met 'an addict' who had become a member of the helping professions. Doing so encouraged her to think about new potential identities for herself. Although she had left school with no qualifications Becky began training in administration skills and was placed at a drugs project where she was eventually employed, and where she was able to observe the work of the counsellors. After successfully attending a counselling skills course, and with backing from her employers, she began to train as a counsellor.

> Starting university…was such a big thing.
> I don't know anyone in my family
> who has been to university.
> The people where I come from,
> and the kind of socialisation [messages] I've had
> are, 'People don't move on.'

I knew I was intelligent
but I did feel like I would struggle academically.

But I am a person that if I want something
I will go and get it,
I'll graft and I don't give up easily
and I am very driven.

As her story drew to a close Becky began to reflect on the meanings of her life and experiences. Her words helped me to understand that adopting a drug-user identity may indeed have been a way of trying to *solve* life's problems, by providing a means for identity construction that others might find in more conventional ways that were unavailable to her.

I don't have any regrets
that I've been a heroin addict.
Because I truly believe
that if I hadn't been brought to my knees by using heroin
I would have engaged in abusive relationships,
trying to always have babies,
thinking that would solve something in me
that doesn't feel right.

It was important to leave my family behind;
leave my home town;
leave Jamie's dad
and make something of my life, I suppose.

If someone had said when I was first in treatment
'What do you want to do?'
I'd have said: 'Well, you know,
I'd like to get married,
I'd like to have some more kids,
maybe go to Spain,
maybe – be a secretary,
or something like that.'

So…I would have sold myself short
compared to what I have today,
which is being able to provide for myself,
being there as a parent,
loving myself,
knowing what I deserve,
and just being independent.

I feel, today – through counselling,
and treatment,
I feel that as a person
I am integrated.

Metaphors of identity transformation

Becky's story of her journey into and out of substance misuse shows how she has made meaning of her life so far, and how her identities have evolved in line with her changing contexts, stages of life and learning.

As I immersed myself in her story I began to notice how the phrases and metaphors she used to describe herself indicated her developing sense of self and identity against the changing backdrop of the events and people in her life. She moved from speaking about herself at different stages of her life as 'defective', 'a joker', 'an ugly duckling', 'a bit of a nomad', 'a magpie', 'a thief', to 'a woman, a mother and an addict'. As she moved through her story she claimed more of her positive sense of identity: seeing herself as more powerful, courageous, worth more, intelligent, and hard working. When we listen to a person's use of metaphor we can see them as the building blocks of meaning, and indirect ways of expressing feelings, values, and personal strengths and resources.

The value Becky placed upon her identity as 'mother', and her desire to provide a different experience of mothering for her child from that which she had experienced herself, seemed to create the disruption required to halt the downward trajectory. After meeting the probation officer, and others who positively influenced her self-esteem, she began to connect with a sense of her own agency and take control of her life. She realised that she too was capable of living a worthwhile life, recognising 'I am a person that if I want something I will go and get it'. By the end of our conversation she was celebrating her 'independence' and 'integration'.

Right from the beginning of Becky's story I heard examples of her resilience: her attempts to ring the police on her toy telephone as a tiny child, and her attempts to avoid the 'end of the world' by storing stolen 'treasures' in the chairs. If we listen to her story from a position of curiosity about what she intended by her behaviours, we can see, for instance, how stealing, which started as a means of gaining positive attention from her teacher and creating safety, later became a means by which she kept up with her 'responsibilities', financing her own and her partner's habits. We can see how her relationship with substances changed over time: from her early use of solvents as a way to 'gel' with others, drinking and smoking cannabis as 'escapism', and heroin use as an attempt to 'alleviate the feeling of being stuck and in pain'.

Impact of social discourses on developing a sense of identity

Threaded throughout her storytelling Becky used concepts that indicated how different treatment discourses, as a client *and* a counsellor, had impacted upon her self-understanding. No doubt her story would have been different told at different stages of her life's progression.

The influence of her first experience of being a client within a humanistic, person-centred relationship, where she was valued and respected as someone who *could* change, was shown through the language and concepts she used, such as 'conditions of worth' and 'inner child'. The influence of treatment based upon the 12-step approach advocated by Alcoholics Anonymous was demonstrated through the use of phrases such as 'co-dependency' and 'being powerless around that drug'.

In other parts of her story there were indications of the influence of the discourses underpinning her integrative training as a counsellor: language related to psychodynamic and person-centred discourses, many of which have become accepted as everyday parlance within western cultures such as 'defence mechanisms' and 'positive regard'. One example of the impact of psychodynamic theories on Becky's self-understanding and revised sense of self and identity was shown towards the end of her story when she talked about a recent conversation she had had with her mother who had been sexually abused as a child by Becky's grandfather – as had many of her mother's siblings:

> I can see now why my mum dismissed me…
> it was easier for her to dismiss me as a female child
> than to get in touch with her own pain
> around what her dad did to her…
> I then unwillingly inherited her 'fucked-upness'
> or inability to parent or be present.
>
> And my dad didn't have no life;
> his mum died when he was three
> and he was brought up by uncles and aunties
> and his alcoholic father…you know.
>
> I don't see this as about me,
> but I did as a child,
> and I think that's what fuelled my using really,
> and putting myself in situations
> where I was going to be abused,
> because I thought that was all I was worth.
>
> I wanted the love from my mum
> but I never felt it.
> I've never had a maternal loving relationship with her
> and I did take that as something defective about me.
> I don't know whether she was scared
> that my dad would do the same to me,
> so maybe that was what was underlying her…
> putting me down my Nan's.
>
> Now…we do have a good relationship…
> we talk to each other…she says to me
> 'I love you. I'm proud of you'
> and I say the same thing to her.

Acknowledgement

A version of this chapter was published in 2006 in *Drugs: Education, Prevention and Policy, 13(3)*, 233–245. Reprinted with kind permission from Taylor and Francis (UK) Journals: www.tandf.co.uk/journals.

Chapter 6

Steven's Story

The London train arrived on time and I anxiously scanned the faces of disem-
barking passengers, wondering if I would recognise Steven. We had met only
once before, more than a year previously, when he came to talk to me about a post
I had advertised for a research assistant. In the end he had decided not to apply
and took a better job. At that first meeting he had talked a bit about his own
history of drug misuse to explain why he had been interested in the research job,
and he agreed to tell his story more fully as a participant once I was ready.

As I drove him from the station to my home we chatted about his new job. As
I made him a sandwich while he settled into the conservatory overlooking our
garden, where we would be taping our conversation, I realised that I felt a strong
maternal tug. Born in 1974, the eldest of two sons, he was almost the same age as
the youngest of my own three sons, and I mused on the differences in their lives
and wondered what it might have been like to watch my child go through what
Steven had suffered.

When I asked him where his story began, he took a deep breath and,
speaking very quickly, launched straight into a potted history of his drug using
from the age of 14 to 20 years.

> I started smoking cannabis when I was about fourteen and then moved onto
> heavier stuff when I was about sixteen. At first it was just recreational, now and
> again, then by seventeen, eighteen it had become quite habitual. By nineteen I'd
> had a breakdown and was sectioned in a psychiatric hospital and was there for
> about four or five months.

As he went back to flesh out the story of his early teenage years his life sounded
very much like any other young person's of that era: into the Beatles, Pink Floyd
and other bands, reflecting the rock and roll lifestyle that included drugs, sex and
alcohol. He linked the music scene with his progressive use of different substances as they became more readily available:

> If I'm honest, I was taking drugs because everyone did: all my friends did. I was
> into the music scene at the time and into drug-related music, drug-related litera-
> ture, and before long discovered cannabis.

I started off into heavy metal and that kind of thing…[then] it was mainly just alcohol. I used to go to gigs, get drunk – it was all just sort of drink-related. Our tastes moved onto…the loud sort of biker-type, heavy metal bands and then we moved on to deeper or…you know, stuff that had influenced that, like Pink Floyd, and Led Zeppelin, and all the '60s and '70s bands that had come before and influenced them. Around that time there was a lot of turning back to earlier kinds of music, and it sort of coincided in the '80s with the Acid House craze, which I guess were the early raves but with LSD. And then in the early '90s it really started to move into the ecstasy scene.

Family life

Steven was born into a close-knit family, living in a 'posh enclave' on the edge of a small town just outside London, between the 'big city' and the surrounding countryside. His family were part of the 'upper working class/lower middle class' who earned enough to move up in the world. He felt fortunate that his parents were still living together, unlike the parents of many of his peers, and fortunate too that his home did not reverberate with violence.

'The Most Unsociable People in the Class' award

He spent most of his social time with his family, especially with his younger brother who was born a year after him. They seemed so inseparable that people thought they were twins. Although he played sport with other children, Steven had only one friend, Joe, who was almost like another family member, staying at his house over weekends, and accompanying them on outings. All of this changed when, at the age of 14, their English teacher suggested that pupils gave awards to the most deserving people in the class. Steven was shocked and dismayed when he and Joe were given the award for 'The Most Unsociable People in the Class'. It had never before occurred to him that his lifestyle might be seen in that way.

> The other kids had loads of friends and they went around in groups, and did all the kinds of 'normal' things that kids do. It's incredible to me now thinking back, but I never went out with my mates when I was twelve, thirteen. So I never sort of said, 'See you later Mum, I'm just going out with my mates.' I didn't go out to play.

Since being in secondary school Steven had been 'picked on' and he coped with that by withdrawing into his own world and becoming 'self-contained'.

> I knew I was 'different'. I worshipped my dad and my family, and it never really bothered me that much, if I'm really honest. And I remember walking out with my dad once – I must have been about eleven, twelve, thirteen, – I don't mean it to sound arrogant, but I think it expresses how I felt at the time about myself – I thought, 'I'm more intelligent than most of the people around me. I've got more insight…more depth maybe.'

Paradoxically, he felt 'stupid' at school, achieving slightly higher than average grades, but not doing as well as might be expected of a boy who was reading material well beyond his years: Hemmingway, H.G. Wells, and classic science-fiction material.

Tribal youth culture

The wake-up call of receiving the award led him to look around at other young people's lives and he began to notice the 'tribal' groups at school.

> I mean, in the '80s, youth culture came into its own really, and of course I was a product of that, so you had different tribes. You had what was called 'the casuals' — the ones who wore the designer clothes, and slicked-back hair, and into the latest music...

He went on to name the other groupings, like 'the hats', who were 'dodgy', and into using drugs before everyone else — they were the 'hard lot' who knocked everyone else around and most ended up in prison for drug dealing and small-scale crime. Steven believes that, at that time, '80 per cent of the kids did drugs — ecstasy was a popular thing to do.'

There were also the 'saps' — the hard working, high performing and well-behaved people — not a group he would feel at home with because he was not performing well enough at school. So he found a place in the 'Motleys' — a collection of 'leftovers' from the other groups, where he became 'whipping boy' for about a year. Steven laughed, but without humour, as he told me that his nickname was 'spastic' and 'gay' and 'vegetable'. This had been 'horrendous' but through sheer bloody-mindedness, and a determination that they would accept him in the end, he began to stick up for himself, and made individual connections with members of the group who, once they got to know him, no longer wanted to treat him badly. People liked his sense of humour and wit, and he became more confident and relaxed — and more popular.

The Motleys were originally a 'male, macho bunch', but around the ages of 15 or 16 they began to mix with girls, who became known as 'The Motley Birds'. He laughs as he remembers:

> When I look back, that was a very happy time of my life really, because we used to do lots of things together. There were inevitably pairings up, but I guess it was the first time that I'd ever done something like that really. You know, we'd go out to the cinema as a big group, we'd have parties and go the pub as a big group, and it was quite cool really.

So Steven was developing social skills, and becoming a more gregarious, outgoing character, although still terrified of girls.

Discovering alcohol

His friends stole whisky which they drank together in the woods but his parents'
reaction to him coming home drunk was tolerant and even amused. He laughed
again as he told me:

> ...they could probably remember the first time *they* got drunk, and it's no big deal
> really. They would roll their eyes and say, 'What are you doing getting drunk?' It
> was just at weekends, or every couple of weekends – we'd all go out and get
> drunk, have a laugh.

Steven's remarks reflect the normalisation of excessive drinking among people in
our society, even today. For young men their first drink is sometimes seen as 'initiation' into manhood, often taken on a visit to the local pub with their father.

It was among this group that he began to experiment with cannabis and from
time to time they would go up into the woods and 'get stoned, have a laugh and
enjoy ourselves'.

He found that drinking helped his growing confidence with girls, around
whom he usually felt 'crippled':

> ...they were from another planet really. They still are from another planet but at
> least I can negotiate that planet a little better than then, when I was just this kid with
> no experience, very, very shy, very crippled in confidence, very sensitive, and girls
> at fourteen, fifteen, they're looking for guys with confidence.

'A' levels split the group

At the age of sixteen most of his peers left school to follow vocational training, to
take jobs or to seek other qualifications, and Steven stayed on with a small group of
peers to do 'A' levels because he did not know what else he should do. He had no
plans to go to university, although his best friend often told him he was bright
enough. He chose English literature, history and sociology – subjects that 'were
very good for me' and at the end of the first year he came top in all three, feeling for
the first time as though he was being 'tested'.

At the weekends Steven went out 'binge drinking' with his 'A' level friends:

> ...getting absolutely plastered, and that's what everyone did, and that's what
> everyone does – even now. I've got friends in their thirties and that's their lifestyle:
> every weekend, and even weekdays, they're getting hammered.

But during the summer, at the end of his first year in the sixth form, Steven began to
spend time with the group who had left school at 16, who by this time had become
'hippies' – a lifestyle that began to seem more and more attractive to Steven.

> I don't know what it was really, but something attracted me to that lifestyle. I was
> really into the music. I knew more about the music scene and the history of music
> than anyone did. We lived [near] the country[side] so – it's so sad now I'm talking

about it – we used to make makeshift camps, and just sit there and smoke dope, looking down into the valley. It was quite nice really, spending hot summer days just putting on the stereo and getting stoned.

As we talked he began to think about why he had lost interest in school during that final year and an interesting realisation unfolded.

I'm not sure what swung it really – maybe it was that the success I was having at school, the success in relationships, was so contrary to what had gone before, and finding out that I was probably very intelligent – not just quite bright, but actually *very* intelligent – and could go to university. I'd never even *thought* about university until the end of this first year when I got these results. I think it probably just scared me, the responsibility of it. It did rattle me a bit. And then maybe there was a real [pull towards] that whole lifestyle these other guys were living: non-conformist, irresponsible – just to drop out, just get stoned...

...during this time, I wanted to be a writer and a music journalist, and I was being told by people who were journalists that, yes, you've got a very good chance. I just threw all of that away...to binge it up with the druggies really. It's hard to say what pushed me in that direction.

Living in a fantasy world

As he explored this theme further he described how, from a very young age, he had created an 'unreal' storied world inside his head, embellished by music. Then, as he began to grow towards maturity, his internal world was challenged by external reality and the adult responsibilities of planning for a future world of work.

Yes, [it was] almost like growing up, leaving the safety of the garden, if you like.

The drugs and his hippie companions offered him a way of escaping back into his preferred 'unreal world' where he felt 'safe' and 'in control' – more so than in his relationships with most of the people he knew.

I had a strong impression that this was new ground and that Steven was making sense of it as we went along.

I found the lives of those going to school around me quite drab and uninteresting. I know it sounds paradoxical – they always seemed almost immature, whereas my mates who were irresponsible, they seemed to have a kind of...coolness, and to be honest they were better people to be with, relating to reality.

This did sound paradoxical but it seemed as if he was saying that, although these friends were escaping reality by using drugs, they were doing so because they were more *in touch* with a reality that they did not like, and therefore needed to escape.

There wasn't the silliness that went with people who were kind of 'university-streamlined'. They were serious, and passionate about music and discussing things, and also because we were taking mind-altering drugs as well, and discussing reality, this was *us* exploring reality *together*. And that to me seemed more exciting and more real than sitting in a classroom and going over some very dull stuff really.

An important relationship lost

And then Steven began to speak of an important relationship he had had with a teacher who had clearly meant a great deal to him.

> I *really* had a connection with him. He *really* encouraged me. He was a great teacher, he really was. You know, you think of one teacher in the world and this guy was it. But he left after my first year [of sixth form], and maybe if he'd have stayed, he might have actually given me the kick up the arse that was needed and actually brought me back on task. But there was no [other teacher] I had a real relationship with, because you've got to remember, I went through school thinking I was thick. The [other] teachers didn't tell me I was wrong.

I began to understand more clearly why Steven's schooling had fallen apart after the end of the first year sixth form, and why he felt disenchanted with school. This teacher had reflected back to him an important part of his identity: as an intelligent person. He began to speak of his sense of betrayal:

> And I also felt betrayed by them [teachers] as well, not because this guy had left, although that was probably part of it, but after coming top of these subjects I remember being so angry at the school, thinking, 'How could I have gone through school, believing that I was stupid, when all the time I was highly intelligent?' Couldn't they have *seen* that, couldn't they have brought that out of me? I've spent my lifetime in these schools failing stuff and not finishing things, and looking quite, you know... I was a dreamer as a kid and I understand that, but nobody ever *really* focused on the abilities I had and brought them out of me. So I felt incredibly betrayed by that, and I think that was another reason for me to go with the non-conformists, and bomb out the whole system. It was 'fuck you' to the whole system.

So it wasn't simply Mr Ryan leaving, but what the relationship had meant. He was the *only* teacher in the whole of Steven's school life who had recognised his intellect.

I felt genuinely shocked when Steven then told me that he had failed *all* of his 'A' levels, not even completing all of the English course work. I wondered how the loss of Mr Ryan as a person had impacted on him.

> I think I felt deserted. He always said that he was going to stay on and to leave a class midway through... He had set out our plan for the two years...in a way that we could see the emergent picture of European history. And we got this other teacher who was just fresh out of teacher-training college...

His passion for history came through with huge energy as he spoke. His father had also been passionate about history and they had shared conversations on the topic throughout Steven's childhood on the walks they took together.

Impact of drugs on family relationships

At that point Steven was using mainly cannabis and LSD, with occasional ecstasy. He began to feel as if he was 'betraying' himself by not pursuing his studies and, about this time, his parents found out he was using drugs. Their reaction, especially his mother's, made him '*so angry*'. He felt pressured and controlled. I asked him what he had wanted from them.

> I wanted them to back off and just leave me to it. But I think I was withdrawing into this fantasy world and they were confronting me with my responsibilities. Well, my dad was, but my mum was on a different level. To her, my taking drugs was a personal betrayal, because it reflected badly on her as a mother.

At that time he felt he wasn't doing too badly but the more he felt pressured by his parents the worse his drug using became, and with hindsight he wonders if he would have simply gone through a drug-using phase, like many other young people, if they had pressured him less.

> But they were continually feeding the fire, continually, continually, continually. But one of the worst things about drugs for me was what it actually did to my perceptions. I began to see reality in a very different way. I started to see my mother's control, her emotional blackmail. I began to see how the 'protection' they were supposed to have provided impacted on me. And I started to see all of the negative interactions that went on in my family. I started to see that you weren't allowed to criticise and question them, but very subtly, but it was all there, and the whole thing of, 'We've been such good parents, and how can you treat us like this?' And, 'We've done our best for you' – which was *true* in a way – but I was starting to see another side to all of this.

> I started to see myself in a different way, and I thought, 'Bloody hell, I'm quite a damaged individual; I'm quite socially inept really.' So going from a 'normal experimentation'…I never knew that drugs would change the way I looked at the world.

I asked him if he might have come to see the reality of his family dynamics anyway, with maturity, or by mixing with others, as most young people do in time. But he seemed very clear that it was his first acid trip that caused a *sudden* 'radical shift' in his perception, rather than it happening slowly, over time, at a pace that allowed him to assimilate new perceptions gradually.

> My first acid trip…changed my view of *everything*. I know it sounds quite extreme. It gave me access to an insight that I was developing and hadn't reached yet – and I wasn't ready for that…I'd never *seen* that before. I started to see human relationships in a very different way and I began to see the negativity and the damage that people do to each other. Suddenly, human relationships became very, very different, very frightening. Maybe they'd always been frightening and I'd just closed myself down to that, and all these drugs were doing was opening up all of those feelings again, and I was seeing it now, not as a kid with the under-developed cognitive abilities, but seeing it as a [person] growing intellectually.

This was shocking to Steven and he didn't know how to cope with his altered view of reality and relationships.

> I didn't know how to be around my family. I thought I loved my family and I realised that I hated the way that they'd created this closed little world for me. I hated the fact that they wouldn't let me go out and, you know…I think all kids go through that, but I think with me the emotional impact…was so strong that it was really hard just to walk away from it all.

He retreated into his world of books: reading psychology, sociology and philosophy which he found 'very exhilarating'. The psychology literature, especially R.D. Laing, began to make a sense of the 'madness' in his family and his feelings towards them:

> The most stunning observation for me at the time was that it's not the overt abuse that drives kids mad – it's the subtle forms of mixed communication that send a kid into confusion and madness. And I could relate to that. And at the time I *knew* that I was unwell, but it was like, 'How do I get out of this?' I never realised when I was taking LSD that I'd end up in a mental hospital.

Recognising his breakdown of reality

His continued use of LSD led him into a state where he 'didn't know who to be, didn't know what to be, didn't know how to communicate properly'. All of the confidence he had built up, his ability to relate to others and interpret his world was 'blown away'. He became 'paranoid', believing that his friends were talking about him behind his back and making fun of him, as they had done in the past.

He appealed to his younger brother, who was also using drugs, but without the same effects, and asked him for help. His brother arranged for him to meet a psychiatric nurse who worked in the drugs field. When Steven suggested that he was suffering from schizophrenia, the nurse asked diagnostic questions and told him that he did *not* have schizophrenia.

> And I went away *devastated*, absolutely devastated, because I felt such an *idiot*. Because I'd built this whole kind of thing in my head: 'I'm mad, I'm mad, I'm mad, and I've got schizophrenia.' *Shit!* I'd got it into my head that I was schizophrenic, and I had been reading about it. Having that confronted just exposed that I was capable of building this world in my head, and it was not actually making contact with reality. It was like the bubble burst by that contact with reality.

After this Steven 'turned over a new leaf' and went back to college for a year to retake his 'A' levels. He had stopped using acid but continued to smoke cannabis. He was unable to function on a social level. He felt '*crippled* inside'. He spent the barest minimum of time on his studies, preferring instead to read Nietzsche, Sartre, Kafka, all confirming the pessimistic, negative, cynical worldview that he'd developed over the last couple of years.

A 'psychotic breakdown'

Steven's behaviour became increasingly bizarre and his friends began to relate to him as a 'mad genius'. He got into trouble with the police, picking fights when he was out with his friends. As he told me about this behaviour he laughed quietly, almost, it seemed, with disbelief:

> ...quite psychotic behaviour really. I got in a fight with a guy...I really beat him up quite badly and got arrested for it. I got bound over for a year, but I could have got done for GBH. I started to withdraw from my friends, spent more and more time in books, and read and read and read, smoked some dope. I was hallucinating on cannabis, but then I started to hallucinate without the cannabis, and the hallucinations were becoming almost like a daily reality. I knew I was hallucinating, but then I thought I was some kind of special, amazing person, a genius – all that kind of stuff. Then I thought, 'Shit. I'm going crazy', and it was like the plug had been pulled and my whole world just collapsed and I knew I was going mad.

> I thought I was carrying the sins of the world on my shoulders. I thought I had confined my whole family to an eternity in hell, and I thought I was actually *in* hell. I'd be seeing spirits, and everything had meaning. An apple would drop and I'd think, 'Oh that's the apple in the Garden of Eden.' I thought I was eternally cursed. It was like suddenly the whole of my future had been taken away from me – my eternal future. I thought, 'My career is lost, I'm going to spend the rest of my life in a mental hospital.' I was 19, and my life was at an end.

Amazingly, at the end of his year at college Steven did achieve the grades he needed at 'A' level, even though he was going through a 'psychotic breakdown' at the time.

Sectioned under the Mental Health Act

Steven had not slept enough for two months because he thought he would die if he slept. His mother had been trying to find help for him but the psychiatrist he saw did not listen when Steven tried to tell him about his misery and despair: instead he gave him a diagnosis of 'depression' and prescribed antidepressants.

> I had long hair at the time, and I was dressing quite eccentrically. I must have looked quite a strange sight. He said, 'I think you should be an in-patient.' And I said, 'No way.' So I walked straight out to the bus stop, expecting them to come for me any minute. At the time I just thought they had the power to do that. And that night, I was drinking endless coffees, and I had a knife, and I thought: if they come for me I'm going to kill myself before they get a chance.

> During that night I think it just reached a climax and it felt like my brain exploded. I cut the side of my arm – I can remember feeling that there was no sensation in my arm and cutting it to see whether that would...but you know, I'd gone psychotic and I'd completely lost it. I was burning my clothes in the house, and it was just wild

exhilaration at the time, feeling like I'd touched God or genius or something. But it was pure madness really. And *that* was when my parents said to me, 'We can't look after you any more and you should go as an in-patient.' So they took me into the in-patient ward. It made me worse, being in there.

Steven was eventually sectioned and remained in hospital for about five months. He was treated with ECT, which deadened his emotions and stole his memory at the time, but it did help him leave hospital eventually. Almost immediately on leaving hospital he went back to smoking cannabis, not wanting to be seen as different by his friends. Cannabis made him feel 'real' and allowed him to feel his emotions again:

When I took cannabis I could *feel* again. And I felt like a dead person. I'd had my twentieth birthday in hospital, and it was the same hospital where I was born. I felt like my life was over. In a very short space of time I had put on about three or four stone, but that was the drugs they put me on, and also the habitual eating pattern.

When I came out I went to work, washing up dishes in the restaurant. And I got back in with the same mates because the alternatives were going to these MIND groups and schizophrenia fellowship things.

He was looking for a group with which he could identify and those groups did not fit the bill.

As Steven was speaking about his time in hospital he became intense and upset. He was clearly reliving some of those experiences and the feelings seemed profound. Later, as we reflected back over the conversation, he told me it had been a surprise to him that he became 'stuck' in this part of the story. It seemed as if he still held some trauma from that experience. He described his treatment in hospital as 'barbaric', made all the worse because it was considered a 'normal' way to treat patients.

Turning points

Feeling a serious lack of direction, Steven smoked cannabis mostly alone, because he would begin to feel paranoid in the presence of others, and after a time he began to meet occasionally with a large group who 'hung out' at a friend's house at weekends, playing music, watching videos, and 'getting stoned'.

Around this time Steven's cousin, also on drugs, had been sectioned under the Mental Health Act and, whilst in hospital, he committed suicide.

It was such a shocking experience, it was like opening it up, and suddenly for the first time, I looked at myself. It was a real re-evaluation. It was like: 'I'm only 21 and what am I doing with my life? What am I doing smoking all these drugs? I should be at university.' And I made a real decision to get my life sorted out.

Steven indicated that he was able to stop simply by deciding to do so. I questioned if that was really possible:

It was for me. It was the shock of seeing what happened to my cousin really, and thinking that could *so* easily have been me. It was the fact that he'd committed suicide while in hospital. So it was quite a heavy experience.

After his cousin's death, as a cynical atheist who was also interested in spirituality, Steven began to wonder if he could find the answers in religion – having unsuccessfully tried to find answers in philosophy and psychology.

Around this time he contacted a girl he 'fancied' who seemed to have disappeared from the weekend gatherings. He discovered then that she had decided to give up using drugs and had gone back to her Christian roots.

I didn't know she was a Christian. And when I phoned her, I got talking to her dad who was quite a leader of the church. I didn't really need any kind of prompting. I started going to their church and meeting people who are very sincere, very open and honest, and very caring in some ways. I thought, 'This is a safe place.' I became a Christian after a year of attending the church and forming a new group of friends. *That* for me was another turning point.

I committed myself to God, and when I made that declaration, that commitment, I said that I wanted to give my life to Christ. I had such an amazing experience of being filled with the Holy Spirit; more powerful than any drug I've ever had. It was like taking drugs but clean, clean drugs, and it didn't have any of that dirtiness that went with LSD or cocaine.

Healed by Jesus

Sixth months after his 'conversion', and feeling he was getting his life sorted out, he decided to train as a primary school teacher and went to college in London, believing that he had been 'healed from mental illness by Jesus'. He was very active in his new church, reading the Bible, and praying, surrounded by a very supportive social network. He lost some of his 'eccentricities' and his 'manic lifestyle' and his life seemed to be going very well indeed. But in this new church he began to see things happening there that he really didn't like:

Going to these churches in London was like going to big school all over again! And I was seeing just what people were doing to each other. The most distressing thing for me personally was going to these churches and seeing a lot of young guys like myself who had been ill, or *were* ill, and getting prayed for, up at the front. You know how charismatic churches are…what they call 'slaying the spirit', supposedly…

And I'd see this happen to these guys and then they'd be put in a mental hospital. And I used to say to people, 'What is all this all about? What's happened to me then?' People in my church were telling me: 'You've been healed by God, and so long as you believe that, you'll be alright, but if you stop believing that you'll get ill again.'

Steven tried to discuss his doubts with the minister who, whilst agreeing that he too had doubts, was not prepared to engage in deep discussion with Steven on those matters. In the face of this Steven began to feel depressed again, not wanting to get out of bed to go to church and having bowel problems. There were things in the Bible he could not believe in and he didn't want to 'pretend he was something' he was not.

Then, he met up with an old friend from his previous church who told him about a 'therapeutic faith community', with a 'Christian slant', where he had been receiving counselling. He explained to Steven that it was a place where people looked at the issues in their life that had stopped them from living the life they wanted to live. Some of the community members had suffered abuse, misused drugs or alcohol, or been psychiatric patients, and everybody worked together to help one another. But Steven was sceptical:

> I had my doubts but I went down there for a New Year's Eve party and I just freaked out. I went to a big party in this house and I had a full-blown panic attack. I think it was because I was with a group of people who were being honest with each other, and actually looking at the issues in their life that they were confronted with.

Coming 'home'

Spending time with those people made Steven realise that he had *not* sorted his life out and neither had he been 'healed by Jesus' as his own church community had wanted him to believe. His friend's new therapeutic faith community had a different message:

> They were telling me, 'Actually that's not true', and probably the only thing *really* holding me together was my belief that God had healed me. That was the only thing I was clinging to, to keep me sane. And here they were saying, 'Well yes, God probably did have something to do with it, but what we've found is that there's a journey you go on – it's not an instant thing.'

> And so, I started to go down to this community in Deal at weekends, to this lovely little town by the sea, and this group of people I could relate to.

> There *was* that shared faith, that belief in God, in Christ, and maybe the core principles of Christian faith. But in actual fact [they] were prepared to be real about things. And I found that hard at first, really shockingly hard. It meant going back to places I didn't want to go back to. And I decided over a time of coming down at weekends, going to workshops, that this is where I want to live, because I had loads of people here, it's a home here, it feels like home.

Having made this decision, Steven moved to Deal and shared a flat with another member of the faith community whilst attending university to study psychology. He had changed the course of his studies after realising that his decision to become a teacher might have been based on fear of doing something that might stretch him intellectually, rather than a real desire to teach.

The Deal church enabled Steven to live in 'the outside world' – still going to university – whilst also belonging to a community, and maintaining a balance between therapeutic work and exploring his relationships with God and other people.

As he moved through his 'journey' in the therapeutic faith community, he began to understand that his illness was not related to his drug use alone, and that an over-controlling mother and family background had driven him into both drug misuse and 'madness'. Their behaviour had made him angry, revengeful, and led him to punish himself with drugs for conforming to their demands; and in another sense, his drug use had been an escape from the reality of grown-up responsibility.

How these realisations are helping now

Steven is on a personal and professional journey, which he views as 'never-ending'. He has come to see how his past relationship with his mother has influenced his attempts to form intimate and long-lasting relationships with other women. He does not blame his mother.

> I began to realise that it's not her fault. But I'd attributed my getting mad to the influence of an over-protective mother, a controlling mother, a mother who had probably given me mixed messages as a child and created conditions for me that *would* send me crazy when I took drugs. So I attributed the negative relationship with my mother as a prime cause of my breakdown. And even very, very recently – over the past two, three years – I was going out with girls, getting to a certain point of closeness and then I'd get really insecure, and effectively push them away and break the relationship.

He realised that, because he had linked his psychotic breakdown with being close to a woman (his mother), he felt threatened whenever he allowed any woman to come close to him, fearing they would try to take over control of his life, as his mother had done.

> It was almost like I felt I'd been cursed: if I had a relationship with another woman I would go mad. And every time I started to get serious, emotionally intimate, it would kick in. Suddenly from being this really sensitive, sweet, intelligent, quite relaxed guy, I would become really insecure, almost suspicious and paranoid. And when I was talking about it in a counselling session I actually started to go into trauma. I had to let go of that trauma, engage it emotionally, and just let it go, just cry it out.

> I'm going out with a girl at the moment – a relationship that broke up last year because of the way I was. And it's amazing, because we've gone back together and it's a completely different feeling now. I'm so much more relaxed with myself. I feel so much more at peace. It's a real change because it's almost removed that barrier, and I'm kind of there, I'm ready for it: I'm not scared of it.

Impact of his parents' sexual abuse on him

Steven had told me earlier that he now understood his mother's behaviour was a result of abuse in *her* childhood – something his father had told him about during his early teens.

> My mother was abused sexually, and in other ways, by her father, and actually, my dad had been abused by *his* father too, which I didn't know until recently. As a result, she's been emotionally blunted by those experiences. I never knew where I stood with my mum as a child. I never *really* got a lot of warmth from her. It was almost like she was always trying, but that warmth was *never* communicated, it was always withheld. So I grew up always trying to grab hold of that love because you could see it but you couldn't always feel it, or connect with it. I used to ask Mum, 'What was your dad like?' She'd say, 'I don't want to talk about him. He was horrible. I don't want talk about it. He was a bastard', which shocked me because I had a really good relationship with *my* dad and I couldn't understand…

> I'd always guessed about the abuse because, as a family, we used to watch the Esther Rantzen programme about child abuse and I'd felt distinctly uncomfortable at the time, and I could feel my dad was uncomfortable, and I could see the expression on my mother's face. So I always knew there was something wrong.

> I was talking to my mum about this recently and she said, 'Why do you have to look at your past? Just get on with life.' And I said to her, 'But it affected me as a child. I knew there was something wrong, and you knew there was something wrong in your relationship with *me*. Obviously, you'd had that experience with *your* father…' And she said, 'But I did the best I could to love you', and I said, 'But on some emotional level you were (I never said this so bluntly: I'm paraphrasing) but you weren't there for me. I *felt* that as a child, and I may not have attributed it to the fact that you'd been abused as a child…but there was always a barrier there, there was always something missing.'

I asked Steven if his father's abuse had created the same problems in their relationship, even though it sounded as if they were very close:

> I think it only happened a few times with his dad…with my mum it was just consistent serial abuse. Her father was the town paedophile. And in those days of course you couldn't talk about it. So, it must have been horrible. And everyone in the town knew about it, and nobody did anything – out of respect for my mum's mum – because she was very popular and very well liked, and she was married to the bastard…

I noticed Steven's apparent minimisation of his father's abuse and gently challenged him by pointing out that, even if it had only happened once, the betrayal in the relationship between father and son would have been huge. I was curious about the intimacy Steven's father seemed able to sustain in *their* relationship and how the effect of his father's abuse did not seem to have prevented that, in the way his mother's had.

Impact on sexuality

His father had told Steven about his own abuse only when his cousin committed suicide. I wondered aloud to Steven if his cousin may also have been abused, and Steven thought that could have been the case. I asked him if he thought his parents' abuse histories might have impacted on his identity as a sexual human being during his teenage years.

> I remember this feeling of shame whenever sex used to come on the TV if my mum was in the room. On the one hand, both me and my brother used to say, 'Oh good.' But then my mum was there…her attitude to sex was very, very puritanical really.

I wondered to Steven what it had been like for his mother, to watch her sons developing into sexually mature males, and his response surprised me in its honesty: 'You see, I never really developed in that way properly.'

Perhaps, I surmised, he was keeping his mother safe in that way? Steven laughed at that:

> I don't think it was necessarily that. I think I'd taken on her fear. I was afraid of sex so I closed right down to emotional intimacy, even by the teenage years, because I never dated through my teens. I went out with this group of girls but I never paired off with anybody. And then of course the whole drugs thing happened and that pretty much blew my life away, and it was impossible for me to even consider a relationship. I almost felt defective. I almost felt castrated in my sexuality. So my sexuality was impotent. It was a sexuality that I could only enjoy alone, because I never would imagine at the time…a girl would actually want me. My brother went the opposite way. He became very sexually promiscuous. I went towards being a neutered male really, sort of an indeterminate gender, whereas he went towards the other end of the scale.

> I don't think my dad knew what to do about my brother, because my dad was also quite promiscuous until he met my mother and then settled down. When I started going down to Deal and began to find my sexuality, my dad didn't know how to take it. He's got used to it now. I think he kind of enjoys the fact that… When they came down to Deal a couple of weeks ago I brought my girlfriend along to meet them and we walked up to them hand in hand and they were just like: 'Cor, blimey! This is nice.' And I'm 30 and it's *sad*, it really is, because I should have been doing this a long time before.

'Work in progress'

As our conversation drew to a close Steven reflected on the process of telling his story to me 'all in one go'. In his community he is used to telling his life story as he connects with new realisations and used to helping others in the community by listening to their stories. He wanted me to know that he sees his story as 'work in progress' rather than a finished 'product'.

I don't want to give the impression that I've come to this great community and now I'm all healed and everything's fine, because it isn't like that. And you know, it's a complete blessing that I found the church in Deal, and that I was able to get the healing that I did. But it is a very painful process and you're constantly learning about yourself, and about other people, and being confronted with what you don't know, which I guess is kind of normal for most people most of the time. But when you've lived outside the normal swing of things, when you've lived a kind of *ab*normal life, which is what I've done, then things that most people take for granted – they're new things.

★   ★   ★   ★

During a later telephone conversation I asked Steven about how he understood the difference between what he had received from the Deal church community and his previous church community. During this conversation he also expanded on what he believed had shaped his identity as a man. I had taped this conversation but unfortunately discovered later that only my side of the conversation had actually been recorded. Steven kindly agreed to write to me about the matters we had discussed on the telephone and his writing is presented below as an ending to his story:

> There are two aspects as to why Christ Church, Deal (CCD) was different to other churches that I had attended. The first was related to my history of mental illness. The churches I had attended before did not know how to deal with mental illness. Although my conversion to Christianity had produced a radical change in my outward behaviour (giving up smoking, drinking, drugs etc., return to college) there was little emphasis on change in the way of inward, character transformation or relational change. The church where I first became a Christian told me that once I had become a Christian the 'old had gone, the new had come': I was now healed. Although this may have been superficially true, I had many issues in my life that were still not dealt with, and were unexamined by the church. For example, I had very little self-esteem, an inaccurate and unhealthy view of my potential (I was unable to achieve much) and was very poor at doing relationships. When I attended the church in London whilst I was studying, many young men with mental illness were attending, but would be in and out of mental hospitals. When I asked 'Why hasn't God healed them as well?', the response was, 'We don't know what to do with them.' When I had recurring problems of mental health, I went to see the pastor who told me to 'just get on with it' and 'you just have to believe, read your bible and pray. Then you will be fine.' This was incredibly unhelpful advice as I was doing all of these things and they were not working! I was eventually told that I was 'no good to Him in this state' and so I decided to leave the church. Again, this was very unhelpful as I know in retrospect that I was going through another breakdown.
>
> In contrast, CCD taught me how to look at the root causes of the issues in my life that had caused my drug abuse and breakdown, and to start to change unhealthy

patterns of thinking, negative self-image, etc. I was given the freedom and space, along with support, to engage emotionally with the issues without judgement or a requirement to conform. I didn't need to fear being sent to see a mental health specialist because I was a bit wobbly. In my own words at the time, 'I could go mad properly.' CCD also became a place where I could learn how to do relationships properly. Most of the relationships beforehand had been quite unhealthy, but at CCD I was able to explore how to build relationships that were positive, honouring and deep, in an environment that allowed me to make mistakes and examine the issues that had caused me to choose bad relationships in the first place. It was almost like an experimental laboratory in which the insights I was gaining about myself could be tested and explored without fear of recrimination.

One of my biggest areas of damage was around manhood, i.e. my identity as a man, what being a man meant, etc. and how this affected all my relationships with myself, other men and women. I think my dad had a very positive influence on my life, but he never taught me how to be a man. Consequently, I went through adolescence without a secure identity as a man. I felt awkward and ashamed of my sexuality. I didn't identify with men who treated women with little respect, but had little awareness of an alternative way to be. My dad always taught me to treat women with respect, 'treat them like ladies', but this meant I didn't know how to hold my own amongst women without being weak or subservient.

In CCD I learnt the values attributed to manhood without giving way to subservience or becoming abusive or sexually aggressive. I learnt to be comfortable being a man, to enjoy my manhood, and learnt that manhood was a quality of being, rather than something defined by outward actions. Part of this was learning to enjoy the friendship of other men, but also to enjoy being a man with women. It was also about looking at the issues that had prevented me from taking up my identity of manhood (e.g. my relationship with my mother) and letting go of the anger, bitterness and revenge that came from having to surrender my manhood to my mother at a very early age. My mother feared, hated and mistrusted men because she was abused so badly by her father, so I learnt from childhood that men were bad, untrustworthy and abusive. Obviously, as *I* was a man this meant I inherited a series of negative associations with men and manhood. Once I had learnt to accept my manhood, once I had let go of the anger and betrayal I felt about my mother, once I had accepted that in many ways my father wasn't always a helpful role-model for being a man in the world, once I had started forming my own image of what a man is and should be (and began living in it), I could start enjoying my identity as a man without the shame, guilt and fear that I had taken on as a child. It also meant the self-destructive patterns of behaviour that I had demonstrated in my teens, linked to revenging my parents, could be replaced by more healthy, life-affirming living.

During Steven's most recent contact with me he shared the good news that he is engaged to be married. It seems his struggle with intimacy, sexuality and manhood has indeed been worthwhile.

Chapter 7

Josie's Story

Josie was the first person to answer my advertisement in the counselling journal. During our initial conversations she was concerned that she might not meet the criteria for the book because her drug of choice was 'only' cannabis. She seemed to be asking if her story was important enough to be included. My own view was that because cannabis use *is* so common, and seen in many circles as less harmful, Josie's story was all the more important. Her life and identity had clearly been shaped by her heavy and daily use of cannabis, her use of 'magic mushrooms', and her role as 'a cannabis dealer'. The traumatic loss that underpinned her story is also commonly experienced: the loss of a father through divorce.

Josie was born in 1973 and was aged 31 at the time of our meeting. She had been married for four years and had a child of 13 by a previous partner. She was brought up as a committed and involved member of a church with which her middle-class family have long been identified, and she has a wide circle of friends. She currently provides drug awareness training for younger members of her church.

Josie now works one day a week as a counsellor in a doctor's surgery and spends the rest of her time working on a farm and caring for her child. She began by telling me how pleased she was to re-tell her story at this point in time, from her current understanding about why she 'got into this mess'. I asked her, 'Where does your story begin?' And she laughed and said, 'Well I guess the thing that's really forefront in my mind is my dad leaving. I have this loop in my head of standing outside my house watching my dad drive away, and that was the end of my world. And it's like that's just dominated everything since then.'

Josie went on to tell me that for a long time she saw this one event as the cause of her problems and then added, 'But I've realised since that my childhood before that time was quite difficult anyway. When I think back to my early childhood I feel tension and kind of walking on eggshells.'

She described a memory of a day that seemed to encapsulate her life at that time. The memory Josie related, whilst moving in and out of the past and present tense, evoked powerful feelings of sadness in me as I pictured this little girl trapped in a double bind.

I really want to love you but I'm not allowed

I have a really strong memory
of when I was about six:
I'd just been given a bin bag full of clothes,
    I had second-hand clothes most of the time,
and I was wearing this dress that I loved,
    it was a knitted dress,
and it was a boiling hot day!

My dad was washing the car
and I was stood watching him,
and I have a feeling with my dad of,
    I really want to love you but I'm not allowed
    so I'll just stand here and watch you.
And my mum was in the kitchen,
    I was a bit easier around her,
    and I felt safer going away from her as well.

There was a feeling of not wanting to leave my dad,
    even before he left,
not wanting to go away from him
in case he went.

Josie was used to her father working away from home, so her fear of losing him
seems to be more linked with him leaving the family than simply working away
from home. It appeared that at some level she was already aware of the possibility
of her parents' separation.

Whatever I did I was going to lose

I remember my dad saying,
    I'm going to the shop.
    Do you want to come?
And me really wanting to go with him.
And him saying,
    Well, if you want to come,
    go and change your dress
    because you can't come in that.

And then, me going in
and seeing my mother and thinking,
    Oh my god, I can't go with him
    because I'm going to have to leave her.
    But if I stay with her
    then he's going to go without me.

And just being completely paralysed
and getting into a right state.

The feeling of that memory is like my life was,
you know,
  I had to choose.
  And whatever I did I was going to lose.

Josie was torn between, what seemed to her, two impossible choices, and with no way to express herself she felt 'paralysed'. She went on to describe a traumatically charged memory of the very day her father left.

It was like he'd gone to the moon

Me and my brother were at a party:
and my mum called us over and said,
  When we get home Dad's going to leave.
  He's going to live in Germany.
And that's all I remember her saying.

And we got home and the car was packed,
and I don't even remember saying goodbye.
Knowing my father now
I can imagine that he just got in the car and went,
  not in an uncaring way,
just because he couldn't bear it.

The feeling I get when I go back to that memory
is of being paralysed and rooted there,
and watching him drive away
off the edge of the world really.
  It was like he'd gone to the moon.

And thinking he's gone because of my mum
  and I can't change it.

And I just couldn't make sense of it.

The kind of paralysis Josie describes here is commonly experienced in response to traumatic events when the perception of threat (experienced in the body), and the inability to discharge the energy released by the nervous system in response to the perceived threat, results in immobilisation. Without any means of release the child experiences a sense of frozen helplessness.

So Josie was left alone to deal with her traumatic loss. Her mother gave mixed messages about being available to support her, telling her on the one hand that 'It's okay to cry, and if you want to talk to me about it, that's okay', but on the other hand, when Josie tried to express her feelings of loss and anger, her mother seemed unable to cope.

I want my dad

I remember just being really upset one day,
and saying,
    I want my dad,
and her saying,
    Well go and have him then,
and just getting really angry with me.

The end of my childhood

That was the end of my childhood really,
    when he left,
and I just spent from eight till about fourteen
feeling like I could not communicate
with anyone.

The world went on at this level
[*hand under her chin*]
and there was all this going on
at this level
[*pointing to her body*]
that I just couldn't express or articulate.

Josie went on to describe how her sense of self was impacted by the beliefs formed by the loss of her father that continued to influence her even after her mother had re-married and she had established regular contact with her father.

The tapes in my head

From when I was about eleven or twelve
it was like I had a tape going in my head all the time,
    My dad left and doesn't love me.
    My mum doesn't want me.
    My step-dad hates me.
    I am stupid and horrible
    and no-one likes me.
    I wish I was dead.

Josie sounded tormented as she described the insistent nature of those intrusive thoughts and ideas. She really wanted help.

I wanted somebody to talk to

From when I was about twelve or thirteen
I wanted somebody to talk to
who would understand how I would feel
    and make me feel better.

I've got letters that I wrote to teenage magazines
    and problems pages,
and I remember pestering my mum
to get me a psychiatrist.
And it's just so frustrating
    the things I did to try and get help
    didn't work.

She had always done well at primary school, getting good marks even when she spent 'half the lesson daydreaming'. It was the one part of her life that was 'predictable' and 'made sense'. But once she went to secondary school 'all that nose-dived', and teachers made comments about her 'not living up to her potential'. However, she threw herself passionately into subjects that involved writing essays and communicated some of her self-loathing and confusion through that work.

Why are you smoking?

I was about fourteen or fifteen,
and this guy who worked in a local shop said,
    Why are you smoking?
and he kind of took me on one side
and had this conversation with me.
And of course it was like,
    Wow, a man, expressing an interest.

So I wrote all this stuff about hating myself
and wanting to punish myself,
    I'm worthless
    so this is all I deserve.

And I showed it to him.
And then I showed my English teacher
and she said,
    If you just change this and this
    you can enter this for your GCSE.

So she was really affirming,
she was kind of taking it seriously.

Shortly after that, and maybe as a response to concerns aroused by her essay, Josie was assigned to a teacher who was involved in 'pastoral care'.

I really trusted her

I was able to talk to her
and I really trusted her,
I remember really enjoying the fact
that she was actually interested
and wanted to know what I was doing.

And by that time I was taking drugs
and she was just happy to listen to it
and I was like,
>   Wow, someone really wants to hear me,
>   this is great.

And then one of my friends got arrested.

She'd told the police what I'd been telling her,
and got him arrested.

That was just horrendous.

Now I look back and think,
>   How naïve!
It was so obvious, what was happening.

We weren't hiding it very well.
I was so *keen* to tell people.
My mum knew I was taking drugs
so they had all the information.

When Josie was 14 her mother gave birth to a baby girl, and Josie believed that her mother would want to: 'let that [previous] family go – because we've got a new family now'. She defined herself then as 'a reminder of a bad time' for her mother.

I was just someone else

I remember going to this party and getting drunk
and going into the toilets
and looking at myself in the mirror
and thinking:
>   I just look the same
>   but inside I feel so different.
>   And the 'voice' has stopped
>   and I feel happy.

That was the drink.

I was so nervous normally,
I was so quiet and introverted,
>   and timid, and scared of everything,
>   scared of boys,
>   and scared of telling anyone
>   how I felt or what I thought.

And then I'd drink and I was totally different,
>   and really popular as well,
>   attractive to boys,
>   felt lovable and loved,
and it was like I was just someone else.

Josie liked the 'someone else' she became when using alcohol so her drinking escalated. She became 'angry and kicking' at home, especially towards her mother and step-father. She continued to drink heavily until she became ill.

If you don't stop drinking...

I became really badly ill with my kidneys,
and the doctor said,
    If you don't stop drinking
    you're going to die.

And I think she was trying to scare me,
    but I *was* very ill,
    and she *did* scare me.

I can't honestly remember
the first time I took cannabis,
but I just remember thinking,
    Wow, I can still get out of it
    and I don't have to drink.

So cannabis gave her an alternative way to keep her emotional and mental distress at bay. Like many young people, Josie first obtained and used drugs in the company of friends who then became the focus of her world. Having for so long felt unable to communicate with others she welcomed the company of people with whom she could identify, whose lifestyle she could share and where she had a sense of being understood and accepted.

Family attitudes to drug taking would also have a part to play in her using at this time. She was aware that two of her uncles were smoking cannabis, which was seen as less harmful than heroin, which was classed as 'bad drugs'.

I'd grown up with this shadow of 'bad drugs'

My mum's brother was a heroin addict
and his girlfriend died of a heroin overdose
    when I was six or seven.
So I'd grown up with this shadow of 'bad drugs'.

And my mother's sister,
then got into a relationship
with a man who'd been on heroin.

And both these uncles were significant for me
    and they still smoked pot...
I used to go to London to stay with my aunt a lot
and both the uncles would be there.
    Though it took me a while to realise
    what they were doing.

So I kind of grew up with this shadow of,
    drugs kill you.
So when these boys at school were taking drugs
I was thinking,
    That's awful.
    I would never do drugs.

At this time Josie was also making relationships with boys in the group.

Looking for my dad

I was desperate for a man to love me,
    you know,
I was still looking for my dad
    who was going to cuddle me,
    and hold me, and love me,
    and make everything alright.

So once I started getting
sexually interested in boys,
that all got mixed up with that.

So it was really lovely to get into this gang.
I could be one of the lads
and they would share their drugs with me,
and it was really nice.

And very quickly I fell in love with one of them.

They were very working class, all these lads,
    and I was middle class,
and they were very angry and violent,
and not afraid to show their feelings,
and it was like,
    Okay, this is real,
    this fits with my reality.
    All that stuff about working hard
    and getting a good job is crap.
    They know what I'm talking about.

And that's when the balance shifted,
and I was paying lip service to school work.

And I remember my teachers saying,
    What are you doing?
    You've got to work,
    you're throwing it all away.

At this time Josie was living between separate worlds. As a single man, her father was taking her as his partner to business functions, but he knew nothing of her drinking and drug taking, or her behaviour at home. Josie felt very 'split', as if she had a battle going on between different parts of herself: one part really keen to do well at school because she wanted to go to university – the part she described as: 'goody-goody, do your work, do what daddy wants' – and another very different part.

Split between two parts

This other part getting more and more angry
and rebellious and wild, from taking drugs,
> Just, fuck it,
> I don't care what anybody else says,
> I'm just going to do what I want.
> I'm angry and the world's a mess,
> and nobody understands.

At the age of 16 Josie fell in love with Jim, one of the young men in the group, a man she perceived as 'damaged' by his upbringing. But he disappeared suddenly from her life. Later she discovered that he had come to her home to say goodbye and had been turned away by her mother. Josie left school and enrolled to do three A levels at college, having achieved good results in her GCSE exams, but after the first term at college she dropped out.

My life was a mess

I'd left home to live on a site with these lads,
in makeshift benders and caravans.
> I wasn't working,
> I was taking a lot of drugs.

My life was a mess.
Taking loads of magic mushrooms
> and drinking a lot
I'd lost contact with all my nice friends

My mum wasn't very happy
because of the company I was keeping.
She said
> You're welcome
> to come and live at home
> if you stop hanging round with them.

I had a couple of relationships
with men living on the site.
One was about 20 years older than me,
> quite a violent person,

he was quite scary…

He just spotted me and said,
    I want you, so,
I just thought if a man wanted me
then I should do what they wanted.

I was so desperate I would go with anybody
I know it's to do with my relationship with my father.
Certainly, there was a part of me
really wanting love and attention,
    a child part of me
    wanting a father figure,
and I was just so desperate I would go with anyone

And then there's another part of me
that was very hard on myself.
That always felt unloved, worthlessness,
and was saying to me,
    Yes, you are worthless,
    you should do what other people want
    and it doesn't matter what you think.
So the two of them combined were quite powerful,
    I just did what men wanted really.

As the only female in the group with men who spent time watching pornographic films, Josie's view of sexuality was heavily influenced by the images she was being exposed to.

Sex is just something for men

That's been a massive problem
    and still is,
because I don't now know what sex is,
    in terms of something that's
    pleasurable and enjoyable for me.
It's just something that's for men.

So, on a physical level
I'm just shut down,
    not interested in sex.
And those first relationships
were just really awful.

Like many young children whose fathers leave home, Josie believed that her father had gone because she loved him. This belief was reinforced when Jim left, believing that her loving him had caused him to leave too.

I'm not nice enough for you

So whenever I really like somebody
I would not allow myself to follow that up.

I remember saying to boys at school,
before I became sexually active,
    I can't go out with you
    I'm not nice enough for you
and just deliberately being horrible to them
so that I would sabotage my attractiveness.

Josie then formed a relationship with Dave which lasted ten months, and after they split up she found she was pregnant, at the age of 17. The baby became an important turning point.

Rock bottom

...it was kind of rock bottom
    from one point of view because,
the baby gave me a conscious reason
to sort myself out.

My father was really pressing
for me to have an abortion,
and then later,
for me to give up the baby when she was born.

My mum was washing her hands of me, saying,
    Well, you can have the baby,
    but I don't want you living here.
    You have to do it on your own.

But it was too important
for me to sabotage,
    the way that I had sabotaged
    everything else I'd wanted...

I've always been really aware of children,
    and how they suffer,
and it's always been really important to me
that I don't knowingly do anything
to cause harm to a child.

After Rebecca's birth, without a stable base, and with the additional responsibilities of single parenthood, she returned to her friends within the drugs world, and was soon back using drugs again.

Selling cannabis

I had a week in hospital,
two weeks at my mum's house,
and then three weeks
with my aunt in London,
    with the hope of living there,
but I really was miserable,
and I came back.

I rented a room from a church member
'til Rebecca was 5 months old,
and in those few months,
I was getting more and more
dependent on drugs,
and more and more
wrapped up in that world,
and I was starting to sell cannabis
to make a bit of extra money.

When her friends began to use heroin, sometimes in the same room as her baby, she realised that she needed to remove herself and Rebecca from that environment.

I can't trust someone who's taking heroin

I felt like,
    it's not enough
    to be doing things on my own,
    I have to get out of this culture
    these people are not trustworthy.
    I can't trust someone who's taking heroin…

Josie moved away from the area for two years. She spent a year living with her uncle, an ex-heroin addict who still smoked pot and drank alcohol on a daily basis. Her mother's parents also lived nearby.

Amazing people

My grandmother is probably
my closest family member
throughout my life.

My grandfather was fabulous with Rebecca
when she was small.

They are both amazing people
who I aspire to being like,
    though [they're] not particularly demonstrative.

During the second year she lived in that area Josie formed another 'unhealthy' relationship – this time with her uncle's friend. Towards the end of that period she left him and took a room in a village where 'there were weird sex scenes going on' and she became involved on the fringes of that.

Weird sex scenes

The man I rented the room from
was about 60 or 70
  and he was very rich
  and he'd go to these parties.

I think he was mostly just watching but
he'd tell stories about it
and buy large amounts of alcohol,
  and have dinner parties
  and encourage us all
to take our clothes off and have sex.

He'd buy me underwear to dress up in.

In a conversation held later, Josie told me she felt prostituted in some ways by those experiences, because her body was being used for sex without her full emotional engagement or consent. She felt, 'That's as much about me doing it to myself as others doing it to me.'

My 'normal' is actually 'abuse'

Yes, at one level,
I was very emotionally immature,
  but at another
I was acting very mature.
I was dressing up in a provocative way,
  and saying and doing things around sex
that implied I was fully aware of what I was doing
and what I wanted.

I didn't ever feel 'pimped'
  but then
  I wouldn't know what that feels like!
I guess I have a stereotype of a pimp
being aggressive and violent.

The old man I lived with
was neither of those –
  he was very generous financially
  and very well mannered.
But he did coerce me into things
I felt uncomfortable about.

So, that's abusive,
and, at some level, involves aggression,
…he used my dependence.

The process of healing
involves me realising that
my 'normal' is actually 'abuse',
'trauma' etc.
It is incredibly hard to see it in that way,
even after years of work.

I still have a voice saying
        Oh, but he did so much for me.
        He paid for all my food,
        didn't charge me rent,
        paid off my debt to my ex
        who wouldn't give me my clothes
        until I'd paid my share of the rent,
        paid for me and a heroin-addict boyfriend
        to stay in the most expensive suite in a hotel.

        Jim wouldn't come,
        said it was too weird.
        He knew!

Josie looked upset as she recounted this part of her story. I was aware of what she had told me earlier about learning about sex through pornographic videos: it seemed her behaviour might have been modelled on what she believed sex to be about.

I checked that she wanted to go on, aware that she might have been struggling with a sense of shame. But she opted to continue.

Can you come and get me?

I went home on a visit,
talked to Dave's brother,
        who was Rebecca's uncle
        a very good friend of mine,
and when I went back I phoned them up
and said,
        This is no good,
        can you come and get me,
and they came down with a van and got me.

This move brought Josie back into closer contact with Rebecca's father, Dave, who she had described earlier as a 'shadowy' figure, 'overwhelmed by life'.

Up all night, dancing

Dave would look after Rebecca while I went out.
I started going to rave parties
and taking lots of magic mushrooms
and staying up all night, dancing.

I was going out a lot with his brother
and I would sleep in his room.
    So we were all in the same house.

That was quite nice for Rebecca
    to be part of a family.
But Dave's dad was an alcoholic
so it's all a bit – it was just…

At this point Josie began to deal in cannabis seriously, in order to pay the rent and other living expenses.

During the two years Josie had lived out of her area she had taken an A level course and now she went back to college again to study psychology in her home town where she met up again with Jim, her first love, and felt the old feelings for him, but she recognised he was 'too damaged', and refused his offer of marriage. At that time the group she had previously hung around with had 'grown up a bit': they were holding down jobs, paying mortgages, even whilst using cannabis daily, and taking acid, speed and ecstasy at weekends. The heroin users had fallen away; some of them were dead.

At this time, still using cannabis, she met Pete at college, someone from 'a nice middle-class family' whose parents were also divorced. The atmosphere in his home was accepting – even of Pete's drug use – and he seemed keen to help her look after Rebecca.

How can I be a good mother?

But that relationship again was difficult.
He was taking cocaine
    on and off
and he was quite violent,
    not to me
    but with other people.

Occasionally he would get angry,
    be a bit scary,
he was very big, strong.

I gave up cannabis.

I remember getting up one day
and watching myself
take over an hour to get my drink

and thinking,
> This is ridiculous.
> How can I be a good mother
> if I'm like this,
and I just stopped.

After giving up using cannabis Josie became overwhelmed, feeling under pressure and responsible for the pain she had 'caused' the two men who wanted to have a committed relationship with her. Without the drugs with which to escape her distress, she slashed at her arms, causing deep wounds. She tried to explain to me her reasons for cutting herself.

Cutting myself as a punishment

I'd been with Jim
and he wanted us to get married
and when it came to the crunch
I didn't actually want to be with him.

And then Pete was really pushing
for more commitment,
> and I didn't want it.
So the cutting myself was a kind of punishment
> for 'leading men on'.
That's the way I was seeing it.

But soon after cutting myself
I got pregnant again and had an abortion
> because I didn't want another child
> whose father I didn't want to live with.
And Pete was too unstable,
> quite aggressive.

The abortion was pretty horrific

The abortion was pretty horrific.
And on top of it,
I had quite frightening hallucinations
in reaction to the anaesthetic.

After we'd split up and I told him
I was going to have an abortion
he was saying,
> You've killed my child
> so I'm going to kill you.
I couldn't go out on my own,
I had to take one of these lads with me.

Pete had already served a prison sentence for assault so, knowing she had to take his threats seriously, Josie served him with an injunction. By this time she had completely lost faith in her ability to make decisions about relationships. Although she was worried about the degree of emotion she had to deal with she never went back to using cannabis, but instead she started using alcohol again, to help wean herself away from drugs.

At this point her godmother offered to pay for her to see a counsellor. Josie's GP had offered her the support of a community psychiatric nurse when she was pregnant with Rebecca, but she had seen that 'as a hoop I had to jump through, to be left alone to take drugs' and had not used it in the spirit that made it useful. This time she was ready to make good use of the counselling.

I suddenly reached out my hand

It's almost like
I suddenly reached out my hand
and it was really important
that someone took it.

I saw her for about four years.
She helped me start to communicate.
I'd been quite articulate with myself,
but never found anywhere to say it.

So I stopped drinking quite quickly
because my therapist said
she wanted me to be completely sober.

I didn't drink for years after that.

I always knew that
I was taking cannabis and drinking
to deal with the emotions and
once I had a support for the emotional stuff...
I could cope with that.
I mean I still wanted it a lot...

* * * *

During her later written reflections on our conversation Josie wrote about both sets of grandparents, all of whom she admired in different ways. Their spiritual and religious beliefs had shaped the ways they lived their lives. Both grandfathers had been conscientious objectors during the war, her mother's father having been imprisoned for his beliefs. She described her maternal grandmother as 'practical, rational, unemotional and unaffectionate'. However, her maternal grandfather was 'a very sensitive man', who 'just got on with it' when he was imprisoned.

Her father, who had attended a church boarding school from an early age, had always struggled with depression and found it hard to deal with the knowledge that his own father had been unfaithful to his mother from when he was eight or nine years old until he was 16, when his father left the marriage and married his lover. I found myself wondering what might have been the impact on Josie's parents of *their* parents' traumatic experiences and ways of coping. And how did her parents' childhood experiences impact on her own? We now know that traumatic experiences in one generation can impact on another generation.

By 'witnessing' the impact on her parents and grandparents of the trauma in their lives, Josie gives herself a chance to witness, understand and change the impact of trauma in her own life, thereby increasing the possibility of developing resilience and limiting the possibility of passing her own trauma onto future generations.

★   ★   ★   ★

Josie responded to reading her story by saying how much she enjoyed seeing her life framed against the backdrop of her ancestors:

> It was something about the fact that my story is part of a bigger picture, there's a kind of template that plays itself out in different ways through the generations, but with a common thread. So my story makes more sense when set in the bigger picture of my family relationships.

Chapter 8

George's Story

George had emailed me in response to reading my advertisement for participants for this book in a counselling journal. He had read some of my earlier work about adult male survivors of childhood sexual abuse and told me how that had helped him in his work with that client group in a prison. He offered to tell me his own story and we began an email and telephone correspondence in preparation for the time when we would meet face to face.

He was working as a musician *and* a counsellor and I was intrigued to find out how someone could manage to balance both those lives. I sensed an enormous energy even in these early communications and was to discover more about that energy as his story unfolded.

George was 50 when we met. He was the third son born to parents who already had a five-year-old and ten-year-old in 1954 when George was born. He had started using drugs at the age of 17 and carried on doing so for at least ten years. Drugs for him meant 'smoking dope, pot, cannabis, more or less every day, and doing other drugs depending on the situation, LSD, cocaine'.

Early childhood in the family

From around the age of five he had known things were not right in his family:

> I always felt like a Martian – from as early as I can remember – totally alienated from my brothers and my father. Just thinking, 'Who are these people, what is going on? This is horrible.' My childhood seemed to have no form. The behaviour of the people around me seemed mad. I couldn't…make any sense of it at all.

> My father was a very unhappy, bitter man. He was very angry, and violent – but not to me, I was too young; it was mainly directed towards my oldest brother Barry.

> I didn't like this man who was my father. I despised him. He obviously never loved me – or maybe he did in his own strange way – but not the sort of love I wanted. I can't ever remember him touching me in any affectionate way, or being affectionate or loving in any way really. [*Pause*]… Just an unpleasant childhood really. I was puzzled by what these adults were doing.

Traumatic loss

I noticed that up to then George had not included his mother in the story and asked if he was also puzzled by his mother's behaviour.

> Well, my mother loved me, it's clear. I was always close to her. I was the youngest: her pet, her baby. She had nearly killed herself in pregnancy because I was unwanted and unexpected and she wasn't happy with my father. But when I was born I had a very bad skin disease: she had to bathe me in olive oil three times a day, and she told me afterwards that this just bonded her to me and she grew to love me intensely.

> My brother, Barry, who was ten years older than me, was too old to connect to. He's a strange man now. He bore the brunt of my father's anger and bitterness, and that scarred him then, and he's scarred now, even in his 60s. He talks about it all the time. He was really, really damaged by horrible psychological cruelty, and physical cruelty too. My middle brother, Jake, [*pause*] he's a fantasist, he lies all the time. I've never got on with him really.

> I don't wish to paint it as though I was a perfect child: I'm sure I was a little brat and that I found ways to manipulate the situation to my own ends.

> What happened was that my mother left, just disappeared, and I was left with them, and I was distraught. She was the only bit of sanity I had in my life and she just disappeared.

I noticed my sense of shock on hearing that his mother had left. George was eight years old when his only 'bit of sanity' had left him alone in this 'horrible' family. Already, I had built up a picture of just how important his mother had been for him; it was hard for *me* to make sense of this, let alone a small boy of eight.

> One day my father said, 'Your mum's gone on holiday. How would you feel if your mum got a job while she's away and didn't come back for a while?'

> I can remember saying, 'I wouldn't like it at all', you know. And I was left there with my father and my brothers, and it was horrible, just horrible. And there were a couple of things that happened with my brother Jake that were very difficult for me, there was mild sexual abuse and...

Sexual abuse

I noticed how he used the passive voice – 'there was mild sexual abuse' – not 'I was sexually abused'. So I asked for clarification: 'Did he abuse you?'

> He abused me, yes, and there was one time when he was suffocating me with a pillow that was quite traumatic for me. Whenever I tell this story, especially now when I work with severely traumatised people, I always hear myself going, 'It's not as bad as what happened to some people.' But of course, to me it was *devastating*. I still remember it – in fact when I think about it clearly, I can remember the pillow; I

> can remember snot coming out of my nose; and me trying to breathe, and thinking I was dying. But I'd always thought it was my older brother [Barry] who did this. It was only when I plucked up the courage to talk to him about this a few years ago that he said, 'It wasn't me, it must have been Jake.' Then I realised that it *was* Jake.

George seems to be drawing attention to well-recognised psychological defence mechanisms of 'minimisation' and 'deflection' – a means of avoiding full connection with painful experiences. However, he seems to catch himself doing this and re-adjusts his story, allowing me, through his sensory memories, to understand his terror, believing he was going to die. By speaking to his brother Barry about his unclear memories he had brought them more clearly into focus.

Traumatised individuals are often too fearful to confront directly the people they believe have abused them, so rarely do they have the chance to check out the details of those events. However, when abusers *are* confronted, they rarely acknowledge their culpability, even when guilty. But in this instance, Barry's denial is not experienced by George as an avoidance of responsibility, but rather as a chance to clarify the identity of his abuser, and to realise that he had never felt safe with Jake.

> I only realised a few years ago that it *was* sexual abuse, you know? I only realised when I started doing my training for working with sexually abused people that what had happened to *me* was sexual abuse.

I asked him how he had viewed those experiences at the time they were happening and he explained that he thought that it was 'normal' – what brothers do when they were exploring their sexual curiosity. He now understands that, when a boy of 12 or 13 engages sexually with a seven- or eight-year-old, the power balance in the relationship is unequal.

> It was mild you know, it was mild in comparison to what happens to some other people, but that's not the point.

As a therapist I was curious about what he saw as 'mild' but as a researcher I wanted to stay with the story so, rather than delving into his experience of abuse, I stayed with a focus on the context in which those behaviours occurred and pointed out that he probably didn't have any other experiences against which to measure that behaviour at the time.

> Exactly! All I had was the hell that my life seemed to become. My mother had gone and there was violence and abuse going on, and no love. And to be fair, Barry did his best.

I asked who had been looking after him during this period.

> I can't remember being looked after by anyone during that period – which seemed like a hell of a long time – but it was probably only four months. She came back and got me. My father…didn't want me, he wanted to get rid of us all, but my mum

took me with her, and Jake went off to a residential school, and Barry, who was eighteen, left home. So my father got married again a year later.

I went with my mum and we travelled around the country, living here and there. This was the early 60s, and quite difficult for a woman on her own. She would get a job here and a job there, around the country as a housekeeper, or silver service waitress.

Trying to establish a secure base

We had a succession of scrapes and episodes. She was a very attractive 40-year-old and she worked as a housekeeper for this bloke who asked her to marry him. He turned out to be a violent man. As soon as this came out we did a moonlight flit. Eventually, she got a job in a boarding school, and part of her pay was that I became a pupil there. I was a working class 'oik' among all the children of poor diplomats. And that was a year of absolute hell for me.

Once again George felt like 'a Martian' – different in so many respects from the other boys at the school. The boys hated him because, whilst they rarely saw their mothers, his mother was 'just down the corridor'. This was where he learned to be 'a good fighter' in order to defend himself.

His mother was trying her best to create a secure base for George by obtaining employment that came with accommodation, but it wasn't working out well and he was extremely unhappy. They moved from pillar to post, trying to find a place to settle. Eventually, when George was ten years old, his mother married, trying to bring stability into their lives.

He laughed as he told me that his mother had great ambitions for him: 'She wanted me to be Prime Minister basically!'

I was very bright at school, academically clever, and I could see how her life became about providing me with a foundation, and paying me back for all the things she felt she'd done to me. So I managed to do a late 11 plus examination and got into the grammar school – which happened to be half a mile from the house of the man she'd married.

In spite of all his disruption, unhappiness and abuse, he had managed to do well academically.

Yes, I was just clever at that sort of thing: my spelling, my maths was good. I was good at geography. I was quite precocious, you know: I would have my nose in books all the time. I can see now it was a way of making a world that was relatively safe, a fantasy world.

His stepfather had few parenting skills and George had no respect for his clumsy efforts to discipline him. He realised as he reflected on his own behaviour that sometimes he had treated his stepfather cruelly, making him look foolish in arguments by using his greater intellect, and outsmarting him at every turn. He visited his biological father for weekends three times a year and his brothers visited occasionally, when he would be pleased to see them. There was no opportunity for Jake, who was by then in the army, to abuse him again.

> It [the abuse] was never in my consciousness... It was only as I talked about my childhood in therapy that I realised what had happened, and how it might have affected me. I'd always remembered the thing with the pillow, and I'd always attributed it to my other brother, strangely. So that took a bit of unearthing.

Early adolescence

So George was on the cusp of adolescence, living in a new home, with a new 'Dad' and a new school, and it sounded as if he was coping well, in spite of his disrupted life. I wondered what had helped him cope. He began to describe a rich fantasy world that became his retreat from reality.

> I would design worlds, you know? I'd have a motor racing world in which I would have Formula One cars and I'd paint them all up, and I'd have books, and keep records, and I'd have an American Civil War world, or I'd fight these complicated war games. I'd make cricket games. I'd design games that I could play on my own because it was easier, more controllable: I wouldn't have this other person, this rogue element, who might do who knows what.

> And I would read, read and read and read – all sorts of things, mainly history and novels. I lived in a fantasy world. It seemed to keep me safe. Increasingly, I realised that I couldn't remain in that fantasy world, and that I had to go out into the big wide world, become an adult, and I had nobody (this is me looking back now), I had nobody to induct me into the adult world.

> My mum was still a child, she was useless, bless her. (That's what you always say when you're slagging someone off, isn't it?) She was useless at inducting me into the adult world, hopeless. My stepfather was hopeless. My father was miles away and I never felt connected to him. So I had no way of being inducted, no rite of passage – as I now see it – to becoming an adult.

> I was a loner. I didn't really have friends. There were a couple of older boys in the same road that I would play with. One played war games with me and the other was into the cricket and football, so that was quite good.

> School was a piece of piss for me. Even with no revision I would always come first, second or third in the class. I was teacher's pet because I was precocious – just one of those kids that was quite on the ball. I was good at sport as well, and I was good at acting, so I wasn't just a swot. I was able to relate to the sporty types, the clever types you know, the artistic types, so I was head boy potential you know. Never got a detention all the years I was at school.

> I was a *completely* good boy until I discovered... Well it was the time of the Beatles, the 60s. I also discovered Jean Paul Sartre and Frank Zappa, and I was just really taken aback by this – and rock music, San Francisco, hippy thing.

Adolescent identity construction

This was the first time George had mentioned the importance of music and philosophy as a means of shaping what was to become an important aspect of his identity: a professional musician. This part of the story seems to tell of his process of separate identity construction during adolescence when, because of biological, cognitive and social changes, the stage is psychosocially set for the construction of identity.

Biological and sexual changes are only part of the emerging picture. Certain changes in thinking may be equally influential at this time, when people think about the world and themselves in highly abstract terms – about what *might be*, rather than simply what *is*, and alternative realities can be imagined and sought out.

The adolescent knows that what he does may not always reflect who he is, that there may be a disparity between the 'me' other people see and the 'real me', inside. This search for identity is initiated and played out in a social context as a young person comes to know who they are through relationships and in social settings, as they move from one world to another.

Ideology is an aspect of identity that becomes a central issue in human lives during teenage years, addressing basic questions about what is right and what is true. A person's ideology functions as a setting for identity, providing the context for their story.

> I learnt to play guitar at a very fundamental level at the age of 11 from a boy in boarding school. I went to see the Beatles around 14 and my mum used to buy me Beatles albums. I loved the Beatles and through that I got some sort of knowledge of music.

> As I grew up, there was this group of people who had long hair and played in a band and I really wanted to be this boy who had hair down to here, because he represented rebellion. He represented the voice of alienation, revolution.

> You know, I can see the naivety of these things, but I can also see the fundamental power and importance of this too, because this is what all human beings feel, or I presume so, at some level. As you grow up you want to change the world; you want to make a mark. That's what I wanted to do and I saw a way of doing that. These people were in a band and I fell in with that bunch, you know, I started playing music.

> The music is vital. It's a vitality, it's something seminal, it's an energy that is here inside me, and it comes out into the world and it's like 'bang', it's free, it's a very childlike way of expressing feeling. I can see now that I was desperate to express feelings and there was a burst of energy that allowed me to do that, and that probably came from getting in with these people, and feeling that I could go from…[one world to another].

I wondered how he had managed to become part of that group, having described himself as 'a loner'.

I got on with people on a certain level. I was painfully shy, but I didn't find it *impossible* to be with other people. And of course, if you're smoking dope it's dead easy because you're bonded by that experience.

Smoking dope was like drinking coffee

At his mention of dope I invited him to tell the story of how, and when, he had come across drugs.

He was still living at home when he started using dope, unhappy with his step-father, unhappy at school, and realising he just had to get out of both places, whilst also being 'terrified' of doing so. Having done extremely well in his exams, he left school at 16:

I was a goody-goody, I was a prefect and at the end of the fifth and going into the lower sixth. I'd got into this bunch of people and discovered smoking dope and I started going off to the Roundhouse in London taking acid, smoking dope. And suddenly school became an absurdity to me, the rules…

I can remember this defining moment: I had all these nice clothes and I went down to Kensington market with my girlfriend and bought an old army jacket. We were walking up the road and I had on this sort of corduroy jacket. I said, 'Hang on a minute, I can't wear this, I'm going back to change.' And I ran back into the house and took off this corduroy jacket and put on this old army jacket. And my hair was growing longer, you know. School were saying, 'Oh, it's over your ears, get it cut.' Shit, you know. And I remember that as a defining moment. I went from being goody-goody to being a rebel – a rebel without a cause.

I met some fantastic people who were smoking dope, and I fell in with them – sort of hippy alternative types – and I just loved this, you know, it was the *alternative*. I saw the world of grown-ups as hell, and I was trying to find a way of avoiding growing up.

Being a musician is a great way of avoiding that, and of course in that world smoking dope, taking drugs is…well, it's almost encouraged. It's part of that creative, open, exploratory world. In the circles that I moved in smoking dope was like drinking coffee, you know? Nobody thought about it as taking drugs really.

So I became sort of a trainee hippy. I wanted to go to San Francisco but I'd missed it by a couple of years actually, and I'd misconstrued a lot of things that Frank Zappa and Jean Paul Sartre had said. Zappa was actually very cynical about hippies. I didn't quite get the level of cynicism and cleverness in his lyrics. Took them at face value in a way. He was actually saying, 'These people are ridiculous', you know. He thought, as I do now in lots of ways, that drugs tend to push you off line. They focus your energy on *doing* the drugs so perhaps a drug might open up your awareness; well then, have open awareness and use that. Don't just seek that experience of enlightenment again and again and again and lose it.

Using LSD

George began using LSD at the age of 16 and that continued for a couple of years until it took him to a place that 'was *more* scary than reality'.

> I think it's like being thrown into a space where you're immediately enlightened *without* being enlightened, without the ten, twenty years of study and meditation. So your perception is stripped of cultural givens and something happens to the brain. It can be a very wonderful place to go, where everything is beautiful and you see *into* things, or at least that's the illusion, but also you have nothing to steer by.

> Initially…it felt like the world was a wonderful, beautiful, subtle, complex, intense place. But there's more to it than that. It is a drug and different drugs will affect you in subtly different ways, depending on your mood. I could be in that space of extremes and then something might happen, and from heaven I would go to hell. High and low: heaven and hell at the same time. I could see how it was both positive and negative for me.

> It was a very formative time – just when I was striking out on my own, or attempting to, and I had a couple of what I can see now were 'nervous breakdowns', when I just fell apart really.

Discovering girls and sex

I enquired about his interest in intimate relationships during this period, when many young people begin to explore their sexual identity. He was 16 when he had his first sustained relationship with a girl he described as 'bohemian'.

> She came from a very interesting family that had money, and she went to a posh school, and mixed with famous people's children. So I got into that world where I went to film directors' houses and met very famous people, and their children. This was like, 'Wow, this is fantastic.'

I remembered how he had told me earlier that he had nobody to introduce him into the adult world but now it seemed as if his first girlfriend was able to offer him that. George seemed a bit distracted at this point and then mentioned that talking about this time had reminded him of his very first sexual experience with a female.

> I just remembered something else actually – my first sexual experience which was about six months before I met this girlfriend. The first time I had sex with this older woman I got gonorrhoea and the crabs. She was the local drug dealer, four years older, around 20 when I was 16.

> She was a very, very, very messed up person. I can see that now very clearly, and I was used in a way. But I was using her in a way too. I was like, 'Oh God, I'm going to have sex for the first time', you know. There are certainly better ways to lose virginity, I can see now, but…

I learned afterwards she was very well known for having sex with anybody. She would *expect* that you would catch gonorrhoea and the crabs from her. It didn't mean anything for her. To me it was really important and it began my first breakdown at that time. I'd thought I had a relationship with this woman and then it clearly wasn't anything like a relationship you know, and...[*laughs*]

I didn't know what was going on. I didn't have anybody I could talk to about it so I had to sort it out myself at the age of 16 – which was a bit tricky. So I went to the doctor's and he was very finger-wagging about it, you know. And gave me antibiotics and it was absolutely horrendous.

I sensed his confusion about whether this experience could be viewed as abusive or not – a confusion that often exists within a culture that socialises young men to feel 'lucky' when initiated into sexual activity by an older woman – a situation that might seem much clearer if the genders were reversed, i.e. a 20-year-old male who involved a 16-year-old girl in sex that led to her developing a sexually transmitted disease.

It was at the time I'd just left home. I was living with a friend who was two years older than me. He said, 'You're obviously not happy at home; you can have one of the rooms in the house.' It wasn't a commune – but there were a few people that lived there, and smoking dope was like having cups of tea, you know. I never questioned it really. I lived with him and then he moved and, you know, he was something to hold on to because I didn't have... Then we moved somewhere else and I moved in with him, some horrible basement flat, and then we moved somewhere else and I stayed with this guy. But unfortunately he drifted, with the other people in the house, into being a heroin addict and I was very fortunate, I didn't want to do that. I tried it once.

I was thinking how this constant moving seemed to echo his childhood experiences. I asked him about his experience of 'having a breakdown'.

I was crying all the time, just sat in my room crying and crying and crying, scared, terrified, just not knowing what to do. Things I couldn't deal with, feelings I just couldn't deal with; shaking, crying, for days on end you know.

Looking back on it I can see several things that might have caused me to feel like that: one was leaving home and the full force of the fact that I had to cope with life on my own – I didn't have my mummy. I didn't have *anybody* apart from the people whose house I was living in. They were doing their best, but of course their lives revolved around drugs, and of course drugs, even dope, which is a relatively [harmless drug]...well, it *can* induce mild psychosis for one in eight people. I've since known three people that have been sectioned through smoking dope. So I can see how maybe smoking dope kicked me into that slight, mild psychosis or – at least – a nervous breakdown or whatever.

I had no ground to stand on. That's what it felt like. I felt the world was a scary place. I'd left school, gone to college to do psychology, and dropped out of college, playing in a band. What was I going to do? This is real life, this is scary. Roll another joint, you know, take another drug. But heroin, I somehow drew back from that. I'm not happy with injecting drugs anyway. Just smoked it once, did the sort of 'chasing the dragon' thing once. I wanted drugs to open me out, and for me, heroin closed things down. It didn't appeal to me somehow, and I saw what was happening to the other people in the house. It wasn't good, two of them died in the end.

Resources to aid resistance to heroin

I wondered how he had managed to keep himself from following his housemates along that path. These were the only people he had to support him at this time and it was the only home he had. What resources did he have to draw upon to keep him safe?

That's an interesting question, how did I manage? [*Pause*] Having a girlfriend actually. She'd say, 'Are you sure you want to do this', and I'd think, 'Well not *really*', and I'd think, 'Look what's happening to these people, do I want to go down that path?' We might go somewhere in the country, it'd be beautiful and I'd go, 'I'm just going to skin up.' She'd say, 'Why d'you need to smoke dope to enjoy this?' Of course, if she had used, we'd have both got stoned.

Also, I saw how destructive it was, and I've always had this thing about wasting time – it felt like a bit of a waste of bloody time to me. I could see how that's partly wisdom and partly a parental voice you know, 'You should be doing something more…' So somehow I managed not to slip into that. I'm very glad I didn't. I existed on the edge of that, and I moved out of the house in the end because money would disappear from my room. I had to get away from it. The girlfriend at the time had a house she was given by her godmother, and we moved into that, and that got me away, luckily.

Impact of early experiences on sexual development and understanding

I asked if this was the same girlfriend he had described as 'bohemian' and this question led him into stories of his 'sexual dysfunction' and difficulties in sustaining intimate relationships:

No, this is a different one – there's been a few! I'm not very good at maintaining relationships. I'm not even a monogamist. I found myself having affairs and going off with women – sexually, very dysfunctional.

At this point he told me more about his mother's reasons for leaving when he was a small boy and why his father had 'thrown her out'. As a small boy, whilst hiding under the table listening to his mother's conversation with a friend, he overheard her talking about her sexual desire for the man with whom she had been having an affair before she left home. As a small boy this led him to believe that sex must be a very powerful thing if it had caused his mother to leave him.

> I discovered sex and masturbation were a way of keeping myself safe and relaxing when I was under pressure. There were the various homosexual experiences that I had with my brother and the abuse that went on, and then boarding school, where there was a lot of sex between the boys there. I've always had a problem with my sexuality: a sort of confusion.

> And when I started reading about sexual abuse, I saw how so much of that was relevant to me, you know? My first sexual imprint was with my *brother*. Ugh, you know. Obviously that's going to cause problems to a child.

I noticed that George referred at this point to his abuse by his brother as a 'homosexual' experience, indicating the mistaken assumption that any male-on-male sexual experience can be labelled 'homosexual'. Before there was a frame of reference for understanding sexual abuse of males, homosexuality was the only way of understanding those experiences, something that created sexual confusion and an inability to disclose such activities at a time when homosexuality might have been, at best, unfortunate and, at worst, illegal and immoral.

At this point George seemed to want to re-visit his story of sexual abuse and having mentioned masturbation I was assuming this was what he had meant as 'mild' abuse. So I asked him if this was the case. He told me that his abuse had involved masturbation *and* oral sex. I noticed my surprise that someone who had studied the sexual abuse literature, and who worked with abuse survivors, was defining masturbation and oral sex on an eight-year-old boy by his older brother as 'mild' and I observed, 'You said it was mild?'

> Well, yes, well, exactly. I mean I know. You see, here I'm being defensive and I'm minimising what happened to me, and I don't need to do that.

I explained that when he had used the word 'mild' I had imagined 'there'd been a bit of showing and a bit of touching'. I was aware of the difficulty for many people in defining male abuse when socialisation messages lead males to believe that anything sexual is OK for 'normal' males.

> Well, I began to realise that it *was* sexual abuse six years ago when I joined an organisation that works with sexually abused people, and started reading stuff, and listening to other men's stories of abuse. I said to someone, '*I* was sexually abused by my brother when I was seven or eight.' And he said, 'Whoa, are you all right?'

> I went into therapy and started looking at this and I realised I *had* been sexually abused.

I asked about the 'homosexual' behaviours he mentioned whilst at boarding school.

I can't remember any oral sex at boarding school. I remember mutual masturbation and just sort of touching and closeness and rubbing and, you know, lonely boys with *no* affection from anybody, with all these hormones and sexuality. It seems perfectly normal to me, you know. But of course, it's a heady mix all that, and abuse, and my confusion over my mother's sexuality.

The story he told then seemed to indicate that his mother had also had a sexual relationship with a woman during the time they were moving around:

We went around the country with what I can now see as a very 'butch' woman. We had to do a moonlight flit from one of her jobs because…I played this game with the guards in this place where Mum was a silver service waitress. I was young, nine or something, and they were saying, 'So your mum, does she have her own bedroom?' I said, 'Oh no, she sleeps with this other woman', you know. 'Oh, they have the same bedroom?' I said, 'Yes, they both sleep in the same bedroom.'

I can see that now…that's been put into context as the years have gone by. So, you know, confusion over sexuality and she would *never* talk about it, nobody would *ever* talk about this with her.

I observed that he had been exposed to complicated ideas and experiences at a very early age that might have been really confusing without anybody to talk to or ask questions of.

Yes. And again, at the back of my mind, when I work with people that have been horribly abused for years, I can see what happened to me was nothing [in comparison]. I can't even talk about it in the same sentence. But of course for me it *was* dreadful.

At this point it felt as if George was acknowledging his experiences as abuse and I wondered if he might be feeling distressed, so I checked out how he was. He seemed to want to continue telling his story so I summarised what he had told me so far, giving him a chance to correct any misunderstandings.

Early adulthood

The age of 16 had seemed a pivotal time in his life: leaving home, leaving school, having a breakdown, girlfriends, meeting people who were using drugs, and living in an atmosphere and group in which drugs were in the very air that he breathed. He had watched people sliding into heroin use, chosen to walk away from them and moved in with his girlfriend. I asked him what happened then and how he was earning his living at that time.

Between the ages of eighteen and twenty-four I was playing in bands, smoking dope and generally failing to enjoy hedonism.

I was earning my money as a musician playing around London and supplementing that with odd jobs, which wasn't a problem in the 70s really. I went into acting in the late 70s when I was around the age of twenty-four to twenty-five. I got an equity card and a job in a theatre group and worked for a few years doing that. Then I was offered a job in a band again with a full-time wage, you know, with a record company and money behind it, and we were nearly huge. So a regular wage for a few years, gave up the acting, got back into music, then another band came along and then another band and I toured round the world, being paid money, being on telly, thinking, 'Oh this is all right!'

By then I was in my late twenties and I'd just got into tai chi in 1982, and I felt this pull, which I still feel right this minute, right this week, today, now whatever, between the two parts of me: the crazy musician – friends of mine call it my evil twin, as a joke – and the serious studious academic. I'm *both* of those things, you know, but I felt the need to develop the other side of me, and tai chi helped release that.

A challenging conversation between two parts of self

At this point George began to describe how he experienced himself as having extremely different parts that together made up his sense of who he was.

I mean, I was, I am, a sensitive, intelligent person who's quite a decent person, you know, a good person. I can give rein to the other side of me, as we all can. It's a choice you know: we're all murderers, we're all thieves. I believe we can all do those things.

So many of the things I've done in my life have been driven by an attitude of 'Oh fuck it', you know? Well the older I get, the less sense that makes to me. How do I make sense of my life but through connection, not through alienation, as I have done for many years? In fact drugs feed into that sense of alienation and being special. In those days we'd call people 'straight' if they didn't take drugs, you know.

Being a musician, you know, artistic, I could exist on the cusp, or seemingly, and then it began to be apparent to me that *nobody* exists on the edge of society. We're all right smack bang in the middle, and *I* make this world the way it is, so everything I do is important. And today that is a sense of great pleasure, and great responsibility for me.

I looked at the drugs and thought, 'This is barmy.' And of course tai chi and meditation helped access that other important *solid* part of me, and it's like, 'Hang on a minute, why do I do this, why do I take drugs? That's a bit weird! Well, yes, to get high. Well, that's OK, yes, every so often', you know. A couple of pints or maybe, every so often, a couple of joints are no problem, but to do it every day...? 'What's wrong with me when I *don't* take drugs, what's wrong with me when I'm *not* out of it? Who am I when I don't take drugs, and who am I when I do? What do drugs do to me that I like?' So I began to look at all these things and the health aspect, you know? I'd go on a cocaine bender for a month and I'd be *really* ill, and I'd think, 'Hang on a minute, this isn't worth it.'

George met an acupuncturist who was also interested in kung fu and he began to practise both of those activities with him. This led to his interest in tai chi which was to become a major part of his life thereafter…

Tai chi

I was 28 when I started doing tai chi and began to get healthy and feel quite good in my body. I felt quite fit, and I could feel the energy, the qi and the sensitivity, and I began to think, 'This is how I can use my sensitivity positively.' And I was good at this. So I became obsessed with it, thinking, '*This* is the answer. I'm not going to be a great musician, I'm going to be a great tai chi master. When I'm a great tai chi master I'll be happy. I'm not going to do drugs any more.'

I found it very difficult emotionally through that very early period of doing tai chi. I just locked myself away in my room and came up against all sorts of stuff that I didn't quite know how to deal with. Fortunately I had a friend who had gone through something similar, and he suggested therapy.

So I began seeing a therapist in 1985. He was a well-known Jungian – sort of transpersonal – and it was perfect for where I was with the tai chi. He worked with my body, with the energies, and I successfully stopped taking drugs, but then there was no way of hiding what was going on from myself. So I began to deal with these things but the circumstances weren't right, various things happened.

I had given up being a musician for about five years, studying tai chi and teaching it on this path of enlightenment and cleanliness, purification, but then I was offered a job playing music again.

Throughout all the years of doing tai chi my body was very open and upright, and when I played the guitar again I found that my body immediately went back into the patterns I'd dropped from the previous ten years. Gradually I did a bit less tai chi, and I stopped doing therapy you know. It was virtually impossible travelling around with the band.

I got married in the summer of 1988 and had my daughter in '89, thinking that would root me even more, you know, 'I'm grown up now, I can handle this.' [*Laughs*] Whoops no, not quite.

He had been finding it hard to make a living from teaching tai chi and his wife was doing a degree. Between them they were trying to manage the care of their child. The marriage broke down when their daughter was three years old.

We had problems in the marriage. I had an affair with somebody down the road, and it was horrible, just horrible, and I left. I can see now that I used my wife to have a child but I *so* regret what I did.

The second defining moment was when I sat on the beach, not being able to carry on any more and wanting to kill myself, and realising I couldn't because I had a daughter and there was no way I could do *that* to her. I love my daughter, and then I remembered my mum saying to me, 'If it wasn't for you I wouldn't be alive today', and so I thought, 'Oh God, my life is full of circles. My life is full of downward spirals and circles and traps and cul-de-sacs and I'm living out something predetermined here. I'm living out a pattern, what's going on? I cannot kill myself; if I'm not going to kill myself I have to do something about that.' And that's when I got into therapy again and from that point I took more power, more control over my life, and I began looking at what drugs were doing to me. I found ways of dealing [with life] without taking drugs.

And I had two years of transactional analysis on a weekly basis and that provided a really important structure to base my life around, to stop me taking drugs. And I found clever ways, skilful ways of dealing with it.

George had been influenced by theories of Transactional Analysis (TA), which is based on the idea that people are made up of three ego states – Parent, Adult and Child – each with its own 'voice' that directs our behaviours and relationships. The aim of this kind of therapy is to become aware of, and balance, all three ego states, recognising that each can be valuable or problematic if allowed to take over. George had applied these theories to explain how they can relate to drug misuse:

I felt very clearly in terms of transactional analysis that drugs decommission Parent voices. They knock them out completely.

The Parent voice influences judgement and control, as well as nurture and protection. So George seemed to be indicating that when Parent is completely 'knocked out' by drugs, then there is neither control nor nurture. This understanding had seemed like 'a major breakthrough', which guided him to find a way of connecting with the emotions he held in his body. He realised that in order to give up using drugs he needed to access the Child ego state: calling upon the pleasure and fulfilment he had felt as a child involved in creating and playing games.

I love games and that's how my Child [ego state] manifests, a safe environment in which I know what the rules are, not like life. Games are contained. So I decided on a game. I said I'd work in four-day periods: on day one I could smoke dope *and* drink; on another day I could *just* smoke dope; on another day I could *just* drink; and on the other day of this four-day cycle I could do neither. And I could choose at any point in that cycle which one of those I would do. And it worked brilliantly, because the first day I'd think: 'Right, what do I want to do today? Do I want to smoke? Well no, not really.' So it broke the habitual use of drugs.

It made me *think* about what I wanted to do. And also, of course, it was quite good fun doing that. So I involved my Child in the decision-making process from a very basic level and it worked.

A wounded healer in a specific way

As George began to move towards the end of his story he began to reflect upon the meaning of his 50 years and what had led him into the profession he works in today.

I can look back and the tendency I have is to think, 'Oh *damn*, I *wish* I hadn't done all that: I wasted 20 years of my life taking drugs.' Well, that's the voice of that extreme part of me, because, actually, I've lived an interesting creative life. Yes, I've hurt some people but I've never done any *bad* things really. I've never killed anybody; I've never really inflicted pain or violence on anybody. I can see how drugs blurred the energy that I *could* have used elsewhere. I got married last summer and I love my wife, she's a fantastic person. I wouldn't be sat here talking to you if I hadn't done everything that I've done, so, you know, I don't regret it but I'm attempting to make sense of it. I'm moving from middle age, into older age, I have to make sense of my existence and this is the way I'm choosing to make sense of it now.

It [my life experience] has enabled me to *work* with people that have been sexually abused and have done drugs, because I understand something fundamental about that. I am the wounded healer in a specific way, so *that* is now making sense of my life, I can take that wound and use it to help other people heal themselves, and that is the focus of the rest of my life.

How do I make meaning out of the first bit of my life now? Well, it's not to dissipate the rest of my life; it's to focus it and use it, that's how I see it.

After I got involved in TA and began reading a bit wider, people would ask me, 'Are you a counsellor?' I'd say, 'No, don't be ridiculous.' They'd say, 'But you know a lot about it, why don't you become one?' And I started thinking, 'Could I? Well, no. I'm too fucked up to be a counsellor. You've got to be sorted to be a counsellor.'

It was only when I realised that of course you don't have to be sorted to be a counsellor, you just have to spot the fact that you're fucked up earlier than anybody else, and then not act on it.

And I thought, 'Could I?' So I did an RSA counselling skills course and I was quite good at it. I took to it. People were reflecting back to me that I had a way of being with people: I was articulate and sensitive. I read every book on counselling I could get hold of, and then I thought, 'Could I become a counsellor?' So I did. And it was fantastic…against all odds really, because I didn't see how I could possibly do this. I had no money, I was travelling around the world, how could I possibly do this?

Well, I know now I *could* do this because I really *wanted* to… So I made it happen. Given a framework to describe my experience through TA and inspired by Joseph Campbell's mantra of *Follow your Bliss*, I began reading and then studying psycho-therapy. I had realised that it was my *responsibility* to use my wound, as well as an opportunity to turn 'negative' to 'positive'. I had looked for meaning in my life for many years – suddenly I realised it was about *giving* meaning, not looking for it.

I took my Child with me, and my Child had always been terrified that if I grew up I would leave him behind and I promised him I wouldn't. And it worked for me you know. And so did the games.

Why did I take dope, you know, smoking dope all the time? Well, part of it was to feel high. I felt high today driving and singing to my stereo you know. I felt just as high as I could feel with a drug. And it's great because that's the energy I have, and that comes from my Child going, 'Yeah, I love this, it's great.' And that needs to be tempered by the rest of me, by doing the hard slog at times. It's not just energy and enthusiasm, but I have a lot of that and I love the work.

★　　★　　★　　★

Following our conversation I received an email from George:

Just wanted to tell you how energised and positive I felt after our meeting on Wednesday. I very much enjoyed talking about myself for two hours (!) and heard myself saying things and expressing them in a way I had not noticed before. Each time I reflect on the narrative of my life, it subtly changes.

Feeling so energised is, for me, an indication that something moved and developed. I know it is connected to my passion for the counselling work that I do and my desire to build on what I have already done.

I was intrigued to know more of George's experience and more of how he understood his positive feelings after our conversation. I also wanted to find out from him how he perceived the research conversation as similar/different to his experience of therapy. He agreed to try and unpick these questions. His responses were:

My experience of taking part in your research project was very positive for me for a number of reasons.

Each time I tell my story my narrative develops and allows me to see it differently. This certainly happened for me on this occasion. The context of research, rather than personal therapy, somehow faced me out into the world rather than inwardly toward myself, thereby altering the dynamic of the experience. There were similarities to therapy in that I felt you were genuinely present, as well as being sensitive to my story and my feelings, but you remained focused on the specifics of the task at hand, which were to facilitate the description of my experience and my thoughts on the development of my coping mechanisms without unduly or specifically delving into, or focusing on, my emotional state.

There was also the simple therapeutic effect of talking about myself to someone who seemed genuinely interested in what I had to say – I am of consequence and my experience has some importance – so much so that someone may even put it into a book! This also ties into the idea of the wounded healer, in that the negative aspects of my trauma may be turned to some positive use and may even help somebody else.

I had an awareness that I was taking part in a project with other people and was therefore one of a community of participants seeking to explore a subject that holds meaning for me.

I fully accepted for the first time that I had been sexually abused in my childhood. I *realised* it. I find it difficult to explain why this should be. I think it may be to do with the 'facing out into the world' that I mentioned above. I described the experience to my wife as, 'Something moved, something changed.' I had always been aware of the events of my childhood, but had always tended to minimise the effect that they had had on me. It was as if, suddenly, the rational and intellectual met with the emotional. As if my Child finally understood what my Adult and Parent had been saying for some time.

Chapter 9

John's Story

John was a year into 'recovery', having previously relapsed several times, when his counsellor told him about my study. Early into our first telephone conversation he told me that he connected his experience of being raped as a seven-year-old with his subsequent drug use, and that he wanted to tell his story now because his feelings about the rape threatened to overwhelm him each time he reduced his drugs intake, invariably leading to relapse. I sensed that he was still emotionally fragile so on the phone before we met, and again at our first meeting, we discussed his readiness to participate.

On first meeting John I noticed he seemed agitated. I made him a drink and asked how he felt about coming to see me. He began to talk about his ambivalence about Alcoholics Anonymous (AA) and the confusion he felt about the causes of his drinking and drug misuse.

He was very aware that the 12-step programme had really helped him and that his regular attendance at meetings generally supported him. He had come to view his substance use as a genetic problem, since his grandfather, mother and probably his father were all addicted to alcohol. However, he had also made the connection that he 'was using on his anger' and that the anger was related to his experiences of childhood neglect and rape.

He had been advised by his AA mentor to keep his addiction 'in one place and put this matter [the rape] in another place'. Once he began to think that his substance misuse might *not* be caused by him being an 'alcoholic addict', but related to unprocessed childhood trauma, he started to wonder if he really needed to go to AA meetings and became resentful about the constraints attached to the AA philosophy on abstinence. It seemed important that we talked about this conflict before he told his story as I did not want to risk confusing him further.

John: My disease starts telling me that I don't need meetings and it's not good really. So I have to keep…that's why I have to get to my meetings before my thinking starts…and my resentment starts building up.

Kim: Right. So does that mean there's a bit of a conflict about…um…?

John: …conflict of interests? Well, yeah – it causes me a lot of confusion really.

Kim: Yes. So you're afraid if you look at your childhood abuse that will in some way take you away from the good work that you've been able to do in AA?

John: …well I've been totally disillusioned, really, in a way.

Kim: Why?

John: Because, I suppose now I've built up a support network around AA and I just think, 'Well, why am I doing it then?', and I suppose I'm thinking I'd have to change my view – and if I could just deal with it, say like through counselling – why would I bother going to meetings if I'm not an alcoholic addict?

Kim: So how would it be to think about the value of both ways of looking at it? You know, that…maybe what happened to you as a child *might* have had some kind of impact on your using – *and* that you've also found AA very helpful?

John: It has been very helpful, yeah.

Kim: So why can't both co-exist?

John: I dunno. When I talked to you the other day on the phone – it just put me in a funny head space…

Kim: Did it?

John: But I think that's my disease saying, 'You don't need your meetings', and then immediately I'm finding things wrong with meetings – and before I know it I would have been drinking or using, you know?

Kim: Before you and I talked on the phone about this…um…your counsellor told you how I was looking for people who were making sense of their using in terms of it being a way of coping with difficulties in childhood, and you were saying, 'Well, that could be my story.'

John: Well, yeah, like I said to you, I think my drinking and my using… I think what happened to me as a kid set a precedent for my using, you know.

Kim: Can you tell me why you think that? Is there some sort of connection there?

John: Well, I just think that feelings of anger, feelings of shame are encompassed in that really. I think I drank and used drugs on that. And I'm still running on anger from it now, I know that.

Kim: Anger from being raped?

John: Yes, when I was seven years old.

★　　★　　★　　★

John had tried to tell this story in various settings but had always been diverted away from doing so. In a drugs rehabilitation centre he had been advised not to deal with the rape until he was drug-free; when he asked for help within the mental health system 'they just wanted to medicate me'; when rape flashbacks occurred during hospitalisation for hepatitis he again asked for help, which at first was offered and later withdrawn. Even his current counsellor within a voluntary mental health organisation told him: 'You've got to put that behind you and leave that there in order to move on.' He went on to tell me, 'There's part of me that thinks – yeah, that's right, but I need to know that I've dealt with it.'

I, too, was unsure if this was the right time and context for his rape story, but by explaining my concerns and taking into account his wishes, we assessed his resources and balanced the risk of his participation in the research with the potential benefits to him. John had good support systems in place: he was currently living in a 'dry house' and was supported by AA sponsors and regular meetings. He was a volunteer for a mental health organisation where he was able to access free counselling and I gave him information about other sources of free counselling specifically for survivors of sexual abuse.

Early years

John was born in 1968, but he looked much older than his 36 years as a result of contracting hepatitis through intravenous drug use. His 'career' of substance abuse had begun with alcohol and solvent sniffing around the age of 13 and progressed to a 'big problem' with amphetamines, acid, methadone and heroin. He spent his early childhood years in London living a 'hippy' lifestyle with his mother during the 1970s when 'dope was like air-freshener' in their home. His mother had left his father when John was a toddler, after she discovered he was seeing another woman, so John only knew his father through other people's eyes:

> He was er…in prison most of the time. I mainly heard bad things about him from my mum. My nan and grandad never liked him. When she left with me he came after her with a gun and my grandad chased him off with a shotgun. But I've never heard nice things about him. He has tried to keep in contact with me, but my mum stopped him.

John told me about the first time he met his father:

> I was starting a three-and-a-half-year sentence for robbery, and he'd just finished an eight year sentence for robbery… He came in to see me and brought me a bit of dope. That was the first time I'd ever seen him.

John was sometimes exposed to the sounds of sexual activity between his mother and her boyfriends behind the curtain that separated their beds, and sometimes he was left alone in their flat.

> …my mum used to go to the pub and, when she'd come back, nine times out of ten I'd have wet myself, you know. Even if I had diarrhoea I wouldn't use the toilet

outside 'cos there was a mad bloke who lived in the bottom [flat] – scary really. The key was left in the door, but I wouldn't go down and use it.

Although he sometimes visited his grandparents, whom he described as 'always there', his contacts with them were intermittent until he moved in with them when he was ten years old. John described his mother as 'an alcoholic' and 'drug user'; his grandfather also drank alcohol to excess; and he assumes his father was also 'a drinker'.

John became tearful each time he mentioned his father and I felt anxious about the degree of distress he seemed to be experiencing. After checking that he wanted to continue I noticed myself gently trying to steer him away from speaking of his father, but in spite of my efforts to 'protect' him he returned to the topic several times during our conversation, apparently confused about whether or not it was *his* responsibility to contact his father, whilst also thinking he had too many other things to deal with at the moment.

John told his rape story about half an hour into our conversation; it was brief and poignant.

> I was out playing one day, in a friend's playground, and I hurt myself. I was outside crying by a wall and a guy pulled up in a van and…I got in. I didn't know any better really. Maybe if my mum hadn't been drinking and using drugs I'd have been better looked after and not out on the streets in London at the age of seven with a key tied round my neck. I tried to tell my gran, yeah, but I couldn't. I said: 'Nan, I seen a man and a boy going down on the floor in the back of a taxi' – she couldn't make anything of that. I didn't know how to say it I suppose.

Moving to the country

When John went to live in the country with his grandparents he found it hard to settle into his new environment, or to relate to children of his own age. He began to mix with older people who were drinking and using drugs.

> So we moved to the country and I didn't want to be there: different school, different sort of policy on education. I think what happened to me [the rape] and growing up in the city really knocked the child out of me to be honest. I just became an adult straight away.

He had done well at primary school in spite of his difficult home life and the rape. He seemed to have a 'natural ability' for reading and athletics:

> I was all right when I went to junior school [in London]. I still didn't feel that I fitted in, but I made friends, and then when I went to secondary school…that was when it [drug use] took off really, that sort of age.

> I used to get the piss taken quite a bit at school. I can remember that [happening] at infant school but nothing like…because my hair used to be quite long, down to my shoulders… And [my mum] used to get me to wear sandals and stuff so I used to

get ridiculed, you know? But... I just used to deal with it really. I gave as good as I got in the end.

I honestly think if we had stayed in London I'd have done a lot better – I don't know. But it's just that the education system's different.

Beginnings of substance use

At 13 he had started using solvents and drinking alcohol – he saw this stage of drug use as 'normal teenage experimentation'.

I enjoyed it really, it took me somewhere I enjoyed being – out of reality – I don't know if, on a deeper level, I was trying to get away from what happened to me [the rape].

I was thrown out of school eventually when I was fourteen for riding a motorbike around the school grounds. But it was everything really...skiving off, you know, I wasn't interested. I could have done it if I'd wanted to, but I thought I knew better really. I was more interested in getting off my head. I thought, 'I can do that another time.' At school I was told, 'You could go to university.'

Without a school with which he could identify, John turned to the group of older youths he had hung around with since coming to live in the country. This group identified with the 'skinhead punk' scene:

This went hand in hand with the glue, and the drink, and then it just led on to pills and...amphetamines... Yeah, amphetamines became a big problem in the end – over everything else really. Amphetamines have been terrible.

Adolescent identity formation

Even as he sought out his identity within the group John felt he was different from the others:

I suppose around that time...I knew I was different from other people [who were] using drugs 'cos I was always the one making weapons. For some reason, I just seemed to be psychologically different. Yeah, [I was] more...angry I think, or full of fear. One or the other – anger *and* fear I think.

As I got older I became aware that something had happened to me that shouldn't have, and the anger started to come through... I was angry with everybody to be honest. I was always carrying weapons and...just angry, always destroying things. And I took a lot of it out on myself by drinking and taking drugs. I wasn't particularly violent to other people... I was quite happy to fight but I wouldn't initiate it.

Thinking about it now, I was going to make sure I was never hurt like that again.

I noticed that like his father and his grandfather John had been involved in using weapons, and I had missed the opportunity to ask him more about his sense of being 'psychologically different' and the link he made with weaponry. I wondered if, as a person who carried an unprocessed sense of powerlessness since the rape, the weapons were both a psychological defence and a physical defence – a means of 'making sure I was never hurt like that again'. I wondered too if John was experiencing symptoms of chronic post-traumatic stress disorder when the body is alerted for an emergency that does not necessarily exist in the present, causing him to feel overwhelmed by anger or fear, being hypervigilant, ready for flight or fight, and at the mercy of intense emotional memories triggered in situations that, consciously or unconsciously, reminded him of the trauma.

Alcohol

John's drug misuse was inter-related with alcohol use and I could hear how much it meant to him to know that one day he would be able to drink alcohol again. However, this desire did not fit with the abstinence model of AA to which he had subscribed in treatment, and which he continued to follow by attending meetings regularly:

> Alcohol just features right the way through it really. When I went into treatment they said to me, 'Do you think you have a problem with alcohol?', and I said: 'No I haven't got a problem with alcohol, I love it!' (*Laughs*). That was how mental [I was]. Alcohol wasn't a problem! I've got to be able to drink again.

> That was underlying it all really, alcohol. I mean, I took amphetamines and they enabled me to drink through the night. I didn't really get drunk but I'd still be taking the alcohol into my system. So I was getting the hit off the alcohol but without the sleepiness.

Describing drug misuse

His drug misuse escalated and he began to deal drugs as he became further involved with a biker's group:

> I did deal speed in the end and I started injecting it. I was on a come-down one day and I met a girl (this is my daughter's mum). She came in and said, 'Here take a few of these, they'll help you come down.'

> I took these DF 118s and that was it – I'd found opiates, and in the end I realised they gave me the energy boost I needed without screwing my head up. There's a psychological effect, see?

> I'd enjoy the buzz of getting my high, but when you come down, the downer is just…horrendous, and the psychological effects are just…paranoia, um, hallucinations…psychosis. I used to get bad psychosis. How can I explain it – I suppose when you've been awake for three or four days and you get locked into a little circle…you get locked into a mental state. You convince yourself that what's going

on in that world is real, and that's all that matters. Just totally cut yourself off from the outside world.

When I was drinking and stuff like that I don't know if I was deluded into thinking that I knew something…but I always felt that I'd be all right.

The biker's group became a substitute family – a group of people where he felt understood and accepted:

I'd found the family I never had. All that mattered to me was what went on inside that club, and I got myself into a mental state where I would have killed, you know, definitely. It was the only thing that mattered. I cut off family and friends. Cutting them off didn't matter. It was like I'd found the family I'd never had, and I didn't want to lose it. I'd found security in all these people. They looked after me, they watched my back and I watched their back. I knew where I stood with everyone and they knew where they stood with me.

I was hooked on methadone before heroin, because methadone was more accessible. I never looked for heroin, it wasn't my scene. The speed, you know, the speed, the bikes, the guns, that was my scene. I never knew what people seen in smack to be honest – people just seemed to sit there with their heads between their legs and…I couldn't relate to that. I had to be doing something, you know?

I did eventually get into it though, because when I'd been ill, physically ill, when I couldn't get methadone – I'd have my speed trips, then on Sunday or a Monday I'd go looking for opiates to bring me down.

I suppose in the end, I did start to get withdrawals off the opiates, and if there was a bit of gear there, and it would stop me being ill, I'd take it.

I was having too much fun really. The party went on until…well, about ten years ago [aged 26], then the party stopped… But then I went back out again and had another party for four years, and that's just stopped again, a year ago.

My life started falling apart really, relationships weren't working; I was in trouble with drugs. It just wasn't fun any more – you know?

But I just carried on with my treatment, got through it, just about scraped through. I did have the odd slips here and there but something stuck in my head, you know. Then I went into secondary [care], used again…went back into primary treatment again.

I just hadn't had enough really [very quietly]. I don't think I'd had enough. Yeah. I've had a couple [of relapses]. But I think everyone's journey's different. Some people stop and that's it, and other people…

Flashbacks

Each time John reduced his drug intake he became tormented by flashbacks and thoughts about the rape. To avoid the distress he returned to using drugs again. It was a vicious circle:

> ...when you clean up...your mind's always going over and over stuff...just obsessing about things...a lot of it around the abuse... It was something that was always just going on in my head. As soon as I cleaned up that would be the first thing...[that happened].

John went on to describe how his body 'remembered' unprocessed fragments of bodily responses to the rape, and the fear he had felt at the time:

> I was in jail and I couldn't sleep in certain positions, and...then it sort of settled down a bit and then when I got out [of prison] again it kept coming up.

With his body in certain positions, and without the 'help' of drugs, John seems to have begun to re-connect with the dissociated fear of his rape.

> That's why I really need [counselling] because I was very aware that the abuse was going to take me back out there...[using].

Being a partner and a parent

John realised that his relationships were badly affected by his experience of rape *and* his subsequent drug misuse:

> As soon as I feel insecure in relationships I bolt, or...smash the house up, things like that. In a relationship with a woman, it's like...I feel like they're taking the piss and I start feeling insecure and start to lose the plot, you know?

> It [the rape] has affected me in many ways I think, but I think that could also be the way I've been brought up...never had security. When I feel like I have some [security] I don't want to lose it, you know?

John had difficulty forming intimate trusting relationships but eventually he tried to settle down with a woman he met through using drugs.

> A lot went on in that relationship. Yeah, we lost a little boy. She had to have him induced but he was fully formed. I was there right until she actually gave birth. I left the room then. But, um, it was quite traumatic. And then, when she was having our daughter I was really worried that this was going to happen again. But it didn't, you know.

> I wanted to be there for my daughter in a way that my parents had never been there for me. I did try my hardest but...drugs...it just wasn't happening really. I wasn't happy in the relationship. I wanted to be with my daughter, but I didn't want to be with her mother, and the only way I could be with Jenny was to stay with her

mother. So I was stuck really, and that was fuelling my drinking and using. I was in an unhappy relationship, and in order to put up with it I drank and used…

Coping style

Earlier in the story I had asked John how he had coped with the traumatic events in his life and he told me:

…an attitude of…indifference, I suppose, not caring…being laid back. I've been laid back about everything even when I was a kid – just not given a shit. I think that's…been my downfall in many ways, but in many ways I think it's what got me through…

Later he came back to this description of himself in a different way:

I just never used to care. I never saw any reason for caring really – about anything really. Didn't give a shit about much really, until my kids came along. That was a real big thing for me, you know. I never had any trust in people, you know…easier not to care I suppose.

[Having Jenny] was a chance for me…to make a difference, and make sure she got the attention I never got, that she got everything I didn't get…that she was looked after and kept safe. And even that had fallen to pieces by then.

Loss of his child

Whilst John was in a treatment centre Jenny's mother had taken her away and refused to allow John to know where she was:

It was like someone had torn a bit of my heart out and I just had a big hole and I was trying to fill with drugs and alcohol, but it wouldn't take the feelings away.

That's when I knew I was in trouble, that's when I knew I had to start dealing with things, because the drugs and alcohol *weren't* taking the feelings away. The loss, you know, the loss. That's when I thought, 'I've gotta do something about this 'cos its terrible…' That's when I started getting better.

I went into treatment in the end, and while I was in treatment, erm…a social worker told me that her mother had been pulling clumps of Jenny's hair out and smacking her and that devastated me. Because at the end of the day I'd thought, 'At least she's safe, she's with her mum. She'll be safe.'

I'd got to about two years clean when I had to go to court and er…she was fostered for quite a while – then she was adopted. I could have fought to get her back, you know. But I wanted what was best for her and, as hard as it was, I thought, 'Maybe it's better she goes for adoption.'

That's the first time I've been in court and the judge has said something complimentary about me. Her mum was using again, I wasn't in a position to have her with me, so the judge couldn't see any other option. But luckily, the adoptive family she went to were part of the same family who fostered her. So she didn't get too much upset, which was good.

They wanted a fresh start, which I could understand, you know. They didn't want me popping up every now and again and upsetting it. And I thought, 'Well, that's fair enough. If that's what needs to be done to give her...a better life...then, I'll have to sit with that.' Well, if I'd gone into court and kept battling away to have her with me it would have been for selfish reasons. And if I'd got her with me I'd probably have taken on more than I could have coped with, and probably would have drunk again.

I had one final visit when she was seven. She's thirteen, fourteen this year.

John's sadness and sense of loss was palpable as he paused in his story. I could also hear his anger at himself for his part in having lost his daughter.

Current strengths and resources

At this point he began to draw attention to his strengths and resourcefulness and speak about how he manages his feelings now:

I'm quite sort of balanced. I've started to sort of level out. Still angry...I'm very aware of that, and sometimes that affects everything – my thinking, everything. But I'm aware of it and I can do something about it I suppose.

I use meditation now so I've had moments of relative calm. So when I'm angry I'm very aware of it, you know. I've had one or two days when I haven't had any anger and I've noticed the difference, you know. I'm sure that my anger affects my thinking. 'Cos my head'll start projecting stuff and...I don't even know someone and I start thinking 'twat'. I think that's my anger.

[I get angry] if I'm feeling I've had my space violated. Do you know what I mean? If people are treading on my boundaries, or if I feel like I'm done some injustice, then my anger kicks in.

I'm a great believer, and always have been, in treating people how I'd like to be treated and...when people are selfish and inconsiderate I deal with it appropriately now, and if it still happens, then I get angry. You have to hold it down sometimes – insecurities, feelings of helplessness.

Health and well-being: an 'inside job'

John then began to speak about the impact on his body of years of drug misuse. He is currently receiving treatment for hepatitis C which he believes he has developed as a result of injecting drugs:

Don't know how long I've had it, but I went in for my tests the other day, and they said my liver's scarred. But at least I haven't got cirrhosis, you know. As long as I

> don't pick up again…I'm hoping…I've got to go in for treatment actually. I'm just waiting to go in for interferon, so hopefully…

> I eat OK – it's mainly your diet, I think. If I eat crap then I get depressed, no energy, but I make sure I eat vegetables every day.

John realises he has to take care of himself, both physically and mentally, if he hopes to recover. He believes he needs to put his health first – a very different attitude to when he was misusing drugs. Even though he works part-time as a voluntary helper in a mental health charity, he knows that a permanent job would cause him stress that could threaten his recovery:

> I did work before when I got clean and…I thought, 'Right, the first thing I've got to do is get back to work.' That's society's view isn't it? Got to be at work, got to have 2.4 children but it's not about that. It's about getting yourself well, and I realise that now. I stopped doing meetings, wasn't working the programme. I thought as long as I had a job everything was all right. But it's not about that – it's an inside job… [*Laughs*]

Need for a healthy environment

However, living in a 'dry house', with other recovering 'addicts', sometimes makes life difficult, so John is trying to find a place of his own:

> I do meditation, that's why I need to get my own space. It's very difficult always running your life around other people. The dynamics of those [dry] houses – it's just too much really.

> I went to see my mate last night and I said, 'I don't know what's going on, I've had a headache for about two weeks.' He said, 'Where are you living?' I said, 'In a dry house.' He said, 'You're picking up all the negative energy.'

> There's a guy in there with depression. There are two guys in there not working the programme, there's another guy about to be thrown out – and that is a lot of negative energy really. And I said, 'I hadn't thought of it like that, you're probably right you know.'

Relationship with mother

John has a limited and strained relationship with his mother nowadays. He realises now that as a child he didn't have enough trust in her to have told her about the rape, not knowing how she would react.

> I told her when I was 25 when I was staying at her place. I thought she needed to know so she can understand my behaviour really. I don't know if I did it appropriately but I thought she needed to know.

> There's still a lot of resentment there. [*Pause*]…I think it probably hurt her more than she showed. I think she was upset. But then she was also very irresponsible…

about me. But I can see it from an addict and alcoholic's point of view. All that matters to them is their…drugs and their alcohol, and having a kid running round your feet all day… Don't get me wrong, it was great for me. I was free…all the time.

I suppose I was just the unlucky one really. Well, you know… [*Long pause*]

Seeking help

John began to talk about the times he had tried to get help to deal with his childhood rape:

See, I tried to get help before, and I've always got so far, and never been able to get any further. And I had a little bit of counselling – when I was in prison. Then another time… Well, what happened was I was in the hospital when I caught hepatitis A, that was when they found out I had hepatitis C. While I was there I told them I was having trouble with [flashbacks], well the stuff that had happened to me, and the doctor down there said, 'I'll get my friend in, you can talk to her.' And she said, 'I can help you.' So I built myself up and it didn't happen. They made me write out a life story – then they came back in and said, 'You're not here long enough…'

I just went back out of there and used again – you know? Here we go again…

★　　★　　★　　★

John's story highlights how difficult it can be to try and put different causal explanations side by side. The first effective help he received was from within an AA treatment model which had shaped the kind of stories he had told himself and others about the causes of his substance abuse and the pathways to recovery. Within AA he had needed to identify with being 'an alcoholic addict' and to accept the disease concept. He had been advised to keep his childhood abuse stories 'elsewhere'.

Among drug treatment workers there is an understandable reluctance to address underlying trauma because they recognise the dangers of re-traumatisation which may lead to relapse, but past traumatic events need to be addressed at some stage if recovery is to be sustained. These approaches can seem to be incommensurable and were clearly felt to be so by John.

Specific training is required for the delicate task of integrating trauma counselling into substance misuse treatment. Sadly specific trauma-related counselling is limited for this client group and in some areas unavailable or costly.

Since our conversation, John has approached one of the voluntary abuse counselling services where I suggested he might find the help he needed, and he has been receiving free counselling for over a year. His persistence has paid off at last, and although taking part in this study was, at times, somewhat distressing for him in the short term, he has gained the long-term benefit of facing his childhood trauma in a safe and professional environment with less risk of relapse.

Chapter 10

Levi's Story

Levi, a 39-year-old mixed race man, offered to tell me his story after hearing me present a paper at a conference about my research on drug misusers' lives. Levi is a counsellor working with young black people in an inner city context and he was studying for a further degree, which included the need for him to undertake research and produce a dissertation. He was interested in my life story approach to research because he intended to use his own story, alongside those of his participants/clients, to underpin an autoethnographic dissertation – a form of self-narrative that places the self within a social context.

He explained that by telling me his story he would be preparing himself for writing it down for his own research, so this seemed to be an instance where reciprocity was possible: by helping me with my research he would also be helping himself. But the potential power and boundary issues inherent in this situation needed to be addressed. It seemed to me entirely possible that Levi viewed me as an authority figure: I was an older white woman, and a senior member of a university. He was a black male, more than 20 years younger than me, and a student. So we agreed to meet to discuss his participation before deciding to work together, particularly focusing on issues related to the power imbalance in our relationship and how that could affect his participation. Levi told me later that this conversation helped him think about the factors he might need to take into account when enlisting people to participate in his own research.

During that first conversation Levi briefly told me the story he repeated again several times during our research conversations when he described a 'self-defining memory' of a traumatic experience that occurred when he was 13 years of age: an experience that challenged his entire sense of who he had known himself to be up to that point in his life. At times during his storytelling he moved between past and present tense, creating a powerful impression that he was reliving his experiences as he told them.

★   ★   ★   ★

Levi was born in 1966 and brought up in London as the youngest child with three older sisters. His father had come from Jamaica 'to fight Hitler' in 1942 when he met and married a white woman. Levi did well at primary school and was 'top boy' at secondary school up to the age of 13. At that point he was using drugs 'recreationally' like 'most of the kids on my estate', until the day his life changed forever:

> I met this man – buying a smoke off him, and he said, 'Your name's Levi, innit?' I thought, 'Oh my God, he knows our dad, I'm in trouble, I'm gonna get a beating!' [*Laughs*] 'Cos if my dad caught me smoking ganja he'd kill me! He said, 'I'll *give* you this, but I won't *sell* you it.' So I've told one of…my big sisters that I met this bloke and [that] he keeps giving me weed for nothing.

> I come home from school one day…and my dad is there, in the kitchen. He was the most hardworking man I know: he worked seven days a week and…never came home till seven o'clock and I'm thinking, 'Oh God…our dad's found out I smoke weed…and he's gonna beat me…and our mum's cryin' because she can't save me…' So I'm actually terrified…an' he said, 'Come in boy, sit down.'

> So I say, 'Dad, what's up?' and he says, 'Well I've got something to tell you. This is a common thing in Jamaica so don't go…don't be too worried, it's no big deal…but I'm not actually your dad, I'm your granddad. That man you've met *now* is your father and your big sister Ellie – she's your mother. But don't look so upset boy, you know, this is…this is just normal Jamaican stuff. We all grew up in separate families…and I'm leaving your mother.' And…with that, he left us. Yeah, they'd bin together since the forties.

> And he told me all that…literally, in the length of time it's taken me to tell you. That's the length of time it took to deal with it. And…that was how I was told that…none of this is real.

> Within about six weeks of that I'd injected diamorphine. I think it was that experi- ence of finding out that most of my life was a lie…that's how it felt at the time – that I'd been lied to a lot of the time. And I think from that point on…erm…my drug taking…went off the wall. So I think that experience of finding out my family wasn't my family – well they *were* my family, but not who they said they were – that my mum and dad was my grandparents really, and my big sister was really my mum, and that man giving me the weed is really my dad – once I discovered all that, my attitude towards drugs changed. It wasn't a 'recreational' thing then…from that point all I wanted…[was to] obliterate my feelings…[*tuts – sighs*]…because I hated life at that point [*very quietly*]. I was really, really angry. I felt lied to and betrayed by all my family…thought everyone was…against me, couldn't trust no-one. So…the only time I felt at ease…in myself, was if I felt off my face.

> That was it. That's it – I just wanted out of me.

In that brief space of time the basis upon which Levi's life and identity had been built was dismantled, almost brutally it seemed.

Levi repeated the story of this episode several times, partly because of my inability to take in what he was saying, but also as if he needed both of us to realise the seriousness of these events. In the telling, Levi repeated two important points:

the *manner* in which the news was imparted and the connection between this event and his changed use of drugs. His repetition of 'the length of time' indicates how the speed with which the news was conveyed increased his sense of shock and trauma. His repetition of 'at that point' and 'from that point' indicates his recognition of that news was a major turning point in his life.

The message from his 'father' was that he should not feel upset or disturbed by the information: so rather than allowing him time to process the news he was left to deal with it alone. The final parting shot was that the man he had known as his father was leaving home – a serious enough blow for any young person to deal with, without the additional assault on his sense of identity.

The sense Levi had made of his life up to then, through the stories he had been told by his parents, sisters and community, no longer made any sense. Levi's trust in his family had been betrayed and the thread of his life story that held him together as a person had been snapped, leaving him confused and adrift.

As well as the loss of his family as he knew them, in that same moment he had to take in the idea of a new and *different* identity, based upon his genetic heritage. Now, instead of his father being a man who would punish him for smoking 'weed', a hard-working, respectable, 'moralistic' man who came to England to fight against Hitler, Levi now viewed his real father as a 'bad man':

> He had dreadlocks when I seen him. He was a well-known figure in the East End…a bit of a legend over there. [Well known] for being a gangster. Yeah, he had a crew, a gang and…[was involved in]…um…um…violent crime…selling weed in large amounts…and prostituting women.

At the age of 13, on the verge of manhood, a son might look to his father as a model of the kind of man he might become, or wish *not* to become. As I heard Levi's story I wondered about the impact on him of the myth 'like father, like son', which was echoing around my head as I listened:

> Me and my real dad…we've got the same birthday: me, him and General Pinochet, all born on the same day – what a gag eh?

> And if you seen us, Kim, you would think, 'How did Levi look at this man and *not* see himself in him?' Because we are…*stamps* of each other. You can see what I'll look like in 30 years.

Not only did he have to deal with his changed view of 'father', he also had to deal with the fact that his mother was no longer the person he had always known her to be. Instead she was 'the sister I didn't really get on with'.

Levi's mother was 15 years old when she gave birth to him, and, like many grandparents in similar situations, her parents cared for him as one of their own children. At the time he discovered his true parentage, his birth mother was 28 and divorced, living with Levi's two half-siblings. He told me:

My brother [born 14 months after him] is blond-haired and blue-eyed, 'cos my mum's mixed race and his dad's white. When I found out, in my head, I was thinking, 'You kept the white one and got rid of the black one.'

The news of his informal adoption by his grandparents has also raised questions about his own racial identity. Instead of his mother being a white woman (his grandmother), his mother was, in fact, of mixed race. His real father, like his grandfather, was Jamaican. The story above seems to indicate that he may have internalised negative messages about his ethnicity prior to discovering his true parentage, and that these messages were reinforced by the news.

For several years after this Levi used whatever drugs he could lay his hands on.

If someone had some amphetamine, I would do amphetamine. If someone had some acid, I did acid. Back when I was about 15, me and my friend hit up micro dots – acid – LSD. No one does that, 'cos the trips come on too much and people are scared it'll send you mad and I didn't mind…I didn't mind the flats turning into scary monsters and things like that, it was weird! The harsher the effect, the more I'd like it. So…after the weed, it would be mostly speed, acid – whatever I could get my hands on – diamorphine, mogadon, you know, prescription stuff – anything to really give you an effect. And I think at some point I realised it was getting out of control.

During the first three years in secondary school I was coming first, second or third in my year. I was top boy. And…at that point I just stopped. Didn't take exams, started coming to school drugged up…um – just didn't care no more. I think it was when I found out all this: I just stopped trying. So around that age I stopped being the top boy, but I was quite gifted so – even though I didn't work hard or try – I could still…get by, quite easily.

So I got this job with the city council and after about a year I got called in to the occupational health person because I'd had 87 days off sick out of 365! It was like, you know [laughing], there's something going on here! Rather than discovering for myself that it was getting out of hand – someone…helped me realise that I'd got a bit of a problem here.

Enlisting in the army

Realising that his drug use was getting out of control and needing a way to escape his drug-using environment he enlisted in the army where he was racially abused:

I realised the drugs was getting out of hand. So I had to save myself, so I went in the army. The army doesn't save you from nothing. The army's a meat grinder…it's like going to a place where the school bully from every area is in one place.

Sat down at a thirty-man table, everyone eating their dinner, everyone got up and just moved to another one – no one sat by me. That went on for weeks – just ignored me, like I didn't exist. I'd ask people, 'Excuse me, do you know how to talk?', and people'd say, 'Sorry I don't talk to blacks', and walk off. And where I come from...being black was a very popular thing – Asian guys had dreadlocks, white guys had dreadlocks. So I'd never experienced this.

He was alienated and excluded from that world. There were no drugs available to him in the army so he coped by drinking alcohol to excess – six or seven pints every night. Surrounded by aggressive and violent men he 'discovered his violent side' and in a rage after 'they'd smashed up my room and they'd written "land of the ape and monkey" on the wall' he attacked several of his sleeping companions with a pick-axe handle. He was given 28 days in the 'glasshouse' for this violence and given an extended tour of duty (18 months rather than the normal six months) on the front line in Northern Ireland, where his job entailed identifying body parts after bombings. He felt traumatised by those duties.

Living a drug dealer lifestyle

On leaving the army around the age of 29 his attitude to the world had hardened and his taste for violence had been established:

> I decided when I got out the army 'sod this for a game of soldiers' as they say...I'm coming out and I'm getting paid. And the world's gonna regret...me.

His life spiralled downwards: using and dealing hard drugs, and becoming involved with the gangster lifestyle, prostitution and extreme violence.

> I'm going out six or seven nights a week, selling in clubs, raves, parties...I would sell whatever anyone wanted. If someone said, 'This party wants a load of Es [ectasy tablets]', I'd get a load of Es. Take a load of Es as well, um... Whatever I sold I used. I'd be my own guinea pig. That was considered irresponsible and stupid. I'd try to cover that with saying it was like a 'quality control' thing! That was bullshit! You know – that was me lying to myself and others. I just wanted to get...high.

> I had a nice flat in Chelsea. I had lots and lots of girlfriends at the time... I'd wake up about 12, go out and get some lunch. It's hard to pick out a pattern 'cos every day was so different.

> One day someone could turn up who'd have a load of clothes that they'd ram raided from a shop...and I'd buy the lot for a quarter of the price on the labels...give them to a mate of mine for a third of the price on the label, and he'd sell them for half. And, you know, that could take a morning...and then maybe – I don't know, uh...meet a biker in the afternoon, go down the pub, buy a load of acid off him, take a couple and sit and chat crap with him for a couple of hours. So...there would be no pattern to my day – but every day was a hustle.

> Every day...I'd think, 'Right [clicks fingers]. I'm gonna earn some money now.' So...even though it didn't have a pattern...the lack of pattern was the pattern. I'd do crime all day. That went on...for eight, seven years...engrossed in that world, around criminals.

Levi described how his moral code eroded whilst he was living this lifestyle. He had grown up in areas where 'girls worked the parlours' and at that time he had judged the punters as 'disgusting' but once he became immersed in the gangster lifestyle he became 'like everyone else'.

> I hardened toward it in the end. Eventually I expected my perks. I didn't expect to pay full whack for things…if I bought a crate of champagne, I bought it nicked. And I bought my clothes cheap. I hadn't been in a shop in years. 'Cos everything I bought had come…from thieves.

A 'drug user' and 'dealer' but not a 'druggie'

However, although misusing drugs himself, his lifestyle was very removed from the usual lifestyle of a 'druggie'.

> I would never even *meet* druggies, um…I would be selling to people, who sold to people who sold to druggies. I was three or four people removed from that… So yeah, I knew the seediness was there…but not around me. There would be…violence would be around my end of the scale – lots and lots of violence.

> 'Cos of my experience in the army – and being a very violent man – I drank a lot, and I would…be quite capable of hurting people. The grimy part of my drugs world wasn't being in a dirty basement surrounded by grime, it would be that you'd have to go round and drag someone out their bed at night, put in the boot and hurt him to get your money. It's horrible – but it's not the low end of the scale, it's the other end…

I asked Levi if he saw his family during these times. His response showed me how much the people in his drugs world had become his 'family' – a family for whom he felt a sense of loyalty and responsibility:

> Nah. Seen the family once every three or four months, if that, um…I was living my life with my people – the people that I worked with, and that was my family, my world. There were people in that world who wouldn't earn that week if I didn't go out and hustle. And some of them had children to feed, and rent to pay. So I had other priorities than my family. I had my new family.

But he also wanted to keep them loyal to him. If he didn't provide them with work, they would 'go elsewhere'. Many of his decisions were financially based:

> It's all money driven. Um…the drugs fuel the chase for the money but it's the money that everyone's coming together for – the prostitution, the stolen goods…the drugs. [The money gave me] freedom. I could live in a flat in Chelsea, I could wear Armani clothes…I could go and eat in the nicest restaurants, drink champagne… It would be a lie to say I didn't enjoy the money.

> I loved that world. Being quite well off – you accepted down periods – people go to jail, people get hurt…but personally I'd been really lucky.

As he spoke of his need for prestige I was reminded of what he had said about feeling worthless when he found out his mother had 'given away' the 'black one' and kept the 'white one'. He told me he was showing the world 'I am of worth':

> ...wearing a Rolex...diamonds in my ears...I wear expensive clothes... My girl-friends were all stunningly beautiful... I was the *best*, obviously, even though maybe deep down inside I never felt that. I was [saying]...to the outside [world], 'Well look, I live like a superstar, everybody knows me...'

> There's prestige in being known as a hood...a certain kind of respect you get out on the street and in nightclubs...you walk to the front of the queue, and people in the queue don't even moan about it 'cos they know you're obviously someone special...special in what way I don't know, but...that was very...intoxicating, very...enticing. And even now that I've left all that behind, to a degree there's still – I don't wanna be a hypocrite here, I'm trying to be totally honest with you, even though on one level I know that that's nothing to be proud of – there's still an element of pride in it.

Loss of relationship as a turning point

I asked Levi what happened to make him give up a lifestyle that had made him feel respected and proud. He began to describe the impact on him of losing people who were important to him, especially Melissa, the only girl with whom he had a long-term relationship. Losing her, along with the loss of a close friend and major injury to another, began a process of re-examining his life. As he spoke about losing Melissa his eyes filled with tears.

> I started to do a lot more of the...heavy end of the business. There were always guns around...stored under my bed: a shotgun at the end of my bed and a pistol in the kitchen. And she...lived with me through the escalation of the crime.

> Melissa was the only one I would call a 'proper' girlfriend – I went out with her for about four years. I didn't see other women [while I was with her]. Before that I would say [to girlfriends], 'I'll see other women and if you don't like it, you blow. It's my world.'

> Melissa said, 'You don't seem to be taking me seriously so, um, I'm gonnna go.' I'd say, 'You can hang with this or you can blow', and she said, 'I'm gonna blow, Levi.'

> She started putting her stuff together and going and...I felt the panic. I didn't want her to go. I didn't want to be on my own. And before that, I wouldn't have...given in to that panic. I'd see that as her making me weak and I'd have blamed her for the weakness in me...

> And she said, 'I know you're trying, you've done everything I've wanted, but this lifestyle, Levi, for the past few years has just worn me down and I don't love you no more. And I'm leaving.'

And…I'd threatened her, 'If you leave me I'll fucking kill you.' She said, 'Do what you want, I really just don't care no more, I'm going.' I was…upset as hell, 'cos I didn't want her to go. That's the longest relationship I've ever had.

So when she left…we were doing a lot more work. But…people started backstabbing against other people. Um…one of our crew shot another crew member in the leg, four times, at the funeral of another crew member who had been kicked to death by…prison warders. Shot him in front of both sets of their children. Crazy stuff…and some part of my self-preservation – a little voice inside my head – said, 'I've got to get out of this.' So I got out of it. But I left it too late for me and Melissa.

Impact of early years on intimate relationships

As he spoke about the loss of Melissa I realised that Levi had said nothing about the years before the age of 13, and I wondered how his early years had been affected by not knowing his real parents.

I always sensed…a difference. I can say that now in hindsight, but I know I always felt…something wasn't right – can't say what. My parents were older than other parents, I knew that, and I'd be a bit embarrassed when my mum came up to the school, 'cos she looked like a granny rather than a mum. I was always aware of that but I don't think that's what…I just felt…we didn't do hugs…there was certain things I didn't get that I noticed other kids got. And I can't put my finger on it and say, 'Oh I realised I wasn't their child', but I always felt slightly different.

I'm very close to my grandma but it wasn't the *same*. So it was a shock [to hear about my parentage] but it made sense of how I'd felt. I'd always felt disconnected [sighs]. There was lots of stuff that didn't make sense at the time I was growing up, but after, I kind of…got it all! But…I think the feeling I had was betrayal, 'You've all lied to me all along, I don't trust no-one now, I only trust me.' And I don't think I really liked me, I think underneath that, 'Sod everyone else, I just trust me', there was a feeling of, 'I'm not really good enough or you'd have kept me.'

I was wondering how much that lack of ability to trust others might have affected his ability to form close and loving relationships as an adult:

I don't think I ever really got what you would call…the emotional…parts of it [relationship], ever. I'd grown up to be quite a hardened person – because I didn't actually know you *needed* that [emotion]. As I got older I'd watch telly – summat like The Simpsons or EastEnders – and there'll be a family unit and people would all be together and…happy, and there's a part of me that thinks, 'Oh, bullshit, turn it over.' But there's part of me that's envious of those families, and part of me that feels separate from that, still. I live on my own…I'm 40 next year, I have no children, I haven't been in a…long-term relationship in ages. Somehow that…attitude [of mistrust] I developed has stayed with me right into my adult life.

And I guess that's something I feel sad about – my inability to form [close relationships], and the fact that I feel on my own most of the time. I'm quite happy with it a lot of the time, but it would sometimes be nice to be more *with* people. So it's affected me that way.

Drugs world as 'family'

But in the drugs world…I felt the first time I had my family…people loved me in that world, because I could always get drugs. There was summat about being black – mixed race – that made it possible for me to move between the black world and the white world.

My dad's a well-known gangster, you know, and through family connections and because of who I am…if I wanted summat on credit no-one would hesitate to give it to me. So in the drugs world that alone-ness, that separate-ness…is an asset, innit? You don't need people, you know? It's a real cut-throat world. So if you don't need people, in that world, I was fine. It felt like I'd finally come home.

I don't think people understand this if they haven't done drugs but when you're drugged up together…there's a real feeling of belonging. We're doing something illegal…that most of society don't really like and we're doing that together. So there's a bond there between me and whoever I'm doing drugs with. A bond…

I was curious about this sense of feeling bonded because I knew that Levi had also used drugs alone, so I asked him about this:

A great deal of the time I done my drugs on my own. I would go and score with people, we'd do a bit together and then I'd go off – but even then, still feeling part of an illegal community, part of a world. I always refer to it as…'our world', like it was separate. There's almost like a sense of pride in it… I know this sounds stupid now…but there's a real sense of…belonging? Rebellious? A bit like an outlaw, breaking the rules. Fuck life – fuck society, I live by my code [*intake of breath*] and I liked the drugs! Some people say they don't like what drugs done to them, but if there was a tablet I could take now that gave me that feeling, and it didn't have long-term effects, I'd still be tempted to take it 'cos I liked that feeling of being blown away. You can really lose yourself in drugs.

As he remembered the effect of using drugs Levi's breathing quickened and he seemed to become agitated. I asked him if he wanted to stop but he continued, explaining what he was feeling:

…it's really weird. Talking about this with you now actually, my heart's racing! It's OK. I'm just surprised. Before you have some drug you usually get excited…and I'm feeling that rush right now. That's surprising me. Um…[*intake of breath*]…my drug of choice was coke…um. I liked cocaine. They describe coke as quite an 'ego' drug. And 'cos I felt like I didn't need no-one – 'fuck the world' and everything – I think that suited me. I did heroin a bit but…I didn't like that kind of…fogginess that it gave you.

[*Big sigh*] When I took cocaine I would think, 'If I could get up off this settee I could do anything in the world.' I felt invincible.

The beginning of the end of drug misuse

At this point I asked Levi again why he had given up the lifestyle and drug use. This took him back to talking about the time after Melissa left when he went back to using cocaine after a four-year break:

> Three things had happened. First, my partner [his cousin] got shot. He didn't die, but he had a shotgun wound in his shoulder – a massive hole, lucky to be alive, you know... This was the month after our other friend had got kicked to death by the prison warders and then Melissa left. He got shot the Monday and she left the Friday. And I was thinking, 'Oh my God, everything's falling apart.'

> I can remember wanting oblivion again [*very quietly*], thinking, 'Man I can't take this, I just wanna be smashed in.' So I started hitting up the coke. And that must have gone on for about...about three or four months. And then I started speedballing – [injecting] coke and heroin. It's a bit like a roller coaster. You fly on the coke, then you smash on the heroin... It's hard on the heart 'cos of the stop-start nature of it. Even people who are heavily into drugs steer away from that.

> Ahhh [*sighs*] it felt good. Just to be blown away. How I loved...that just...out of my skull feeling and that was the most out of my skull feeling I think you can get.

Recognition of 'addiction'

On realising that he still wanted drugs the morning after having had a 'dirty hit' and feeling extremely ill, Levi could no longer avoid the truth that he was addicted:

> ...so I'm having a bad time, probably convulsing. A friend comes over to make sure I'm OK but I won't let him ring an ambulance 'cos I don't want it on my record that I'm a junkie. So I survived that night... I wake up the next day and I feel like some drugs again. And then it hits me...[inaudible]...I thought, 'After what you went through last night...[inaudible]...I'm in a bad way.'

> So um, I ring my real mum where she lives at the seaside and I say, 'Mum, can I come and visit you?' And she's over the moon. She's always happy to see me. And I say, 'Well I don't mean to come up for a weekend, I mean to stay for a while.' So they come and collected all my belongings...and I moved in with them.

> Um we've talked about it since and she's said, 'I'd never seen you upset like you were when Melissa left you. You just stayed in your room for about two weeks and you didn't talk to no-one.'

> Couldn't tell her. Ashamed. Disgusted that I'd let myself become...hooked. That was for punters. That was for other people. That was for weak people. That was for stupid people. I'm better than that. I was the boss. I'd been on holiday with

Melissa to the Masai Mara and we're looking out over Africa, clinking our cocktails and I said, 'God bless the punters.' I wasn't meant to end up one. They fed my life.

I wasn't meant to get hooked. So it was the shame – the realisation that…I'm under this – this has got me. Uh – that was shocking. That was, just…to me the worst… I didn't deserve to talk to no-one about it, 'You deserve to sit in your room and suffer, and tough it out. Take the pain.'

Me, like that, hunched up, and feeling sick and can't move… I never wanted my mum to see me like that: my mum least of all, my God, the shame. My mum sees me as a together, tough, strong boy. She knew I was into crime but she wouldn't know what kind. She had a safe, and I'd go and leave a few grand with her. I'd had no job in years, and I'm going off on holidays round the world – she didn't ask questions. None of the family members really asked…none of 'em would have really approved. I lived my own life by then. If they'd questioned me I would have punished them…by not letting them see me. They would know that 'cos of things I'd said in the past.

Detox

Levi stayed alone in a room in his mother's house until he had 'detoxed' by going 'cold turkey'. He described it as 'the worst flu you've ever had, but no worse than that':

It's like you ache, and it's bad. Mentally, it's tough – physically it's not that bad. Having said that, I wouldn't want to go through it again. So it wasn't great…but I'd imagined worse.

I took about £15,000 with me, and I'd think, 'I can just get in a cab, go home, get me some kit and take this pain away.' That's the mental bit. But I couldn't do that – 'cos if I didn't stop then, I felt as if I'd never be able to stop.

I was worried…I had heard stories. I was driving around with a guy I used to buy heroin from – he's got a convertible Mercedes…Del Boy, his name – covered in gold, living large – he pointed out a guy who looked like a bum, on the street. And he said, 'That's the guy who got me into the game.' I said, 'What, him?', and he said, 'Yeah man – he got me into the kit.' I was thinking, 'Wow!' So I know people who'd had it all and ended up with nuttin' because of the kit [heroin].

The drugs took the money. So I knew that that was possible…but I just didn't think it could happen to me. And I think my fear now was that this could happen to me. I could end up…toothless…I mean, you know – living in a squat. And that was a terrifying thought.

Embodied addict identity

Some of his friends had recognised his slide into addiction, but he had ignored them. For a long time they had noticed the change in him:

I lost loads of weight. I went from about 13 stone down to about 9, really looked terrible. Clothes hanging on...very expensive clothes, but hanging on...like a clotheshorse and um...I've gone to get, um, loads of tests. I thought, I must have a disease, like leukaemia or cancer, or AIDS or something.

I'm on the way over to get my tests...and building myself up, thinking, 'Get yourself ready for bad news', and I get the results and I've got nothing wrong with me. And I've gone to see my friend and said, 'Look, you know, I was all worried, nearly in tears, thinking I'm dying...and they say there's nothing wrong with me.' And he said, 'D'you think it might be the drugs, Levi?' and I laughed and said, 'Don't be so fucking stupid.' I still had no concept that it could be the drugs.

Looking back, I cannot understand how I could delude myself so entirely. If I look at the pattern of my...taking from the start, I can see I was out of control. Even the drinking, I've said several times, even recently, 'I'm not a drinker.' But I've drank...from the age of 13...up until now, harder than most people would...you know, it just didn't feel out of control, you know. So I'd have four or five vodkas through the day... Looking back, at the time I had no concept of that. I considered myself as someone who didn't drink. And I drank all the way through – with the drugs. I don't understand how I could delude myself entirely.

Levi stayed at his mother's house for six weeks, although the detox took only a week.

But I was frightened to come back 'cos I thought I'd do the drugs again. And it wasn't till I got bored with the seaside – it's a retirement place and there's no black people...so I'd walk along the beach, alone again! In my own little bubble. It's like, 'God, I always end up back here. On my own!' So, yeah, I got my shit together as much as I could on my own, and then I decided, 'Right, I'll come back, get back on the game, be around drugs and all that still, but not take 'em. That's the plan.'

Self-searching

It was weird, because while I was living at Mum's I spent loads of time looking at stars and real...self-searching, asking, 'What am I all about? What's gonna become of me?', that type of stuff, really questioning myself for the first time. And didn't have answers. Just thought, 'OK, I'll still sell drugs and be involved in crime, but not take 'em. Save loads of money and...uh.' I really didn't have much of a plan, except not taking the drugs. 'Don't inject.' Um...still planned to maybe pop a pill here or there...but just not injecting, basically.

But that's...not a lot had changed actually, now I'm saying it, yeah! Just thinking the injecting was the bit that was bad.

So then I've come back – done a deal, got ripped off, and I thought to myself, 'That's because I've lost it. People can sense it.' So I got revenge on the guy, and I hurt him. And a couple of months later I heard that he was trying to pay more than half of the money he'd robbed from me for someone to shoot me. And the only reason it didn't go down is that the guy he was trying to employ to do that was a friend of mine. Just blind luck, you know, he could have asked someone else who didn't know me, or didn't like me, and I could have got it.

I suddenly realised the madness of the world I lived in. 'You're gonna rob my money...I'm gonna hurt you over it...and so you're gonna pay over half my own bloody money to get me killed. Is this fucking mad, or what?' And I just thought, 'I can't do this no more.' Without the drugs, that realisation came...quite quick.

Feeling the fear

Levi was afraid to take the drugs that had made it possible for him to live in that crazy, dangerous world, having realised that 'drugs have fucked me up'.

That stayed with me. That's...still with me – that if I'd misbehaved or...went on a wild week bender...I more likely wouldn't come back from it now. I don't feel I've got that strength to go down one last...tough it out. I think it'd just have me. I'd never had that fear before, look. I didn't feel no drug...nothing that grows out the ground could be more powerful than me – and my willpower so...

I was just fed up with crime...what do I do? This is all I've done for so long, and that was...almost as hard...that made me feel like...doing the drugs again. This was the only way I'd known...and I was...a top player at this. I could always get work. People would trust me, with thousands of pounds' worth of stuff...

Becoming aware of fear, the fear of what the drugs could do to his life, fear of the dangerous world in which he was trying to operate, left him vulnerable. His very existence was threatened. He realised that, if he wanted to survive, it was not enough simply to give up using drugs, he would also have to give up his lifestyle. But like many others who reach this point, Levi had no other way of living – no other way of earning money, and no other way of earning respect.

At this point he decided to use his money to get advice from a career guidance organisation who, after testing him with various psychological tools, advised him to educate himself, either as a social worker or as a counsellor! At this point Levi demanded his money back, thinking, 'They're taking the piss.'

To appease him the career guidance organisation paid for him to attend an introductory counselling skills course at a local college, to which he reluctantly agreed. Levi went on to study the field of counselling and gained a professional qualification six years ago. Since then he has been working with inner city young black people as a dedicated and committed counsellor. He has turned his life around.

★　　★　　★　　★

Levi and I met for a second conversation, which began with his responses to reading the transcript of our first meeting. He seemed shaken by the realisation of how his drug misuse had been shaped by family events. When he first offered me his story Levi had seemed to have already made that connection so I was surprised at his shocked responses to reading the transcription.

Kim: So…any responses to reading it through?

Levi: Um…it was strange – reading it through. Uh…because I've never looked at…how I got into drug-taking so much. So that was the shock. I'd always known it was linked around…um, family – but I didn't realise how much. So that…that was quite heavy – reading it. When I first read it through [I knew] you wanted me to write some responses down the side, and I haven't put any down. Initially, it was just so difficult to know anything 'cos I was so…

Kim: You were…shocked?

Levi: Shocked, yeah. So it almost felt as if it was…two-pronged. It was about my drug taking but it was also about my family – that felt just as…prevalent. And reading it, I could feel the power in it. So that was the bit that really stood out.

Kim: What surprises me is that…when I explained what I was doing you said, 'Well that's *my* story'…um, and it was like you knew that already.

Levi: It's something about telling it. Maybe I had accepted it mentally – compartmentalised it, and forgot. It didn't feel powerful. Whereas talking about it with you…it felt powerful.

Kim: Was there one particular story that…was most powerful or significant in that respect?

Levi: It was the…family lie.

Kim: The family lie? Finding out, like you did…

Levi: Yeah, yeah. That's the part.

Kim: …who you were?

Levi: I was not who I thought I was. That seems to be…the real key turning – a…fork in my life. That feels like wow…particularly re-reading it. When I was telling you I was just 'in the moment' but re-reading it, I'm also looking at it through a therapist's eyes. I was aware of the damage that could have been done to me by what happened – which I think I've always known, but not *felt*, you know – it's different allowing yourself to feel it. It just felt totally linked to why I did drugs. If that hadn't happened – would I have just experimented with drugs – like other kids on the estate – and then grown out of it? And maybe drugs would not have become…a daily part of my life. So that's…that's quite a shock.

But it was surprising – I always thought drugs were fun but now it feels like I was medicating myself, using drugs to anaesthetise the anger, the confusion – the pain…y'know?…it obliterated some of…the pain. So I really don't think I would have ever made that link… I would have…looked at drugs as something you did on the estate – and it was fun, and I grew into it and liked it more.

Part 3

Thinking across the Stories

For each of us…a multitude of discourses is constantly at work constructing and producing our identity. Our identity therefore originates not from inside the person, but from the social realm, where people swim in a sea of language and other signs, a sea that is invisible to us because it is the very medium of our existence as social beings.

(Burr 1995, p.53)

Chapter 11

Impact of Trauma on Selves and Relationships

In this chapter I will focus on what the storytellers told me about how they came to define themselves as young children through their interactions with other people and the discourses that shaped and informed those interactions. Additionally I will examine how their self-definitions were impacted upon by the traumatic events in their lives and influenced their construction of a 'drug user' identity.

A child's sense of self, which forms the basis for identity construction, is formed through relationships with early care-givers whose influence is crucial in the development of trust, which in turn will influence other relationships throughout the person's life.

Trauma, selves and human relationships

> Traumatic events call into question basic human relationships. They breach attachments of family, friendship, love, and community. They shatter the construction of the self that is formed and sustained in relation to others. They undermine the belief systems that give meaning to human experience. They violate the victim's faith in a natural or divine order and cast the victim into a state of existential crisis. (Herman 1992, p.51)

Although Herman's work has informed my thinking in many important ways I view selves and identities as plural and constantly reconstructed. Therefore, whilst acknowledging the importance of the above statement, I do not use words such as 'shatter', which seem to indicate that 'self' is a discrete entity, but prefer to use 'disrupt'. However, for ease of flow I will sometimes refer to 'self and identity' rather than selves and identities.

Each storyteller in this book recognised that, at some stage in their childhood, they had been traumatised and that their drug misuse was related to those experiences. Children who are securely attached to adults who support their development and show regard for their individuality, dignity and personhood develop a sense of agency and separateness within those relationships (Herman 1992; Meares 2000) and a sense of who they are. Trauma violates that sense of agency, often at a level of bodily integrity, particularly when sexual or physical abuse occurs, or when children are abandoned or neglected by their carers. Loss of control over traumatic events can give rise to shame and humiliation. The child learns that their wishes count for nothing and they come to believe that they cannot maintain a separate sense of themselves whilst in relationships with others, leaving them with a sense of inferiority, doubt and uncertainty, and fear of closeness and intimacy. In this way trauma disrupts connections between the child and others, and between the child and communities of others (such as family) — something that is especially difficult when the trauma involves betrayal of relationships with people upon whom the child depends.

In a chronically abusive environment children have nowhere to turn, recognising that the adults around them do not protect them from harm. Nevertheless, they need to find ways to develop a sense of basic trust and safety which may require them to form attachments to abusive, neglectful or rejecting care-takers and to trust people who are untrustworthy or unsafe (this is particularly clear in Hannah's story). They have to find a way to maintain a sense of agency with people who override their wishes and ignore their basic needs, and to soothe themselves where no solace is offered. From an early environment where relationships are damaging, the child needs to learn how to create and sustain satisfying intimate adult relationships (Herman 1992).

Childhood identities

Children (and their care-givers) are subtly exposed to powerful societal discourses that underpin certain versions of events and present them in a particular light. Those versions inform our construction of self/ves and identities and have implications for what we can and should do (Davies and Harre 1990).

In our society, for example, there are certain culturally available discourses about what it means to be a 'good child' or a 'bad mother' or 'drug addict' against which we measure our own experiences and construct our identities. Burr suggests that 'identities are achieved by a subtle interweaving of many different threads' (1995, p.50) that may be to do with age, class, ethnicity, gender, religion and so on. But for each 'thread' there are a limited number of discourses available out of which to shape our selves, and such limits may depend upon the position adopted by carers whose identities have, in turn, been shaped by family, cultural and historical ways of thinking that were available to *them*. For example, parents whose range of understandings of 'child abuse' were limited by knowledge available prior to the 1970s, before feminism expanded knowledge about the prevalence and effect of abuse, may have interacted differently with their children to parents who have been exposed to more recent concepts such as 'trauma'.

Selves and identities are therefore constructed between people. Once we begin to take up a position within the categories of 'person' to which we have been allocated and see ourselves as belonging to (e.g. 'bad child' or 'good child'), we develop an appropriate system of morals, ideas, appearances and behaviours about what is possible and impossible (Burr 1995, p.146). Those ideas and morals provide us with metaphors and other ways of speaking about ourselves which reinforce and commit us emotionally to identities we have adopted.

However, because identities are defined within interactions with others and the social discourse available, some may be more temporary than others, always dependent upon the changing flow of positions negotiated. In order to renegotiate preferred identities, however, we must first identify the discourses that have shaped us and stand back from them in order to view alternatives.

So in this chapter I focus on the kind of language and metaphors used by the storytellers that indicate the influences that may have shaped the ways they viewed their experiences during childhood and contributed to their fashioning of selves and identities. In doing so I hope to raise some questions and open up some spaces in thinking for people involved in the drugs field, whether they be 'clients', practitioners, policy makers or service providers, and to invite them to think about the discourses that shape *their* interactions and to listen to, or read differently, drug users' stories.

I invite the reader to notice evidence of the influence of a wide range of discourses in the following excerpts from the stories presented earlier in this book (with some additional use of material from the transcripts which may not have been used in the stories), particularly concerning gender, religion, ethnicity, culture, class, education, power, drug use and misuse, mental health, trauma, family, 'normal' teenage behaviour, difference, appearance, popular and media discourses, for example 'like father, like son', and psychological and treatment discourses.

Levi's self-descriptions

During his early years at school Levi had developed a sense of himself as 'top boy' and 'gifted' in response to his successes, but on learning at the age of 13 that his parents were actually his grandparents he began to realise that 'I was not who I thought I was'. Instead of his father being 'a hard-working man…who came to this country to fight Hitler' he discovered his father was a 'drug dealer', 'a pimp' and 'a gangster' who had impregnated his 15-year-old mother and then abandoned her. Additionally, believing that his birth mother had rejected him – having kept the two 'white' children subsequently born to her – he viewed himself as 'not worth much'. The traumatic loss of his early sense of identity, and of feeling valued, became a double burden to him on the brink of adolescence – a crucial time for identity construction. The basis upon which he had constructed his sense of self and identity had been dismantled. Levi also told me that the news helped him to make sense of his lifelong sense of 'disconnection'.

After hearing the news Levi felt he could trust nobody: 'So…the only time I felt at ease…in myself, was if I felt off my face…' This experience took his 'recreational' use of drugs to a new and problematic level within a matter of weeks.

The loss of a 'secure base' described above has been said to be 'possibly [the] most damaging psychological trauma' a young person can be exposed to (van der Kolk 1987, p.32), in that it damages the capacity to trust, and therefore the capacity to form intimate, trusting relationships.

RELATIONSHIPS WITH OTHERS

Levi told me he felt unable to form intimate loving relationships during adulthood and that most of the time he experienced himself as 'living in a separate world'. For much of his life as a drug user Levi's sense of separateness did not trouble him. Indeed, he valued it as a means whereby he could operate in that world: '…in the drugs world that alone-ness, that separate-ness…is an asset. You don't need people…'

Levi's basic need for connection with other humans was also satisfied within that world: '…the first time I had my family [was in] the drugs world…when you're drugged up together…there's a real feeling of belonging… So there's a bond there between me and whoever I'm doing drugs with'.

As he spoke I remembered that he had also talked about using drugs alone, so I asked him: 'So where was your feeling of belonging [then]?' His reply helped me to see that being part of the 'drugs world' was not only about a sense of personal or individual connection, but rather a sense of feeling connected in a wider sense, to a community. '…feeling part of an illegal community – part of a world. I always refer to it as "our world" – like it was separate. There's…almost a sense of pride in it…there's a real sense of belonging.'

Hannah's self-descriptions

Hannah saw herself during childhood as a 'good girl' who was 'really, really quiet', and 'really pretty'. During adolescence when she realised that she had been a victim of her uncle's sexual abuse since she was a tiny child, and a victim of her parents' neglect and betrayal, she realised that despite being a 'good girl' bad things had happened to her. In trying to take control of her life and stop the abuse Hannah changed her appearance from 'really pretty' to being 'a goth': deathly pale, dressed in black, black eye make-up and 'mad hair'. Her behaviour changed from 'good' to 'bad': at school she 'crossed over' from being bullied to 'being the bully'. She lost interest in learning, and having been in the top group for maths she 'dropped from A grades to ungraded'.

At 13 she stopped going to school regularly and started hanging around with people who introduced her to alcohol and drugs: 'They'd pick you up in stolen cars and you'd go joy riding and…drug taking', all of which led to her mother's judgement of her as an 'evil child'. From that point in her life she 'performed' an identity of a 'bad girl', whilst believing she was 'like the devil'.

Hannah saw herself as being 'on her own' in the world – an idea that was reinforced by her abuser's frequent assurances that her family knew about and condoned his abuse of her, and that she would be responsible for destroying her family if she made a fuss.

Abandonment by parents is often resented by abuse survivors even more than the abuse itself (Gold 2000) and this is demonstrated throughout Hannah's story, her parents' failure to prevent or stop the abuse being just one of the *many* ways in which they had negated their responsibilities to nurture and safeguard her.

After her first suicide attempt, at the age of 14, she was 'sent' to see a child psychologist: 'on my own'. After a second overdose, at the age of 19, Hannah asked her cousin and closest friend to support her to disclose the abuse, but once again she was told to keep silent, 'and I knew at that point that I was *really* on my own'. When her father refused to accompany her to the court case she realised 'I was very much on my own with that as well'.

During the court case Hannah's behaviour was offered by the defence lawyers as a means by which she could be defined as 'a prostitute' and 'drug-using whore', and in spite of her attempts to offer a different discourse – 'because I wanted to forget…what he had done to me' – the case resulted in a hung jury and her abuser walked free.

At one point in the conversation I asked Hannah what had helped her to survive, and her answer surprised me by turning the concept of 'being on my own' on its head. After a long considered pause she responded, 'I'm a strong person, and I've always been on my own…there's just something that's different in me… I won't ever…lay down and take it…' Hannah seemed to be saying that being 'strong' meant being alone, that being alone, whilst terrifying and lonely, was better than being abused and betrayed – but it had required the use of alcohol and drugs to maintain that position.

RELATIONSHIPS WITH OTHERS

Hannah's adult relationships with men were also influenced by her uncle's abuse. While she was being abused she survived by creating 'a picture of my dad being this real *strong*…man' who would come to the rescue. Still seeking a rescuer and protector, she formed relationships with men who were like her father, but once in those relationships she discovered 'they were horrible, they were abusing me in their own…way'. Her experience of prolonged sexual abuse had led her to believe that 'it was their right to do that'. This fitted with what her uncle had told her, 'This is what you're here for' (i.e. to be abused).

After a successful attempt to quit drugs she relapsed when she 'fell in love with this bouncer…he just looked so much like my dad, and he was so strong…he said he'd look after me – protect me'. This man 'spiked' her drinks and once again she became hooked on drugs.

Hannah was finally able to form a relationship with a man who supported her to disclose the abuse and she now maintains a loving relationship with her partner by living separately from him with their child:

> …he is there whenever I need him, and he comes round nearly every night. I've enjoyed being on my own – I've enjoyed looking after myself and my daughter on my own – 'cos before I was…just so scared of being on my own… I've never *really* been on my own – I had drugs or drink or something.

It seems as though Hannah is trying to find out what it is like to *choose* positively to be on her own rather than being on her own through fear of abuse *or* fear of being alone.

Omar's self-descriptions

Omar 'stuck out like a sore thumb' as a Pakistani child in his all-white primary school but nevertheless he saw himself as 'leader of the pack' and one of the 'stars of the school play' and 'good at sports'. He saw himself as 'one of the extroverts' during those 'heydays' at primary school.

However, he also described himself as a 'quiet child' and 'not much of a talker'. Omar remembered too that he was a 'very anxious child', an 'obsessive child'; he suffered nightmares and felt 'there was something wrong' with him.

At home he and his siblings were physically abused by both parents, as well as being heavily criticised by them – being labelled 'failures', 'bad kids' or 'the worst kids in the world'. Nevertheless, Omar saw himself as 'Mum's favourite', and he stayed close to her, trying to make up for the disappointment she felt about her older sons' behaviour, and to ensure his own safety.

At secondary school Omar was called 'dirty Paki' and he felt humiliated when he allowed his peers to ridicule his mother's ethnic dress. He rejected his Asian cultural identity which he experienced as shameful and he 'felt pretty much lost'. Still seeking a group with which he could safely identify Omar was attracted to a group of black youths: 'I got into this whole black culture – wanting to be part of them, dressing like them, sounding like them, and getting involved with a lot of crime with them. I thought it was cool, and I felt safe.'

RELATIONSHIPS WITH OTHERS

Omar spent much of his time during late adolescence trying to find ways of staying safe and he managed this by attaching himself to 'the toughest kid in the school'. As a child whose ability to feel safe whilst in relationship with others was limited by his mistreatment, Omar needed to seek out protective attachments, thereby accommodating his need to be in relationships with others to alleviate his sense of vulnerability, alongside his *fear* of being abused by others.

Omar found a positive connection with others through AA meetings during his travels in the USA, following a period of rehabilitation.

The connection that I got with the American fellowship was fantastic: that's what I needed – to be with people, to overcome that fear. That's one thing that was missing in my recovery… I've always been pretty independent, and feared being co-dependent. I needed that kind of being with people to get a balance really.'

Becky's self-descriptions

Becky was born into a large Catholic Maltese family who had come to live in the UK after the Second World War. They were a 'very well known' and 'very good looking' family. Her early memories were of large Maltese community gatherings where ethnic food was shared, but Becky believed that 'being Catholic was probably more of an identity [than being Maltese]…being a member of the Church…going to a Catholic school'.

Before the age of four Becky viewed herself as being part of a 'normal' family, living with her parents and brother. She felt connected to her father even though he drank heavily and behaved violently towards her mother and brother: 'I could see that he was more human, more in touch with his emotions… So we could have that connection, whereas with my mum she was *so* shut down and so void.'

In spite of experiencing herself as her father's 'favourite' she formed the idea that 'there was something defective' about her that led to her being sent to live with her grandmother, her 'schizophrenic alcoholic' uncle and suicidal aunt when she was four years old. Her sense of being defective was reinforced by the shameful realisation that she was no longer part of a 'normal' family – rather that she was living without her parents and brother in a household where several of the adults had been diagnosed with mental illnesses. Physically, she felt 'quite noticeably different', and 'ugly' because of a scar over her eye and teeth that were 'fucked up' by a fall. At primary school she 'hid behind humour' and took on the role as 'joker', entertaining the other children as a means to gain popularity and keep shame at bay.

RELATIONSHIPS WITH OTHERS

She described herself at the age of 13 as 'a bit of a nomad', moving from one group of friends to another, constantly seeking affection and 'love', using alcohol and solvents and 'having a laugh' – something she saw as 'normal teenage experimentation'. This behaviour, whilst ensuring that she could fill the void left by the loss of her parents and brother, led her to a traumatic abortion at the age of 14. That experience was impacted by feeling she was being controlled by others, notably her Catholic school who tried to support her to keep the pregnancy, and her mother who was insistent that she did not, after which she became 'more focused around drinking, smoking cannabis and my shoplifting really took off'. Having always defined herself as 'a thief' and 'a magpie' Becky's stealing and drug use took on a different purpose: she then needed to 'earn' the money to pay for drugs for herself and her boyfriend for whom she felt responsible.

As an adult Becky has struggled to maintain intimate sexual relationships, although she has many good friendships which are important to her, and a good relationship with her child, and also, nowadays, with her mother and brother. Her affiliation with Narcotics Anonymous (NA) provides her with opportunities for giving and receiving friendship and creates a supportive alternative 'family', even today, many years after becoming abstinent.

Meares (2000, p.30) suggests:

> People whose development has been disrupted may show competent attachment behaviour with their children, affiliation with friends, but have a failure in the sphere of intimacy, living out a relationship in alienation and isolation with a marital partner with whom, nevertheless, sexual relations are maintained. They live in relationships characterised by non-intimate attachment.

At this point in her life Becky chooses not to live in the kind of non-intimate relationships she has had in the past, but rather to focus on her career and her child's education and welfare.

Steven's self-descriptions

Both of Steven's parents had been sexually abused during their childhood. In their need to protect him from harm they kept him close to home and all of his social needs were met through his family. He defined his family as 'lower middle-class, upper working-class'.

He went through his school life believing 'I was thick' whilst at the same time realising that he was probably 'more intelligent' than most people, and that he was 'different' from other children. He was 'picked on' by his peers, and called 'spastic'. He coped with this by withdrawing into books, building a fantasy world into which he could escape, seeing himself as 'a dreamer' and 'very self-contained'.

RELATIONSHIPS WITH OTHERS

After being labelled as a 'most unsociable person' by his peers at secondary school, he began to realise that, unlike most of his peer group, he had no friendships outside of his home. Being 'very shy, very crippled, very sensitive' around girls and unable to relate to them, Steven was additionally labelled 'gay', 'spastic' and 'vegetable'. However, by using his considerable intelligence he worked out that by allowing people to get to know him better they could change their views of him. His determination and 'bloody-mindedness' won through and he became the 'most popular bloke in the group'. He recognised that he had 'a very good sense of humour, and a very good wit...I could be very funny'.

At this point he started using alcohol and cannabis which he viewed as part of being 'a product of the 80s youth culture' – binge drinking at weekends and smoking cannabis occasionally.

Steven's ability to make and sustain friendships improved but his long-held habit of withdrawing into a world of his own, through reading and philosophising, exacerbated by his misuse of substances, eventually created a 'psychotic breakdown' characterised by aggression and paranoia. Steven's attitude to his family changed at this time, believing them to be the cause of his problems, especially his 'over-controlling' mother.

> Over two or three years I was going out with girls, getting to a certain point of closeness and then I'd get really insecure, and effectively push them away and break the relationship.

> I felt I'd been cursed: that if I had a relationship with a woman I would go mad. And every time I started to get serious, emotionally intimate…suddenly from being this really sensitive, sweet, intelligent, quite relaxed guy, I would become really insecure, suspicious and paranoid.

John's self-descriptions

John did not know his father, and his drug and alcohol-using mother neglected his welfare: he was also raped at the age of seven by a stranger. John believed that he 'was the unlucky one' and that his experience of rape, and of growing up on the streets of London, meant he became 'an adult' straight away, having had the child 'knocked out' of him. He adapted to this lack of care by becoming streetwise and independent.

During his primary school years John would 'get the piss taken' because he wore his hair down to his shoulders and sandals, probably reflecting his mother's lifestyle as 'a hippy'. John's ability to 'not give a shit' enabled him to maintain relationships with other children and give 'as good as I got', being 'quite happy to fight', although he would not normally initiate violence. He told me: 'I was good at sport, I was good at English, enjoyed art… I had a reading age of 13 when I was about seven.'

However, on moving to live with his grandparents in the country he 'didn't get on' with his new peers, preferring instead to be with much older drug-using members of a biker's club who became his 'substitute family'. John described himself as 'psychologically different' from other drug users in the club, being 'more involved with weapons' and 'full of anger and fear'.

John explained that he coped with his life by having 'an attitude of…indifference, not caring… I think that's…been my downfall in many ways, but in many ways I think it's what got me through…just not really caring.'

His indifference and disconnectedness seem to have been a necessary means of dealing with his distressing life. His use of alcohol and drugs supported that disconnection, protecting him from fear, rage and loss, whilst also excluding him from any chance of being cared for in intimate relationships, or caring for others.

RELATIONSHIPS WITH OTHERS

As an adult, in his relationships with women, John was constantly on his guard against being emotionally hurt or neglected again: 'As soon as I feel insecure in relationships I bolt, or…smash the house up. In a relationship with a woman, [if] I feel like they're taking the piss…I start feeling insecure and lose the plot.'

John believes that the rape has 'affected me in many ways…but…that could also be the way I've been brought up…never had security. When I feel like I have some [security] I don't want to lose it, you know?' He responds to his fear of losing security with rage.

Josie's self-descriptions

Josie was brought up in a 'middle-class family'. The traumatic loss of her father, and the sense she made of that, contributed to a dramatic disruption in her sense of self. Once her father left home Josie felt 'alien to everything'. She described herself as 'nervous, quiet, introverted and timid – scared of everything'.

Going to school 'made sense' to Josie because it was 'predictable'. As a 'naturally very intelligent' child, she could 'spend half the lesson dreaming' and still achieve high marks for her work. At secondary school she used her writing ability to support herself and communicate with others. She wrote about 'hating myself and wanting to punish myself'; she wrote about feeling 'I'm worthless'. Like Omar she felt there was 'something wrong' with her and tried hard to find people who 'would understand how I would feel and make me feel better'.

From the age of ten Josie felt she had 'a tape in my head' that told her 'my dad's left, nobody loves me, everyone hates me, my step-dad hates me, I hate my step-dad… My mum doesn't want me…', and on the birth of her step-sister when she was 14 Josie saw herself as 'a reminder of a bad time'. The torment of those negative self stories was only quieted by excessive use of alcohol and, subsequently, cannabis.

RELATIONSHIPS WITH OTHERS

Josie's stories are characterised by her struggles to form relationships with men. Like Hannah, she repeatedly chose to be with 'damaged' men in her search for male affection, driven by her need for protection and care, and haunted by a fear of abandonment or exploitation (Herman 1992, p.111). Josie's longing for nurture and care made it difficult for her to establish safe and appropriate boundaries with men. Her belief that she should please others, and her habit of self-denigration and obedience to anyone she perceived to be in a position of power or authority, added to that vulnerability.

George's self-descriptions

George was an 'unexpected' and 'unwelcome' third son in his family. However, because of a skin condition that required his mother to massage him with oil regularly he grew to be 'her pet', and he knew she loved him dearly. This close connection was severely disrupted when she left the family home for four months when George was eight years old, resulting in a sense of alienation and disconnection from others: 'I always felt like a Martian…'

The additional trauma of physical and sexual abuse perpetrated by his brother during his mother's absence increased his sense of vulnerability in relationship with others. George described himself as 'a loner' who was 'painfully shy' but in spite of that he was able to 'get on with people' socially, although not at a level of intimacy. As a child he preferred to play on his own: 'It was easier, more controllable. I wouldn't have this other person, this rogue element, who might do who knows what.'

RELATIONSHIPS WITH OTHERS

George's first sexual relationship was with 'an older woman…a local drug dealer' who infected him with sexually transmitted diseases. He told me with some signs of distress that the relationship 'didn't mean anything for her: to me it was really important and it…began my first breakdown at that time.'

His later relationships with women seemed guaranteed to limit the level of intimacy possible and thereby kept him 'safe': 'I found myself having affairs and going off with women – sexually, very dysfunctional.'

As well as feeling alienated from others, George seemed to experience a degree of alienation from different parts of himself, describing one part as 'a sensitive, intelligent person who's quite a decent person', and the other side, which was described jokingly by his friends as 'the evil twin'. This 'split' can also be seen in several other stories, especially Josie's.

George's story also resonates with John's attitude of indifference towards relationships with others: 'So many of the things I've done in my life have been driven by an attitude of "Oh fuck it", you know?' But as he began to understand the impact of trauma and drug misuse in his life he asked himself: 'How do I make sense of my life but through connection, not through alienation, as I have done for many years?'

Experiences of schooling

During the early years children spend much of their time at home or at school, or engaged in activities that are supported by one of those arenas. For the storytellers 'home' was not a positive environment; rather it was a source of trauma, abuse or neglect. In spite of that, for most of them, primary school was a positive experience. Omar described those early years as 'heydays', even though at home he was being abused; Hannah had loved school and had a dream of going to university; for Josie primary school was 'the only part of life that was predictable and made sense'; George found learning easy, being good at academic subjects, as well as sports, art and drama; John felt he did 'all right' at primary school, having 'natural ability in reading and sports'; and Levi was 'top boy' up to the age of 13 until his world fell apart.

Only two of the storytellers did not include stories of 'doing well' at primary school: Becky's memories of that time focused on stealing other children's belongings which she would 'miraculously find again' in the hope of gaining reward from her teacher; Steven's stories of school were heavily focused on his secondary years, almost to the exclusion of the primary years.

In spite of all the stories of doing well at primary school, stories of secondary schooling were very different. Hannah, Steven and Omar were bullied at secondary school, and George described his time at boarding school as 'hell' – a place where he learned to fight to protect himself. John and Becky were expelled at 14 and 15 respectively – John for riding a motorbike around the playground and Becky for stealing the school cash box, although both had been truanting 'and messing around' for some time prior to committing those offences. Omar was expelled twice: the first time for dealing cannabis during the sixth form and the second time for being drunk and disorderly at college. Both Josie and Steven lost interest in their studies around the age of 17, preferring to be with drug-misusing friends. So it is clear to see that, in spite of their ability, few were able to benefit fully from education during their secondary years. However, all of them have continued their education as adults, and most have studied at university.

Seeking connection, bonding and 'family'

Without a positive connection to school or family, or any other mainstream organisation with which they could identify during their teenage years, the storytellers, as social beings, needed to connect with others and create a sense of belonging. In every case they sought out affiliation to, and identification with, groups that led them to their inclusion in a 'drug subculture'.

The stories show clearly, in line with other published research (Miller and Plant 2003), that drug use began as a social activity, even though in some cases it became a solo pursuit later on. Many adolescents encounter drugs routinely, and early substance use can be part of a 'normal' leisure activity with groups of friends. Indeed, some of our storytellers had parents who used drugs and/or alcohol and all told of how they were introduced to drugs through friends, peers or siblings.

Group relationships

All of the storytellers were drawn towards groups that satisfied their need to 'belong', since they were no longer spending time with old friends and family, either because being with them was a constant reminder of feelings they were trying to escape, or because of their need to avoid the censure, shame and stigma of other people's judgements.

These groups provided a new social identity and membership of a subculture with its own language, lifestyle and out-groups (Anderson 1995) and social norms that further isolated them from non-users and 'normal' life. The illicit nature of recreational drug use further bonds the group, and 'getting out of it' is a shared secret between members, hidden from parents (Aldridge *et al.* 1998). Measham (2000, p.168) suggests, 'There is great store placed on observation, conversation and the role of drugs stories – tales told and retold among young people', strengthening a sense of group membership and reinforcing a sense of distance and difference from other friendship and/or family groups.

Omar, who was being racially bullied at his first 'mainly white' secondary school, had difficulty accepting his Asian identity. Around the age of 14 he moved to a new secondary school which had more of a racial mix and he began to hang about with the 'Asian kids' who worked hard academically but were seen as 'nerds':

> They used to get bullied by the white kids *and* the black kids. I was quite confused. I didn't like the idea of getting bullied again, and then it was that whole 'embarrassed to be an Asian thing'…not wanting to be Asian.

In his need to feel safe, Omar formed a relationship with a

> white kid who was the toughest in the school…smoking cigarettes, cannabis…taking amphetamines…[he] was selling…cannabis, small amounts… It's a way in, isn't it – cannabis? It's almost like it gives you some sort of identity and you fit in.

John began using solvents and alcohol around the age of 13 after moving to the country from London. After being expelled at 14 he spent his time with members of a biker's club: 'It was the only thing that mattered. I cut off family and friends… It was like I'd found the family I'd never had, and I didn't want to lose it.'

Levi also described his membership of the 'drugs world' as being with his 'family': 'I was living my life with my people…in my world…I had my new family.' This 'family' filled Levi's need for belonging left by the void created by his rejection of his own family. In this 'world' he felt respected and loved 'because I could always get drugs. There was summat about being mixed race that made it possible for me to move between the black world and the white world.'

Group affiliation for George and Steven came through their interest in music. I was struck by many similarities in Steven and George's stories: both of them were precociously intelligent; both coped by withdrawing from the 'real' world through reading and fantasy; both were 'loners' as children; both were very knowledgeable about, and influenced by, the music scene even though they were born 20 years apart; and for both of them music and drugs went hand in hand.

Steven described how he had created an 'unreal' storied world inside his head, embellished by music. Having made a deliberate attempt to make social contact with his peers during adolescence he began to enjoy being part of a group: 'We'd go out to the cinema…we'd have parties and go to the pub as a big group, and it was quite cool really.'

Having stayed on at school into the sixth form he began to realise he needed to prepare himself for the adult world of work: 'I wanted to be a writer and a music journalist... I just threw all of that away...to binge it up with the druggies really.'

Several of his peers who had left school at 16 were living a 'hippy lifestyle' and he began to feel a 'real [pull towards] that whole lifestyle...non-conformist, irresponsible – just to drop out, just get stoned.' The drugs and his hippy companions offered him a way of escaping back into his preferred 'unreal world' where he felt 'safe' and 'in control' – more so than in his relationships with most of the people he knew.

George had also coped with his disrupted life by creating and living in a fantasy world:

> It seemed to keep me safe. Increasingly, I realised that I couldn't remain in that fantasy world, and that I had to go out into the big wide world, become an adult, and I had nobody...to induct me into the adult world.

When he was 15 he met

> some fantastic people who were smoking dope, and I fell in with them sort of hippy alternative types – and I just loved this... I was trying to find a way of avoiding growing up... Being a musician is a great way of avoiding that...in that world...taking drugs is...almost encouraged... Nobody thought about it as 'taking drugs'.

From the age of 13 Hannah would leave home for several days when she heard her abusive uncle was coming to visit, and stay with the people 'hanging around the shops on council estates' who were using drugs and alcohol. These people called her 'posh'. She described how she moved from one 'level' of substance abuse to the next:

> ...as you're growing older you're able to move up to the next territory and the next like, set of...shops... They'd say, 'Do you want to come for a drive?'...start skinning up... They'd all have flats or know somebody with a flat and you could all just stay round there...

Josie was attracted to a 'gang of lads' from another school who hung around where she lived:

> It was really lovely to get into this gang... I could be one of the lads and they would share their drugs with me... And very quickly I fell in love with one of them. They were very working class...I was middle class, and they were very angry and violent, and not afraid to show their feelings, and I [thought] OK, this is real, this fits with my reality.

At the age of 13 Becky started 'hanging around the park' until 4 am, 'hiding out and drinking... I'd just get pissed, being sick...moving within a different circle of people…yeah, puffing – so that was quite normal, to be drinking and smoking cannabis…'

Individual relationships

Although all three women storytellers were drawn to groups of drug users, their stories were different from those of men in so far as they quickly became sexually involved with violent men within those groups. Hannah was sexually abused at the age of 13 by a 28-year-old man who expected her to 'pay' for drugs with sex, and she continued to be used sexually by men throughout the period of her drug misuse. Josie and Becky both became sexually involved with men they described as 'scary' and with whom they used drugs. One of the men in Josie's group was 20 years older than her – old enough to be her father. She told me, 'He said "I want you", so I just thought if a man wanted me then I should do what they wanted.'

Involvement with a drug-using male may appeal to females who have experienced, and therefore fear, rejection. It has been suggested that by entering into a relationship, and eventually a shared addiction, women make themselves indispensable to their partners by providing support for them and their drug use when others are less keen (Eames 2004).

Although George was taken advantage of sexually by an older female, and John felt let down by the mother of his children (also a drug misuser), Levi, George, Omar and Steven seemed to view their relationships with females as helpful in their resistance to drugs. George was particularly clear on that point. When I asked him how he resisted being drawn into heroin misuse with his housemates, after a long pause he responded: 'Having a girlfriend actually. She'd say, "Are you sure you want to do this?", and I'd think, "Well not *really*"… Of course, if she had used, we'd have both got stoned.'

Levi and Omar had been rejected by their girlfriends *because* of their misuse of drugs and alcohol, and Steven was attracted away from his drug-using group of friends by his desire to find a girl who left the group and returned to her Christian beliefs – an event that began his journey towards transformation.

★   ★   ★   ★

Whilst writing this chapter I have been remembering my own early years and reflecting upon the discourses that shaped my own selves and identities. Having been brought up to believe I was 'the only girl' with seven brothers, this idea formed a core notion of my identity. Like Levi, this sense of identity was severely disrupted during adolescence when I gradually realised that there were two other females (my step-sisters) among my father's children from his earlier marriage. But I had grown up to feel that I was 'special' and my father's 'favourite', and whilst knowing that this position kept me safe from the violence he showed towards my brothers, I was also aware that it kept me separate from them – in that they would be punished by my father if I hurt myself whilst playing with them. I was viewed as a 'troublemaker' by my mother and my brothers, an identity that has shadowed me throughout my life, especially since trying to speak out in my family about childhood issues they would prefer to forget – I am 'the person who speaks the unspeakable'.

Confusingly, as well as being treated as 'special' by my father and being disliked by my mother for that, as a Catholic female child in an Irish family I was trained to serve others, including my brothers and especially my mother, and to view my very existence as 'God's gift' to her for her old age. From an early age I was groomed to believe that I would take care of her and that my brothers would not be expected to do so in any way other than financially.

Part of being 'special' included my being sent to a private convent preparatory school, by grace of a scholarship where, like George at his boarding school, I stood out as 'different' from the other girls whose wealthy parents could afford the fees. I also stood out as 'different' in my local community, wearing uniform to school, and taking a bus to travel there.

However, whilst acknowledging the additional problems this created, I also took pride in being 'special' and in being 'different' and I gained a great deal from the learning and environment of my prep school (Etherington 2003) which, in turn, fed into a grammar school at the age of 11 for those of us who passed the 11 plus scholarship. Unlike the storytellers in this book I was also able to maintain and enjoy my affiliation with mainstream organisations – my church and secondary school – which involved me in sports, at which I was successful, and membership of a Girl Guide group attached to my church, where my qualities of leadership were recognised and nurtured, and my relationships with affirming people supported my developing sense of self and identity in ways that were not conditional upon their needs of me. Those relationships provided me with examples of supportive adult relationships against which I could measure my expectations in future relationships.

However, I believe that as a teenager growing up in the 1950s, as well as having those affiliations through which I could construct more positive identities, I grew up with no awareness of drugs, either locally or nationally, and as I have researched the lives of ex-drug misusers I have wondered how my life might have been had that not been the case. However, I *was* aware of alcohol and its misuses, but this was kept outside the home (except at Christmas) and, in my family, was seen as an entirely masculine preserve.

Without drugs and alcohol I found other ways to deal with my childhood trauma – through illness and depression: a story that is told elsewhere (Etherington 2003).

In conclusion of this chapter I am left wondering about the frequency in the stories of mention of a sense of 'difference' which, like my own sense of difference, can be celebrated. Do we all feel different? Is a sense of 'being different' related to a person's tacit knowing that they are indeed being shaped by the discourses surrounding them – that they are being expected to fit into a 'hole' of a certain shape that is not their own? Is feeling different a recognition of resistance and resilience that speaks of standing out against discourses that do not match a person's values and desires for their life? John recognised that his anger and fear made him 'different' from other drug users. Hannah told me that being different means she won't 'lay down and take it'. Josie recognised her attraction to the lads living in a bender was that they were not afraid to show their feelings and that their anger fitted in with her 'own reality'. Steven also spoke of being drawn towards his hippy friends whose reality 'seemed more real than sitting in a classroom'.

However, by becoming identified with other drug-users, borne out of a desire to belong and reduce their sense of alienation, storytellers were left with little to prevent them from sliding further and faster into an 'addict' identity and lifestyle (Etherington and Barnes 2006), which will be explored in the chapters that follow.

Chapter 12

Problematic Drug Use and Turning Points

In the previous chapter I examined the role of trauma and discourses in the construction of selves and identities and in the formation of individual and group relationships. This chapter continues to weave those threads to show how storytellers came to a point in their lives when their drug-using lifestyle became problematic which, in turn, eventually led to them transforming their lives.

Storytellers indicated that the adoption of a 'drug-user' identity provided them with access to groups of people with whom they felt accepted and understood, and with whom they had a shared reality, thereby lessening their sense of alienation from 'normal' society. At that stage drug use was not necessarily experienced by them as problematic, although it may have been viewed as problematic by others. The drugs used by storytellers included cannabis, cocaine and crack cocaine, LSD, acid, ecstasy, heroin and benzodiazepines. All of them used more than one drug at a time, and some people were willing to use anything at hand. But what was also very noticeable in the stories, although I did not ask about it, was the storytellers' relationship with alcohol.

Inter-relationship between alcohol and drugs

A major feature in all of the stories was the part played by alcohol in the drug-using lifestyles. Even though the focus was on drug misuse it became clear as their stories unfolded that alcohol was part of a taken-for-granted 'norm' among their family and friends and in their own lives.

Alcohol is widely accepted and associated with socialising, relaxing and pleasure and is a known and familiar way of reducing inhibitions. Used in moderation alcohol can be beneficial to health – a fact that is frequently used by people who drink to excess to explain or excuse their use of alcohol.

Omar began to drink heavily whilst still at school as a 'kind of real release from everything'. After the breakdown of his relationship with his girlfriend his drinking increased: 'I remember *really* drinking heavily after that – a young lad drinking a lot of spirits, vodkas, heavy, heavy drinking.' His use of alcohol to bring him down from cocaine clearly shows how both substances were inter-related and his statement that 'I sobered up into the drugs world' further defines his view of the connection between both substances.

Hannah, who had grown up with an alcoholic mother, told me how using alcohol led her into using drugs. Whilst truanting from school, in order to avoid going home, she would hang around with a gang of young people who were picked up in cars by older men: 'They introduced me to drinking first, and, and then drugs…cider, to start with and then Special Brew…and…Thunderbirds… I got into really bad states with that, that is the first thing I started with really…'

Josie was drinking 'quite a lot' by the time she was 14:

> I was going into town with this girlfriend… And we'd go to the pub and dress up, and they'd let us in and we'd get drunk, and we'd flirt with men and they'd buy us drinks. And I got into quite a few scrapes doing that, thankfully nothing too awful, but several times I ended up with a man in a back street wanting to have sex…

Although she was normally 'quiet and introverted, and timid, and scared of every-thing', she found that she became like 'someone else' when she drank alcohol: 'I'd drink and I was totally different, and really popular as well, attractive to boys, felt lovable and loved, and it was like I was just someone else.' But her excessive drinking at such a young age led to a warning from her GP that she was ruining her health. On discovering that cannabis allowed her to still 'get out of it' without having to drink she drank less and used cannabis more often. But alcohol continued to feature in her life even after she quit using drugs, when she went back to using alcohol to cope with the emotions that had been hitherto suppressed by drugs. Alcohol was the last substance she was able to give up.

Steven also pointed out how 'normal' it was to drink at weekends with his 'A' level friends emphasising how, even today, it is still 'normal' behaviour in our society: '…getting absolutely plastered, and that's what everyone did, and that's what everyone does – even now. I've got friends in their thirties and that's their lifestyle: every weekend, and even weekdays, they're getting hammered.'

He recognised that his involvement in the 'music scene' had been instrumental in his use of substances: 'I started off into heavy metal and that kind of thing…[then] it was mainly just alcohol. I used to go to gigs, get drunk – it was all just sort of drink-related.' I enquired about his parents' reaction to him coming home drunk, which he described as 'tolerant and even amused'. He laughed again as he told me:

> …they could probably remember the first time *they* got drunk, and it's no big deal really. They would roll their eyes and say, 'What are you doing getting drunk?' It was just at weekends, or every couple of weekends – we'd all go out and get drunk, have a laugh.

Steven's remarks reflect the current trend of 'binge drinking' which was said to be costing £20 billion a year in a government report published in the UK in 2003

(Prime Minister's Strategy Unit 2003). The report states that 17 million working days are lost to hangovers and drink-related illness each year, at an annual cost to employers of £6.4 billion, while the cost to the NHS is in the region of £1.7 billion. Billions more are spent clearing up alcohol-related crime and social problems.

In addition to the effects of binge drinking, alcohol-related problems were said to be responsible for 22,000 premature deaths each year, at a conservative estimate. The report found that there are 1.2 million incidents of alcohol-related violence a year and that around 40 per cent of admissions to accident and emergency departments are alcohol-related, rising to 70 per cent between the hours of midnight and 5 am. Around 150,000 people each year end up in hospital because of alcohol-related accidents and illnesses and up to 1.3 million children are affected by parents with drink problems.

Those children, like some of our storytellers, are also more likely to have a range of problems later in life. It has also been recognised that young people reared in home environments that have permissive attitudes to alcohol use (not necessarily 'problematic' alcohol use), and who are introduced to alcohol at an early age, are likely to be more vulnerable to alcohol-related problems in adolescence (Fergusson, Lynksey and Horwood 1994).

John told me he was 'fed whisky and sugar on a spoon…when I was teething…to ease the pain' and had grown up with his mother and grandfather 'drinking heavily' during his early years. He had 'got consciously drunk' for the first time whilst on holiday with his family in Spain at the age of ten, and started drinking regularly at the age of 13. He saw this as 'normal teenage experimentation'. The idea that he may never be able to drink again is one that John rejects, even though that is the underlying premise of the AA movement to which he is attached.

> Alcohol just features right the way through. When I went into treatment they said to me, 'Do you think you have a problem with alcohol?', and I said: 'No I haven't got a problem with alcohol – I love it!' [*Laughs*]. That was how mental [I was]. I've got to be able to drink again.

He explained the inter-relationship between alcohol and drug misuse, seeing alcohol as

> underlying it all really. I mean, I took amphetamines and they enabled me to drink through the night. I didn't really get drunk but I'd still be taking the alcohol into my system. So I was getting the hit off the alcohol but without the sleepiness.

During our first meeting Levi only referred to using alcohol excessively during his years in the army, when alcohol was very much part of the culture and there were no drugs available to him. During a second meeting he told me:

I've said several times, even recently, 'I'm not a drinker.' But I've drank…from the age of 13…up until now, harder than most people would… It just didn't feel out of control, you know. So I'd have four or five vodkas through the day…

Looking back, at the time I had no concept of that – I considered myself as someone who didn't drink. And I drank all the way through – with the drugs. I don't understand how I could delude myself entirely.

George made no reference to using alcohol until he came to the point in his story that described the 'game' he invented to help him quit using drugs. He had devised a four-day plan which seemed to indicate that he saw alcohol misuse to be as much of a problem as drugs: 'on day one I could smoke dope *and* drink; on another day I could *just* smoke dope; on another day I could *just* drink; and on the other day of this four-day cycle I could do neither.'

Becky grew up surrounded by alcoholic adults: her father whom she described as 'an alcoholic' was the son of an alcoholic; her mother's father had been an alcoholic who sexually abused several of his children; and she lived with 'an alcoholic schizophrenic uncle' when she went to live in her Nan's house from the age of four. By the age of 13 she was 'hiding out and drinking' in the park until the early hours of the morning, going to 'these house parties…where I'd just get pissed, being sick…that was quite normal, drinking and smoking cannabis', and by the age of 14 she had also experienced a traumatic abortion. Becky told me: 'That's when I started drinking more, still managing to go in to school…but I was more focused around drinking, smoking cannabis and my shoplifting really took off.'

Having successfully detoxed from drugs, and having ended her relationship with her violent boyfriend, Becky was constantly on the alert and fearful that she would bump into him again: 'I started to drink really heavily, started taking pills, going out raving – just drinking really, really heavily all the time.'

So for each of the storytellers alcohol had been a central part of their lives and an integral part of the journey towards drug misuse. On reflecting on the evidence of the inter-relationship between alcohol and drug misuse depicted in these stories I notice the effect of the normalising messages concerning the use of alcohol in our homes and society, which is in stark contrast to our attitudes to drugs. Although negative public attitudes and the stigma attached to drug misuse can be viewed as additional and unhelpful burdens upon already marginalised people (Etherington and Barnes 2006), the current permissive attitudes to alcohol consumption could be seen as equally unhelpful. Research published in 2002 (Gossop, Marsden and Stewart) investigating the inter-relationship between alcohol and drug dependence concluded that alcohol use is an important and under-rated problem among drug misusers and needs to be separately assessed and treated.

The trauma literature also shows the acceptance of the idea that the use of alcohol (as well as drugs) is a well-recognised means of coping with unprocessed trauma (Navjavits *et al.* 1997; Porter 1994; Ravndal *et al.* 2001; Rohsenow *et al.* 1988).

Problematic drug use

Drug use was identified as 'problematic' by some storytellers when the motives for using changed, rather than when the amount they used increased (Etherington and Barnes 2006; McIntosh and McKeganey 2000a). For Omar, Levi and John, who had been injecting heroin, and Becky, who had been smoking heroin, that shift had occurred after a difficult period when the substances took over, leading to physical and psychological reactions that required constant 'medication' to avoid feeling ill. When that happened there was a shift from being 'the person they were before' towards the development of a new 'addict' identity and lifestyle, characterised by a range of behaviours to fund their habits, or as a result of their drug use, that were not in tune with their previously held values and moralities. Levi and Omar also had to accept that addiction had altered their physical appearance in ways that identified them as drug addicts, with the accompanying stigma attached.

Their use of drugs also became problematic when they were identified as the cause of psychological distress or mental ill health. The long-term mental health risks for those who have been exposed to childhood abuse and trauma have been well documented and the links between trauma and subsequent drug misuse has been made clearly in Chapter 2 (Briere 1992; Browne and Finkelhor 1986; Finkelhor and Browne 1985; Kendler *et al.* 2000). Judith Herman (1992) argued that 'many, or even most, psychiatric patients are survivors of child abuse' (p.122). A study by Read proposed that it is not only mild or moderate adult dysfunction that is related to childhood abuse, but also some of the most severe dysfunction (Read 1997). In an international literature review concerning the links between mental health and childhood abuse Read found that, among patients with 'severe mental illness', 76 per cent of women and 72 per cent of men had been sexually or physically abused in childhood (Read 1998, p.360).

Substance misuse may become a means of self-medication to deal with the distress of severe anxiety, depression, self-destructive urges and suicidal feelings caused by unprocessed trauma. Josie suffered tortuous ruminations which could only be silenced by alcohol or drugs; George experienced two 'breakdowns' in his mental health; others spoke about suicidal ideas and attempts, depression and self-harm. But it is difficult to separate out how many of their symptoms were experienced as a result of trauma and how many were the consequences of drug-taking. It would appear that it is less clear cut than that: Steven, who was sectioned under the Mental Health Act, initially believed that his experiences of grandiose delusions, aggression and hallucinations were caused by his use of drugs. Later he suggested that his upbringing created the conditions in which his drug use would inevitably lead to psychosis. John ascribed his severe psychotic breakdown, manifested by sleeplessness, paranoia, hallucinations and a sense of being 'cut off from the outside world', to his use of drugs. So in some cases drug use was perceived as problematic when it was identified as the cause of a breakdown in mental health.

Hannah, Josie, George and Steven, who had not used heroin (although both Hannah and George had used it briefly and had been able to draw back from 'going down that road'), did not speak about themselves as 'addicts' but rather spoke of their drug use as being problematic when they experienced psychological torment that led them to experience an existential crisis (see Chapter 2 for definitions). Although for Hannah and Josie there was a similar sense of their drug-using behaviour and lifestyle having reached a point beyond which they did not want to go, their decision to change, like George and Steven's, seemed to be most influenced by their realisation that if they were to survive, mentally and physically, they would need to stop. Steven told me, 'I never...I never realised when I was taking LSD that I'd end up in a mental hospital.' He spoke of his decision to stop using drugs as 'self-preservation' after hearing about his drug-using cousin's suicide. Josie, who had begun to cut herself, and feared harming herself further, told me, 'I got stuck in my head and I forgot how to get out and talk to people...' George told me, 'I walked to the beach...I was going to drown myself.' Hannah, having attempted suicide twice, and trying to deal with terrifying flashbacks, said, 'I couldn't bear the pain. I'd just had enough.' These crises catapulted them into making a decision to stop – and they were all successful in doing so, like Levi, without conventional treatment interventions. The means by which they supported themselves to give up using drugs and transforming their identities will be addressed in Chapter 13.

Reaching rock bottom

Although all of the stories showed evidence of the events that led to rock bottom or existential experiences (Biernacki 1986), only four of the eight storytellers came to view themselves as 'addicts'. Here I will focus on the stories told by Omar and Levi, two of the men who resisted identifying themselves as addicts until they hit 'rock bottom'. These stories highlight the impact of stigma, racial identities, drug dealing and the dual use of heroin and cocaine on their sense of self and identity.

Omar used drugs and alcohol from the age of 15 without viewing that as problematic: his use of substances gained him entry into a group with which he could identify without having to embrace his Asian identity. However, from the fringes of the drugs world he discovered that there *were* some Asians, including his brother, who were respected by others: these were the drug dealers. Having discovered an Asian identity that was linked with 'respect', Omar wanted 'to be...almost like a gangster... I wanted what he had – respect...being flash around it, leather jacket, designer clothes, enjoying it with other people.' Around the age of 18 he was taken 'under the wing' of a drug dealer and began to 'do well' for himself whilst also starting to use cocaine which 'came hand in hand with that'. At this time he also began to sell heroin.

Many drug users view their ability to resist becoming an 'addict' as a source of pride. Omar, like several other storytellers, felt superior to heroin users, whom he described as 'smackheads', and he told himself, 'I'd never do that.' The stigma connected to heroin use, in particular, and the stereotype of the 'typical addict', causes people to distance themselves from that identity, allowing them to maintain some sense of self-worth through recognising that there were still things that they believed to be morally wrong. If a positive identity is not easily attainable in other ways, then criticising the negative qualities of others and comparing themselves positively may provide a measure of self-worth (Sulkunen 1992).

Larkin and Griffiths (2002, p.301) draw attention to how the particular stigma attached to heroin use becomes a way of describing the whole person, rather than the behaviour as one aspect of the person: 'one is no longer a "user of heroin" (a particular kind of "addict") but simply an "addict" (a particular kind of person – identified by a particular kind of relationship with – potentially – many kinds of behaviours).'

When Omar first began to use heroin he saw himself as 'doing quite well' in terms of his lifestyle, but he was using cocaine heavily: '…everyone was doing it and it'd make you feel really good. I'd need a heavy drink to come down. And heroin did that [as well].' When he eventually began to use heroin he told me, 'I remember not liking it at first, but after getting used to that kind of escapism – it was perfect for coming down off of cocaine.'

However, using heroin was not a problem for Omar all the time it was available, and he had enough money to keep himself 'topped up'. But after using heroin for a year he ran into debt, and to avoid his debtors he went to Pakistan where he first experienced withdrawal symptoms: 'I never knew about cold turkey, physical dependency, until…I got over there…'

Levi, who described himself as mixed race, had a similar story in that, even though he was heavily using many different drugs, and alcohol, he did not see himself as 'a druggie'. Having seen himself as 'someone who would use drugs at weekends' like most of the kids on his estate, his attitudes to drug using changed after hearing the news about his parentage. He began to use drugs as a way to escape from his unbearable reality, and later as a means whereby he could survive in the drugs world.

As he became further immersed in that world, like Omar, Levi's drug use became inextricably linked with dealing drugs and involvement in a criminal lifestyle. Also, like Omar, Levi had been racially abused and treated disrespectfully and he spoke about the respect he gained from dealing drugs and living that lifestyle: '…there's prestige in being known as a hood…there's a certain kind of respect you get out on the street.' Even though he was using large quantities of drugs during this time he still did not view himself as an 'addict' or 'druggie': '…it wasn't a…druggie's life where you were burgling…houses to get the money – it was on a big scale.' It seems as though the stereotype of 'drug addict' did not fit with his experience of himself or his lifestyle: 'I would never even *meet* druggies like that… I would be selling to people, who sold to people, who sold to them.'

Although he used various drugs he described his 'drug of choice' as coke, which supported him in feeling that he was 'capable of anything' and that he 'did not need anybody': heroin made him feel 'fuzzy' rather than omnipotent.

The big shift for Levi came after experiencing several relationship losses, and in his need to protect himself from being overwhelmed by his grief he began to use heroin *and* coke – a practice called 'speedballing' which is known to put severe strain on the heart and, in some cases, cause death. After three months of this dangerous practice Levi was badly affected by using 'dirty' heroin, which caused convulsions. On realising that even after such a bad experience he was still craving for heroin, he acknowledged that he was 'in a bad way' and that he was no longer in control of his use of drugs.

At this point Levi accepted with self-disgust and shame that he was 'hooked'. His self-disgust was underpinned by the stigma and stereotypes that abound related to 'drug addict'. His words indicated the struggle between the person he was previously and the person he believed he had become: 'That was for weak people. That was for stupid people… I'm better than that. I was the boss.' The realisation that 'I'm under this…this has got me' was humiliating and shameful: he felt he 'didn't deserve to talk to no-one about it…just…tough it out – take the pain'. Levi's words seem to suggest that the stigma surrounding heroin use reinforced a negative self-image and contributed to difficulties in seeking help: his fear of being viewed as 'weak' and 'a dirty junkie' and his loss of self-respect led him to view himself as undeserving of care and support.

His story, like Omar's, also shows how a changed appearance has an effect on the person's embodied sense of self and identity, which draws attention to their state of dependence on drugs, and leaves them more open to the discrimination that stigma attached to drug misuse invites. Levi told me: 'I lost loads of weight…really looked terrible. Clothes hanging on…very expensive clothes, but hanging on…like a clotheshorse…'

Existential experiences

Here I will focus on Hannah's story which shows how she reached and faced an existential crisis which led to her decision to change. Her story shows powerfully how denial and oppression can silence victims and lead to the experience of a double-bind where in the end something has to give, thereby generating some form of bodily reaction to the unspeakable dilemma.

A child who is sexually abused over a long period of time, from a very early age, within the family, and without any means to soothe herself, may turn to self-harm and/or suicide as the only way out of an unspeakable dilemma. There is a great deal of evidence to show the increased risk of mental ill health and suicide attempts among survivors of child abuse (Itzin 2000, 2006; Kendler *et al.* 2000; Read 1998).

For many years Hannah had prayed to die in her sleep. 'I used to…pray "Please don't let me wake up" and I'd wake up with…pain and sadness each time: "Oh, I'm here again."'

By the age of 14 her life and drug use felt out of control: 'I'd taken *so* many drugs…ecstasy had come in at that point…and acid.' Although she did not make a conscious decision to end her life she felt, 'I don't feel I'm going to be here that much longer', believing that the drugs would kill her or that she would inevitably take her own life.

At this point she took an overdose which was unsuccessful in killing her and also unsuccessful in drawing her mother's attention to the fact that she was a deeply unhappy child. Instead of asking why she had taken the pills, the adults around her accused her of upsetting her mother. Hannah's pain was evident as she repeatedly asked me, 'Why did nobody ask me why?'

Her drug misuse escalated further, and by 16 her life seemed to be spiralling out of control again. She was by then 'tooting the dragon' (sniffing heroin from foil) and her peers had started to inject. She had been 'doing sexual favours' for drug dealers who were paying her and plying her with a range of drugs.

The realisation that she had reached a point beyond which she did not want to go gave her the necessary impetus to leave the UK and start a new life abroad, away from the family and environment that had been the context for her drug use. In her new home she remained drug-free for two years, not feeling the need, even though drugs were available, because she felt 'less pressure…free of [the abuser]'. But the abuse continued to 'haunt' her and she returned to the UK to disclose to her aunt that both she and her cousin had been abused by her aunt's husband. Whilst preparing herself to face her aunt, and back living with her mother, she was reintroduced to drugs by a boyfriend who spiked her drinks.

As the pressure to disclose built up within her, and the pressure from her family to keep silent increased, Hannah was plagued by flashbacks of the sexual abuse and once again she became suicidal. She told me, 'I couldn't bear the pain… I was having the nightmares again, it was…every day it was like reliving [the abuse] – 'cos I could feel him there…and it was just tearing me apart.'

Hannah is not describing the cognitive memory of abuse but a 'reliving' of the abuse, as though it was actually happening, with all the accompanying sensations. Whilst being abused, children may survive by means of disconnecting parts of the experience to protect themselves – and thereby survive. During 'flashbacks' the person experiences the disconnected part *without* the defence of dissociation. It could therefore be said that they are feeling the experience for the first time. This is commonly a dangerous time for survivors, when suicide is viewed as perhaps the only way of avoiding extreme pain and distress.

Without the support of caring people to whom to disclose, Hannah experienced an existential dilemma between 'disclose or die' and, left to deal with it alone, she 'couldn't bear the pain. I'd just had enough.' She explained that for her family she did not exist: '…they look at me but see right through me…'cos if they looked at me too long then they're going to see my pain and...they can't bear that... That's why I took drugs because...*I* have to bear it.'

For all storytellers this stage of crisis was characterised by self-questioning and 'self-searching'. George asked himself:

> What's wrong with me when I *don't* take drugs, what's wrong with me when I'm *not* out of it...? Who am I when I don't take drugs, and who am I when I do? What do drugs do to me that I like?

Steven described this time as:

> like opening it up, and suddenly, for the first time...I looked at myself: it was a real re-evaluation, it was like, I'm only 21 and what am I doing with my life? What am I doing smoking all these drugs?

Levi told me, 'I spent loads of time...walking on the beach and looking at stars and...really self-searching: "What am I all about? What's gonna become of me?"' Omar described his 'strange' experience in Pakistan: 'I didn't know what was happening to me, I started praying again. I was really lost over there...I was on this spiritual journey'. Josie told me:

> I really believed that God was there, and somebody, somehow, was holding me all through, he's holding me and watching over me. And more and more, as I watch...a lot of my friends from that time are dead now...one hung himself, and one shot himself, quite a lot overdosed on drugs. And another one...is a heroin addict...just a mess, and I just think, 'Why did I survive and they all died?'

For some of the storytellers the self-questioning was related to becoming a parent when they became aware of the values most dear to them, either reclaimed from before their drug using or newly emerging at a different stage of life. Their desire to give their child a better experience than their own seemed to provide the motivation for change.

John, who had had no model of 'good parenting' upon which to draw, became fearful when his second child was about to be born, having experienced the death of his first. His lifelong attitude of indifference, which had helped him survive, had been dismantled by that experience of that loss: 'I didn't give a shit about much really, until my kids came along.' But although his second child was healthy, his drug-using lifestyle resulted in her being given up for adoption, her mother also being a drug addict. John told me: 'I knew I had to start dealing with things, because the drugs and alcohol *weren't* taking the feelings [of loss] away... That's when I started getting better.'

Josie became pregnant whilst living in a bender with a group of drug users. She told me, 'It was kind of rock bottom...in my head I started to think, "What can I do to sort this out?" The baby gave me a conscious reason to sort myself out.' Her previously held values in relation to children caused her to question how she could care for a child whilst still using drugs:

> It's always been really important to me that I don't knowingly do anything to cause harm to a child… I remember getting up one day and watching myself take over an hour to get my drink and thinking, 'This is ridiculous, how do I think I can be a good mother if I'm like this?', and I just stopped.

The conflict between her 'drug-user' identity and her 'mother' identity made her realise that using drugs was now too problematic and gave her the much-needed impetus to stop.

The same conflict emerged from Becky's story, as she told of how she began to review her behaviour and sense of self dramatically once her child was born: 'I'd take Jamie with me to…all these…dirty dealers, you know?… I just felt the guilt and shame around Jamie… I just felt bad because…I was a woman, a mother, a drug addict.' Becky told me towards the end of her story, 'if I hadn't had Jamie I wouldn't have got into recovery at the age of 20. I just wouldn't have been entertaining the idea of a life without drugs or alcohol now.'

The common motivating factor was to lead a non-drug-using way of life with 'normal' roles and lifestyles. Once the decision to stop was made, the journey towards transformation could begin, but the journeys were never straightforward: conflicts between their using and non-using worlds continued to cause problems, which often led to lapses. As well as managing cravings, the changes in self and lifestyle were also problematic, particularly in the light of the stigma and labelling that drug users encounter within families and society.

Chapter 13

Transforming Identities

Trauma survivors strive for health...they seek the restoration of
meaning and wholeness to personality and the process of living.

(Wilson 2006, p.xxiv)

In earlier parts of this book I have focused on the negative impacts of traumatic
experiences on a person's construction of self and identity, and the additional
distress caused to themselves and others through using drugs to cope. Although
an important part of developing a non-using identity involves examining parts of
a drug-using lifestyle for its negative consequences (McIntosh and McKeganey
2000a), it is also important to examine a person's life stories for what positively
helped them build a more rewarding sense of self and identity, in order to
build upon and reinforce those strengths and resources and support necessary
behaviour changes (Larkin and Griffiths 2002).

There is an increasing literature nowadays that recognises resilience in
trauma survivors (Ayalon 2005; Joseph, Liney and Harris 2005; Tedeschi and
Calhoun 1995; Tennen and Affleck 1999) and the positive growth possible after
facing what has been described by Wilson (2006) as the 'Abyss Experience',
when a person confronts the possibility of their own death and/or disintegration.
It has been recognised that trauma that has been overcome and integrated as part
of a person's identity can increase a sense of continuity, coherence, connection,
autonomy, vitality and energy and lead to transcendence of self (Wilson 2006,
p.3), thus transforming the adverse effects of trauma and drug misuse and, in the
process, transform the person (Wilson 2006, p.401). Bearing in mind that
previously I have shown how trauma creates a sense of *dis*continuity, a chaotic
sense of self, *dis*connection, over-control, and lethargy and fatigue, this is indeed
transformation.

So in this chapter I intend to focus on aspects of the stories that show us how
the storytellers' behaviour and their beliefs about self, the world and others
changed over time in ways that helped them transform themselves from drug user
to non-drug user. All of them drew upon their personal strengths and resources,
as well as on supportive relationships that were already available to them or newly
created as part of the reconnections they made on their journeys towards
transformation.

Identity transformation

For some of the storytellers it was possible to reconnect with or extend an existing identity as 'daughter' or 'son' which had been relatively untouched by their drug-misusing behaviour. Josie's story shows how the support she needed was available through her extended family and members of her church who had stood beside her throughout her journey. Levi had also maintained his relationship with his mother by keeping her in ignorance about the source of his wealth (from drug dealing) and thereby managed to find a safe haven in her home during his detoxification. George needed to separate out his preferred and pre-existing identity of 'musician' from his 'drug-misuser' identity, even whilst recognising one as part of the other, so closely bound together were both behaviours.

Becky, John, Hannah and Josie were enabled by the emergence of a new identity as 'parent' which gave them the necessary impetus to change their drug-using lifestyle. Steven adopted a new identity as 'Christian', and Levi made a conscious decision to leave behind his 'career' as a drug dealer and user and found a route that led him towards becoming a member of a helping profession. Omar also began to identify with a 'helper' aspect of his identity when he was taken on as a member of staff at the rehabilitation centre at which he had been treated.

Leaving behind their environment and lifestyle

The sense of alienation and disconnection experienced as a result of trauma had led all of the storytellers to identify with a drug-using sub-culture. Paradoxically, once they realised the need to change, they began to realise they needed to experience themselves as 'separate' once again, but this time to make a conscious decision to separate themselves as a means to discover who they might be without the drugs. All of them knew that it was not enough simply to give up using drugs, but that they also needed to leave behind their drug-using environment and culture.

Omar escaped his drug-misusing environment by visiting his family in Pakistan where he experienced 'cold turkey' for the first time. Levi visited his mother's seaside home and locked himself away in a bedroom for a week whilst he faced his physical and psychological dependence on heroin: he stayed away from his drug-misusing environment for six weeks questioning his lifestyle. Josie left her home town for two years in an effort to protect her child. George left his shared house once his friends began to use heroin. Hannah spent two years abroad and remained drug-free during that time. John went into a treatment centre. Steven was admitted to a psychiatric hospital for four months after a psychotic break-down. Becky's first opportunity to separate herself from her environment and abusive relationship came through imprisonment for shoplifting where she was able to detox successfully for the first time. However, on her release she found that nothing had changed: she was coming out 'to the same flat, him [her partner] still on the gear', and she soon went back to using drugs.

However, the initial period of separation, whilst a necessary and important stage of transformation in terms of creating a space in which people could examine their lifestyle from some distance, was not in itself enough to avoid lapses or create long-term identity reconstruction. Omar returned from Pakistan to *more* serious drug misuse and became homeless. Josie went back to using cannabis and alcohol on her return to her home town. Hannah became seriously addicted again on moving back to live with her mother. John 'went back out again' after leaving the treatment centre 'and had another party for four years' until his 'life fell apart'. Steven went back to smoking drugs until his cousin committed suicide. Levi decided he would continue to sell drugs but not inject them, but without the emotional numbing of drugs he became too fearful in that world and eventually left again. Becky went out 'drinking really heavily...taking pills, going out raving', until she was re-arrested and referred to the probation worker.

What helped Becky most was a referral to a mother and baby treatment centre at a distance from her home where she was supported 'to leave my family behind, to put some distance between myself and them...leave Jamie's dad and that baggage there and make something of my life'. But Becky also emphasised that what was most important to her success was that she was able to take her child with her to the rehabilitation centre, and that he was given his own carer who could focus on his needs. Important, too, was the opportunity she was given to learn parenting and life skills. Research has shown the benefits of parenting training in residential substance abuse treatment (Baker and Carson 1999; Camp and Finkelstein 1997). All too rarely are parents offered rehabilitation programmes that include their children, even though it has been recognised that children of drug misusers are among the most at risk in our society; exposed as they may be to physical and emotional neglect or harm, and a whole range of poor developmental and social outcomes (Barnard 2005, 2007; Barnard and McKeganey 2004; McKeganey, Barnard and McIntosh 2002). In a recent study of the children of problematic drug users many children stated that they would have welcomed intervention that took their needs into account (Barnard 2007). Sadly, the centre where Becky and Jamie were cared for no longer admits mothers with their babies. There is also a dearth of information about how to support drug-using parents generally (Clark 2005).

Role models – the wounded healer

Becky and Omar described the importance of meeting a role model. It is interesting to note how many drugs workers have themselves been problematic drug users in the past, adding credence to the concept of Carl Jung's archetype, 'the wounded healer', that originated with the Greek myth of Chiron who was physically wounded and, by way of overcoming the pain of his own wounds, became a compassionate teacher of healing.

Becky told me, 'I think the biggest therapeutic tool in my recovery is people who believe in you and who are able to spur you on when you sometimes get in to those old maladaptive beliefs of: I'm a piece of shit and I'm not worthy' – beliefs that were formed through the internalisation of societal stereotypes attached to drug addiction, and reinforced by her GP, who told her, 'If you come here again and say you've used heroin I *will* take your kid away.' In contrast to that, the 'probation guy' who treated her respectfully and asked 'Do you want help?' was the first person 'who'd empathised with me and who believed…that I could do it'. This man also provided her with hope for her future when he disclosed that he was himself 'in recovery': 'From when I first started seeing that guy who got me into treatment, I'd say *I* want to be a probation officer, I'd had that dream.' And although Becky never became a probation officer, she did become a helping professional.

Omar was also helped by the disclosure of a drugs worker who approached him on the street and said, 'You look like you're in trouble, do you need help?' Omar told me: 'This was the first heroin addict in recovery that I've ever met…she works as a social worker…she actually explained about her being a heroin addict. It was fairly normal in her country – so it's an amazing story.' I asked him what it had meant to him that she had also been addicted:

> It was really nice to talk to somebody who actually understood. And I trusted her…almost immediately…she was saying, 'This is a *really* good one [rehab] – you should try it.' I'm not sure I'd have trusted the person or their judgement [if they hadn't been an ex-user].

This kind of respectful, trusting, collaborative relationship remains the cornerstone of transformation where human connection is restored and agency remains central to the recovery process. Problematic drug users are sometimes suspicious of the motives of others and find it hard to trust people who approach them to offer help (McIntosh and McKeganey 2000b) so when workers disclose their own history of drug misuse they begin to create a more equal relationship which demonstrates the potential for *all* of us to occupy the roles of helper or the one in need of help, thus undoing some of the stigmatising and totalising identity of 'drug addict'. Becky told me how, during her recovery when she had been offered an administrative placement in a hospital, she had burst into tears and said: 'But I'm an addict and I've got a criminal record and I can't go and work in a hospital.' She added, 'I wasn't ready', indicating that she knew at some level that one day she might be ready to shift from that position and connect with the 'helper' within herself.

George, who had found his own safe haven within a therapeutic relationship, also struggled to accept the possibility that he could be a helper, but his ability to listen to others was pointed out to him by people who asked him if *he* was a counsellor. He told me:

I'd say no, don't be ridiculous, but [they'd say] you know a lot about it, why don't you become one? [I'd say] go on, don't be ridiculous... And I started reading and I started thinking, could I? Well no, I'm too fucked up to be a counsellor – you've got to be sorted to be a counsellor. Only when I realised that of course you don't have to be sorted to be a counsellor, you just have to spot the fact that you're fucked up earlier than anybody else...and then not act on it... So I did an RSA counselling skills and...people were reflecting back to me that I had...a way of being with people, I was articulate, I was sensitive. I read every book I could get hold of on counselling, and then I thought, could I become a counsellor? So I did. And it was...against all odds really because I didn't see how I could possibly do this. But I really *wanted* to do this, so I had to make it so.

Six of the eight storytellers trained as psychological therapists: Josie, Levi, Omar, George, Steven and Becky. This is not surprising when I had sought out storytellers via a counselling journal. However, there is also evidence that there is an increased rate of trauma survivors among the ranks of helping professionals in general (Elliot and Guy 1993; Etherington 1995; Follette, Polusny and Millbeck 1994; Schauben and Frazier 1995). John does voluntary work for a mental health organisation and Hannah plans to work in an administrative capacity for the abuse survivors' organisation that provided her with counselling. Omar has been a provider of supported accommodation for people leaving a treatment centre and is working towards creating a charity that provides for others what he most needed himself. Steven has worked as a researcher in the field of mental health.

Resilient trauma survivors use their own experiences to reach out to help others. By helping others they help themselves maintain a continuous sense of self-transformation; they give of themselves in nurturing ways without expectations of immediate benefits (Wilson 2006, p.379). Hannah recently told me, 'I want to use everything that I've experienced, to help other people... I just have this...strength...like a drive to change things...'cos it was so horrible for me', and for this reason she also plans to write about what she learned from her own experience of taking her abuser through the criminal justice system.

Making meaning and connection

Following the period of self-questioning, during their separation from their familiar environments, answers began to emerge in the struggle to find meaning and connection with hitherto out-of-awareness aspects of themselves, as well as connection with others, the natural world, and systems of belief, God and the universe. Wilson (2006, p.411) states that 'there is a direct relationship between a sense of connectedness to *external* sources of meaning (e.g. one's culture, group membership, religion, nature, beliefs in a Higher Power) and an *inner* sense of continuity and well-being'. Several storytellers showed how they experienced the awe-inspiring vastness of the universe whilst also reflecting on their internal state: Levi spoke of looking at the stars whilst questioning his lifestyle, George sat looking at the sea whilst thinking about suicide, and Omar wandered in Pakistan, and later in the USA, whilst feeling a sense of disequilibrium that is frequently a forerunner of fundamental change processes. In comparison to nature, a person might feel humble or insignificant, aware that their life is finite and, to some extent, dependent on the whims of something greater and more powerful than oneself.

Josie made meaning of her survival through her lifelong relationship with God, having been brought up within a faith community. She told me, 'I really believed that God was there and...was holding me all through...and watching over me...a lot of my friends from that time are dead now, you know.' Omar had also been brought up to believe in God and when I asked him what he believed had helped him survive he told me: 'I do remember praying at one stage and just asking God to get me out of this. It was almost like there was *something* there keeping me going, this little glimmer of something...'

The realisation that 'everything in life is transitory and filled with uncertainty', as stated in the teachings of Buddha (Wilson 2006, p.406), connects a person with their inner sense of vulnerability, which may have been suppressed in order to survive their early experience of trauma.

Trauma survivors sometimes defend against their experience of vulnerability by forming a belief that they are totally in control. However, having faced a rock bottom or existential experience, they come to see this as an illusion and recognise the wisdom of letting go of things that are beyond their capacity to control. Levi was only able to let go of drugs when he recognised their destructive potential: 'I had believed that...nothing that grows out the ground could be more powerful than me and my will power', but his acceptance of the destructive power of drugs connected him with fear: '...first time I think I've actually...ever...respected drugs...and that is still with me... If I went on a wild week bender...it's more likely I wouldn't come back from it now... I'd never had that fear before.'

Steven was led to his external source of meaning, a Christian God, by his attraction to a girl:

> I committed myself to God, and...I wanted to give my life to Christ...it was such a powerful experience, more powerful than any drug experience I've had...and you could feel it positively. Because the thing with drugs is that you know you feel dirty afterwards...but this wasn't dirty...

Some time after this initial conversion experience Steven joined with a different group of Christian people in a therapeutic faith community who, as well as having belief in Christ, and the principles of Christian faith, were also able to explore their life stories and the issues that had shaped their experiences. Although Steven found that 'shockingly hard' at first, he eventually decided to live as part of that community which by then had become 'like home'.

It was through the exploration of his life stories with those people that he was able to create meaning in terms of the 'intergenerational transmission' of trauma (Buchanan 1996; Leifer, Kilbane and Kalick 2004; McCloskey and Bailey 2000), as was also mentioned by Becky and hinted at by Josie and John – the ways in which his parents' unprocessed and un-integrated trauma had impacted negatively on his own life. Adults whose capabilities to form loving attachments or bonds have been impacted by trauma/abuse sometimes struggle to create or sustain the kind of closeness and intimacy needed by their own children. Such parents are sometimes described as 'distant', unaffectionate, or 'not there'.

Steven's mother, who had been sexually abused throughout childhood by her father, was experienced by him as 'emotionally blunted by those experiences... I never really got any warmth from her... It was almost like she was always trying...you could see it but you couldn't...connect with it.' Becky's mother had also been sexually abused as a child by her father and was described as '*so* shut down and so void...so rigid and controlled and angry...silently angry, or she was just asleep...she could not relate to me as a child – a *female* child'. Several other storytellers told of less than positive experiences with parents who were physically and emotionally abusive or unavailable, and although stories of their parents' childhood experiences might not have been available to or related by their offspring it might be safe to assume from what they *did* know of their parents' lives that their parenting behaviour was also influenced by unexplored trauma in their past.

Neither Steven nor Becky judge their parents, even whilst acknowledging the harm that was done. Rather, they recognise the various influences that shaped their parents' lives, including the fact they were once children too, reacting to family pressures. Barbour suggests that trying to imagine the parents' point of view requires ethical assessment:

> They do not simply excuse their parents from moral evaluation, however, or present them as passive victims of fate; rather they consider how their parents might have responded differently to the influences on them, what alternatives they had, and what it would have taken for them to act in other ways. (Barbour 2004, p.90)

Towards the end of their stories both George and Becky reflected upon the meaning they ascribed to their drug use and found positive ways of integrating those parts of their lives: George explained:

> ...the tendency I have is to think, 'Oh *damn*, I *wish* I hadn't wasted 20 years of my life taking drugs'...but I've lived an interesting creative life, yes... I wouldn't be sat here talking to you if I hadn't done everything that I've done so, you know, I don't regret it, but when I'm at the point of attempting to make sense of it... I am the wounded healer in a specific way...*that* is now making sense of my life. I can take that wound and use it to help other people heal themselves, and that is the focus of the rest of my life... It makes complete meaning out of the first bit and now...well it's not to dissipate the rest of my life, it's to focus it and use it.'

Becky told me:

...in some respects I don't have any regrets that I've been a heroin addict because I truly believe that if I hadn't have picked up heroin and been brought to my knees, I would have engaged in abusive relationships, always trying to have babies, thinking that would solve something in me that didn't feel right – or I would have been a alcoholic... I would have sold myself short...compared to what I have today, which is being able to provide for myself, being there as a parent, loving myself, knowing what I deserve... I feel, today – through counselling, through treatment – that as a person I am integrated. I don't feel today as if I'm a fragmented person.

Storytelling as meaning making

Narrative psychologists believe that people make meaning of their lives by reflexively ordering them as life stories (Bruner 1990; Giddens 1991; Hanninen and Koski-Jannes 1999; Polkinghorne 1988). A coherent self-narrative is particularly important during change as it helps maintain a sense of continuity and allows for visions of the future (Hanninen and Koski-Jannes 1999), because some events from our past take on extraordinary meaning over time as their significance in the overall story of our lives and times is realised. This indicates the importance of counsellor involvement during recovery to help clients establish a coherent and functional story that provides positive orientation for the future (Hanninen and Koski-Jannes 1999).

When we reflect on our lives in adulthood we do so from a wider perspective, being able to place our childhood experiences in the larger context of adolescence and adulthood. When our interpretations of our lives and experiences have been shaped during childhood by cultural conditioning, with maturity we are able to distance ourselves from that culture and examine its influence. This is how both individuals and cultures evolve (Zohar and Marshall 2000, p.186). When the discourses that have shaped our sense of selves and identities are examined and expanded, or recognised for simply being one among many different ways of understanding and explaining people and their lives, this allows us to describe, explain or interpret events in different ways and therefore alter our responses (Gergen 1999, p.115). It also creates possibilities for people to engage with alternative identity projects that allow opportunities for 'creative re-engagements with their own histories' (White 2001, p.66), offering cause for hope – and an antidote to despair (White 2001, p.67).

From our early years we are all exposed to story or narrative form, and are usually more prepared to connect with learning through stories than abstract arguments (Gergen 1999). While listening to stories we generate images, thrive on the drama, suffer and celebrate with the speaker. When other people listen and ask curious questions we learn that our stories are worth listening to: when people are moved by the stories that we tell, our suffering is affirmed.

Although storytelling is usually an intrinsic part of counselling and psychotherapy, opportunities for storytelling are not limited to those contexts. Steven told of his experience in his Christian therapeutic community where storytelling was part of the culture: 'we're constantly telling our stories to each other. You know, we'll go up the pub, and say, yes, I saw this about myself today, and bloody hell…that's why I'm doing that… And you kind of build each other's narratives.'

Research as meaning making

Other storytellers had told their stories in counselling or psychotherapy or as part of their groupwork in treatment centres. However, although those opportunities in some cases contributed greatly to their recovery, it was noticeable that the kind of stories told were limited by what was expected within those contexts. All of the storytellers explained that before telling their stories for this book they had never before been invited to make the healing connections that might be possible by reflecting upon how their early childhood trauma and later drug misuse might be linked, so they had not articulated those connections, even whilst, at some level, knowing they were there. Nicola King points out: 'The ability to tell a coherent story of our life…seems synonymous with our concept of identity…the telling of a story in which past and present are brought into connection is clearly a necessary and therapeutic process for many' (King 2000, p.23).

Several of the storytellers responded to my invitation to provide me with self-reflective comments on the process of being involved in the research, as noted at the end of their chapters. In most cases, their involvement seemed to have allowed them to make sense of their life experiences in ways that have extended their experience of therapy. The therapeutic value of research has been commented upon by researchers elsewhere (Etherington 2001; Gale 1992; Rennie 1994; Skinner 1998; Wosket 1999), and White (2001) provides one explanation that seems to fit with what George, Omar and Levi told me about their experience of being involved in this book:

> It is largely in the reading of our lives as lived through the structure of narrative that we are afforded the purchase to stand back from our lives. The reading of our lives through narrative structures provided the opportunity for us to render meaningful that which previously wasn't, and to re-conceive of that which has already been rendered meaningful. This generation and regeneration of meaning allows for a sense of narrative authority, and for an experience of living that people describe as akin to stepping in and out of the flow of life. (p.23)

However, the fact that each one of the storytellers volunteered for this research seemed to indicate to me evidence of their sense of personal and community ethics, their intentions being to join with the lives of others as a force for positive change. Personal agency, related to energy and vitality, is also shown in the ways storytellers position themselves towards their future ideas and intentions that demonstrate their values, hopes, visions and dreams for the future, and reflect their changed sense of selves and identities.

Towards the end of her story Hannah told me, 'I am proud of myself now, very proud of myself and…I'm proud of…the energy in me, that keeps me going. I feel like burning my bra and…wanting…to change things.'

George finds his energy through his work and his music. He told me: 'the music is vital… I felt that last night, clearly, playing music. It's a vitality…it's an energy that is here [*points to chest*] and it comes out into the world and it's like bang, it's free.' However, trying to manage both aspects of his life, as a member of an international band and as a counsellor, was becoming increasingly demanding.

> I love the work…and I *know* that I'm the sort of person that if I put all my energy into counselling and therapy I would develop something and manage to make it work, but in order to do that I have to leave the band…because they cannot any more exist side by side. So I have a big decision to make.

During my latest communication with George he told me that he had now made that decision and informed the band of his intention to leave.

Personal reflections

As I draw towards the end of the final chapter of this book I realise that this journey has been something like a visit to a 'foreign culture', although our shared history of childhood trauma linked me with the storytellers and helped me to understand and empathise somewhat. However, as this was the first piece of research I have undertaken where I had no personal experience of the topic of enquiry (illegal drug misuse), I felt at times lost – perhaps reflecting what many of us feel when faced with the behaviours of problematic drug users. I wondered what I was doing here in this unfamiliar land, remembering my response back in the late 1980s when asked during my counsellor training which clients I would not want to work with, a question posed to expose some of the assumptions, stereotypes and myths concerning a range of different client issues we held as trainees. For me the answer came readily: I did not want to work with people who had drug and alcohol problems.

Having now been involved in the field of drug addiction as a supervisor and consultant for many years, and more recently as a researcher, I had clearly changed those views, but I still noticed a reluctance to get too close to those stories. I had made *some* sense of this reluctance by acknowledging the impact on myself, my mother and my siblings of my father's misuse of alcohol during my childhood, and I have never since been comfortable around people who become affected by the amount of alcohol they drink in ways that remind me of those days, but I had no experience of drug misuse during childhood, neither my own nor anybody else's. However, it was not until I realised that my own experience of trauma (which I had expressed somatically through pain and physical illness) had, to some extent, created in me a degree of dependence to major painkillers that I connected with the shame of that acknowledgement, and understood my reluctance to 'go there'.

That realisation allowed me to face and bear my own shame which, in turn, enabled me to draw close to the storytellers' shame without a need to defend myself.

Gergen (1999) reminds me that

> explorations of other cultures draw us into questions of similarity, and difference. We are fascinated by what we share, and the ways in which we are alien. However, all such distinctions are drawn from our own vernaculars, the conventions of construction with which we attempt to make sense of the other. And such distinctions are necessarily saturated with the values they sustain. Thus every telling of similarity and difference – every assay of the other – is not so much a reflection of the real as it is a reflection of our own modes of being. To read the other is to make manifest our own existence – how it is we construct the world and with what end. And herein lies opportunity to move beyond. (p.107)

There were times when listening to and working with Levi's story that I was aware of fear – the fear he felt and the fear I felt for him – knowing that the consequences of his gangster lifestyle could still catch up with him one day. Being immersed in Hannah's story created a sense of sadness at her family's inability to give her what every child deserves, and anger at the injustice that she and other women are dealt through our current criminal justice system. Steven and Becky's stories put me in touch again with the pain of knowing the impact of my own parents' inability to deal with their trauma history which they therefore passed on to me. Levi and Omar's stories reminded me how little I knew about the lives of people of mixed race and Asian identity, and brought my own racist attitudes to the fore, whilst at the same time providing me with an opportunity to challenge them and learn more. They also helped me recognise the effects of racial abuse on the sufferers' attempts to reclaim respect and raised questions for me about the wisdom of the government's recent attempts to 'shame' young offenders rather than deal with their already profound sense of humiliation. Steven and Josie's stories made me think about the value of my own relationship with God, nurtured throughout my Catholic convent school days, whilst also causing me to wonder how I keep my relationship with God alive having rejected the church which no longer holds appeal for me. John's story caused me to feel a huge sense of sadness, recognising the neglect and sense of loss in his childhood, whilst also marvelling at his determination to find what he knows he needs.

John was the only storyteller who asked me not to contact him, having handed over his story to me: he is out there somewhere, still struggling with his recovery. His request that I should not keep in touch with him went against the grain for me as a researcher, believing as I do that research participants have a right to see how we use the material they offer in good faith, and that their responses to the ways their stories are represented enrich the process and the product of the research. But John made a clear request which I needed to place above my own priorities. I can only hope that the manner in which I have represented and interpreted his stories feels honourable to him. Maybe one day he will read this book and let me know.

So I set out to discover different ways of thinking about a person's journey into and out of drug misuse that could be put alongside existing concepts related to drug misuse such as 'disease' and 'personality' – based upon essentialist and 'fixed' views of the Self – ideas that seem pre-determined. I have done this by entering into the lived experience of the storytellers, gathering, representing and interpreting their life stories whilst viewing them as the 'experts' on their own lives and being aware of my own preconceptions.

New images of the person can emerge from stories when we listen in ways that challenge the stigmatising stereotypes that are often internalised by problematic drug users, and affect the ways they (and we) think about them – ways that might hold them back from seeking help, in the expectation of judgement and rejection. It is hard to judge people when we truly understand them, although we might continue to judge their behaviours negatively. By listening to drug users' stories in ways that invite them (and us) to understand better the effects on their sense of self and identity of the trauma in their lives, rather than trying to fit them into pre-conceived notions about 'addiction', we can hear examples of valued 'practices of living' (White 2004) that counter the 'identity diminishing' self-stories (Payne 2006) that have dominated the person's sense of who they are. By addressing the *impact* of the trauma on the person's sense of self and identity, rather than eliciting detailed stories of the trauma itself, there is a reduced risk of re-traumatisation which can result from more traditional interventions. Once the person has developed a stronger sense of self and identity, further trauma work can ensue, if necessary, once a safe place has been found.

I hope the stories affect you, as they have me, emotionally and intellectually, raise new questions for you, and maybe move you to action of some sort. The stories have challenged my assumptions and sustained my interest, as I hope they will yours.

Life stories like these may be hard to read, as the lives they tell of have been hard to live. They might shake our faith in humanity, disrupt our sense of security and heighten our sense of personal vulnerability. But most of all, my hope is that Hannah, Omar, Becky, Steven, Josie, George, John and Levi have shown the ways that ordinary human beings can transform themselves even in the face of some of life's most difficult challenges, thus demonstrating the wonderful resilience of the human spirit.

References

Ainscough, C. and Toon, K. (2000) *Breaking Free Workbook*. London: SPCK.

Aldridge, J., Parker, H. and Measham, F. (1998) 'Rethinking young people's drug use.' *Health Education, 5*(August), 164–172.

American Psychiatric Association (1980) *Diagnostic and Statistical Manual of Mental Disorders*, third edition. Arlington: American Psychiatric Association.

American Psychiatric Association (1994) *Diagnostic and Statistical Manual of Mental Disorders*, fourth edition. Arlington: American Psychiatric Association.

Anderson, T.L. (1994) 'Drug abuse and identity: linking micro and macro factors.' *Sociological Quarterly, 35*(1), 159–174.

Anderson, T.L. (1995) 'Towards a preliminary macro theory of drug addiction.' *Deviant Behaviour, 16*(4), 353–372.

Atkinson, P. (1997) 'Narrative turn or blind alley?' *Qualitative Health Research, 7*, 325–344.

Ayalon, L. (2005) 'Challenges associated with the study of resilience to trauma in holocaust survivors.' *Journal of Loss and Trauma, 10*, 347–358.

Bailey, J.A. and McCloskey, L.A. (2005) 'Pathways to adolescent substance use among sexually abused girls.' *Journal of Abnormal Child Psychology, 33*(1), 39–53.

Baker, P.L. and Carson, A. (1999) '"I take care of my kids": mothering practices of substance-abusing women.' *Gender and Society, 13*, 347–363.

Barbour, J.D. (2004) 'Judging and not Judging Parents.' In P.J. Eakin (ed.) *The Ethics of Life Writing*. Ithaca and London: Cornell University Press.

Barclay, C.R. (1994) *Composing Protoselves Through Improvisation*. Cambridge: Cambridge University Press.

Barnard, M. (2005) 'Discomforting research: colliding moralities and looking for "truth" in a study of parental drug problems.' *Sociology of Health and Illness, 27*(1), 1–19.

Barnard, M. (2007) *Drug Addiction and Families*. London and Philadelphia: Jessica Kingsley Publishers.

Barnard, M. and McKeganey, N. (2004) 'The impact of parental drug use on children: what is the problem and what can be done to help?' *Addiction, 99*, 552–559.

Batmanghelidjh, C. (2006) *Shattered Lives: Children who Live with Courage and Dignity*. London: Jessica Kingsley Publishers.

Bernstein, D.P., Stein, J.A. and Handelsmans, L. (1998) 'Predicting personality pathology among adult patients with substance use disorders: effects of childhood maltreatment.' *Addictive Behaviours, 23*(6), 855–868.

Biernacki, P. (1986) *Pathways from Heroin Addiction: Recovery without Treatment*. Philadelphia: Temple University Press.

Bowlby, J. (1969) *Attachment and Loss: Attachment* (Vol. 1). New York: Basic Books.

Bowlby, J. (1973) *Attachment and Loss: Separation, Anxiety and Anger* (Vol. 2). New York: Basic Books.

Briere, J.N. (1992) *Child Abuse Trauma and Treatment of the Lasting Effects*. Newbury Park, CA: Sage.

Brown, P.J. and Stout, R.L. (1996) 'Posttraumatic stress disorder and substance abuse relapse among women: a pilot study.' *Psychology of Addictive Behaviours, 10*(2), 124–128.

Browne, A. and Finkelhor, D. (1986) 'The impact of child sexual abuse: a review of the research.' *Psychological Bulletin, 99*, 66–77.

Bruner, J. (1986) *Actual Minds, Possible Worlds*. Cambridge, MA: Harvard University Press.

Bruner, J. (1990) *Acts of Meaning*. Cambridge, MA: Harvard University Press.

Bruner, J. (1994) 'The "Remembered" Self'. In U. Neisser and R.E. Fivush (eds) *The Remembering Self: Construction and Accuracy in the Self-narrative*. New York: Cambridge University Press.

Bruner, J. (2002) *Making Stories: Law, Literature and Life.* New York: Farrar, Strauss and Giroux.

Buchanan, A. (1996) *Cycles of Child Maltreatment: Facts, Fallacies and Interventions.* Chichester, UK: John Wiley and Sons.

Burr, V. (1995) *An Introduction to Social Constructionism.* London: Routledge.

Cain, C. (1991) 'Personal stories: identity acquisition and self-understanding in Alcoholics Anonymous.' *Ethos, 19,* 210–253.

Cameron, C. (2000) *Resolving Childhood Trauma: A Long-term Study of Abuse Survivors.* London: Sage.

Camp, J.M. and Finkelstein, N. (1997) 'Parenting training for women in residential substance abuse treatment.' *Journal of Substance Abuse Treatment, 14,* 411–422.

Clark, A. (2005) *Who is There for Lucy? An Attempt to Discover the Availability of Care, Counselling, or Support for the Children of a Single Parent, if the Parent Wants to Start on a Recovery Programme.* Bristol, UK: University of Bristol.

Cloitre, M., Morin, N.A. and Linares, L.O. (2004) 'Children's resilience in the face of trauma.' *New York Child Study Center Newsletter, 8*(3), 1–6.

Daiute, C. and Lightfoot, C. (eds) (2004) *Narrative Analysis: Studying the Development of Individuals in Society.* Thousand Oaks, London and New Delhi: Sage.

Davies, B. and Harre, R. (1990) 'Positioning: the discursive production of selves.' *Journal for the Theory of Social Behaviour, 20*(1), 43–63.

Dembo, R., Williams, L., Wothke, W. and Schmeidler, J. (1992) 'The role of family factors, physical abuse and sexual victimization experiences in high-risk youths' alcohol and other drug use and delinquency: a longitudinal model.' *Violence and Victims, 7,* 245–266.

Denzin, N. (1989) *Interpretive Interactionism.* Newbury Park, CA: Sage.

Downs, W.R. and Harison, L. (1998) 'Childhood maltreatment and the risk of substance problems in later life.' *Health and Social Care in the Community, 6*(1), 35–46.

Eakin, P.J. (ed.) (2004) *The Ethics of Life Writing.* Ithaca and London: Cornell University Press.

Eames, C.S. (2004) 'Heroin use among female adolescents: the role of partner influence in path of initiation and route of administration.' *American Journal of Drug Use and Alcohol Abuse, 30*(1), 21–38.

Elbaz-Luwisch, F. (1997) 'Narrative research: political issues and implications.' *Teaching and Teachers Education 13*(1), 75–83.

Elliot, D.M. and Guy, J.D. (1993) 'Mental health professionals versus non-mental health professionals: childhood trauma and adult functioning.' *Professional Psychology: Research and Practice, 24*(1), 83–90.

Ellis, C. (2002) 'Being real, moving inward towards social change.' *Qualitative Studies in Education, 15*(4), 399–406.

Erbes, C. (2004) 'Our constructions of trauma: a dialectical perspective.' *Journal of Constructivist Psychology, 17,* 201–220.

Erikson, E.H. (1968) *Identity: Youth and Crisis.* New York: Norton.

Etherington, K. (1995) *Adult Male Survivors of Childhood Sexual Abuse.* Brighton: Pavilion Publishing.

Etherington, K. (2000) *Narrative Approaches to Working with Male Survivors of Sexual Abuse: The Client's, the Counsellor's and the Researcher's Story.* London: Jessica Kingsley Publishers.

Etherington, K. (2001) 'Research with ex-clients: an extension and celebration of the therapeutic process.' *British Journal of Guidance and Counselling, 29*(1), 5–19.

Etherington, K. (ed.) (2003) *Trauma, the Body and Transformation: A Narrative Inquiry.* London: Jessica Kingsley Publishers.

Etherington, K. (2004) *Becoming a Reflexive Researcher: Using our Selves in Research.* London: Jessica Kingsley Publishers.

Etherington, K. (2007) 'Working with traumatic stories: from transcriber to witness.' *International Journal of Social Research Methodology, 10,* 85–97.

Etherington, K. and Barnes, E. (2006) *The Southmead Project: Practices and Processes. An Exploration of Drug Misuse, Treatment and Aftercare and the Processes Involved.* Bristol: University of Bristol.

Felitti, V. (1998) 'Childhood trauma tied to adult illness.' *American Journal of Preventative Medicine, 14*(6), 245–258.

Fergusson, D.M., Lynskey, M.T. and Horwood, L.J. (1994) 'Childhood exposure to alcohol and adolescent drinking patterns.' *Addiction, 89*(8), 1007–1011.

Finkelhor, D. and Browne, A. (1985) 'The traumatic impact of child sexual abuse: a conceptualization.' *American Journal of Orthopsychiatry, 55,* 530–543.

Larkin, M. and Griffiths, M.D. (2002) 'Experiences of addiction and recovery: the case for subjective accounts.' *Addiction Research and Theory, 10*(3), 281–311.

Leifer, M., Kilbane, T. and Kalick, S. (2004) 'Vulnerability or resilience to intergenerational sexual abuse: the role of maternal factors.' *Child Maltreatment, 9*(1), 78–91.

Levine, P. (1997) *Waking the Tiger – Healing Trauma.* Berkeley, CA: North Atlantic Books.

Lieblich, A., McAdams, D. and Josselson, R. (eds) (2004) *Healing Plots: The Narrative Basis of Psychotherapy.* Washington DC: American Psychological Association.

Lubit, R., Rovine, D., Defrancisci, L. and Eth, S. (2003) 'Impact of trauma on children.' *Journal of Psychiatric Practice, 9*(2), 128–138.

Mair, M. (1989) *Between Psychology and Psychotherapy: A Poetics of Experience.* London: Routledge.

Marcenko, M.O., Kemp, S.P. and Larson, N.C. (2000) 'Childhood experiences of abuse, later substance use, and parenting outcomes among low income mothers.' *American Journal of Orthopsychiatry, 70*(3), 316–326.

Masten, A. (2001) 'Ordinary magic: resilience process in development.' *American Psychologist, 56*(3), 227–238.

Masters, A. (2005) *Stuart: A Life Backwards.* London and New York: Fourth Estate.

McAdams, D.P. (1993) *The Stories We Live By: Personal Myths and the Making of the Self.* New York and London: Guilford Press.

McCann, I.L. and Pearlman, L.A. (1990) 'Vicarious traumatisation: a framework for understanding the psychological effects of working with victims.' *Journal of Traumatic Stress, 3*(1), 131–149.

McCloskey, L.A. and Bailey, J.A. (2000) 'The intergenerational transmission of risk for child sexual abuse.' *Journal of Interpersonal Violence, 15*(10), 1019–1035.

McCormack, C. (2004) 'Storying stories: a narrative approach to in-depth interview conversations.' *International Journal of Social Research Methodology, 7*(3), 219–236.

McIntosh, J. and McKeganey, N. (2000a) 'Addicts' narratives of recovery from drug use: constructing a non-addict identity.' *Social Science and Medicine, 50*, 1501–1510.

McIntosh, J. and McKeganey, N. (2000b) 'The recovery from dependent drug use: addicts' strategies for reducing the risk of relapse.' *Drugs: Education, Prevention and Policy, 7*(2), 179–192.

McIntosh, J. and McKeganey, N. (2001) 'Identity and recovery from dependent drug use: the addict's perspective.' *Drugs: Education, Prevention and Policy, 8*(1), 47–59.

McKeganey, N., Barnard, M. and McIntosh, J. (2002) 'Paying the price for their parents' addiction: meeting the needs of the children of drug-using parents.' *Drugs: Education, Prevention and Policy, 9*, 233–246.

Mead, G.H. (1934) *Mind, Self and Society.* Chicago: University of Chicago Press.

Meares, R. (2000) *Intimacy and Alienation: Memory, Trauma and Personal Being.* London: Routledge.

Measham, F. (2000) *Locating Leisure: Feminist, Historical and Socio-cultural Perspectives on Young People's Leisure, Substance Use and Social Divisions in 1990s British Pubs and Clubs,* unpublished PhD. Manchester: University of Manchester.

Miliora, M.T. (1998) 'Trauma, dissociation, and somatization: a self-psychological perspective.' *Journal of the American Academy of Psychoanalysis, 26*(2), 273–293.

Miller, P. and Plant, M. (2003) 'The family, peer influences and substance use: findings from a study of UK teenagers.' *Journal of Substance Use, 8*, 19–26.

Mishler, E.G. (1991) 'Representing discourses: the rhetoric of transcription.' *Journal of Narrative and Life History, 1*(4), 255–280.

Mishler, E.G. (1999) *Storylines. Craftartists: Narratives of Identity.* Cambridge, MA: Harvard University Press.

Morrill, A.C., Kasten, L., Urato, M. and Larson, M.J. (2001) 'Abuse, addiction, and depression as pathways to sexual risk in women and men with a history of substance abuse.' *Journal of Substance Abuse, 13*, 169–184.

Najavits, L.M., Weiss, R.D. and Shaw, S.R. (1997) 'The link between substance abuse and posttraumatic stress disorder in women.' *American Journal of Addiction, 6*, 273–283.

Neisser, U. and Fivush, R. (1994) *The Remembering Self: Construction and Accuracy in the Self-narrative.* New York: Cambridge University Press.

Northrup, C. (1998) *Women's Bodies, Women's Wisdom: The Complete Guide to Women's Health and Well-being.* London: Piatkus Publishers.

Ochberg, R.L. (1994) *Life Stories and Storied Lives.* Thousand Oaks, CA: Sage.

O'Donoghue, W. and Elliot, A. (1992) 'The current status of posttraumatic stress disorder as a diagnostic category: problems and proposals.' *Journal of Traumatic Stress, 5*, 421–439.

Payne, M. (2006) *Narrative Therapy: An Introduction for Counsellors,* 2nd ed. London: Sage.

Follette, V.M., Polusny, M.M. and Milbeck, K. (1994) 'Mental health and law enforcement professionals: trauma history, psychological symptoms, and impact of providing services to child sexual abuse survivors.' *Professional Psychology: Research and Practice, 25*(3), 275–282.

Forsyth, A.J.M. and Barnard, M. (2003) 'Young people's awareness of illicit drug use in the family.' *Addic Research and Theory, 11*(6), 459–472.

Frank, A.W. (1995) *The Wounded Storyteller.* Chicago and London: University of Chicago Press.

Frank, A.W. (2000) 'The standpoint of storyteller.' *Qualitative Health Research, 10,* 354–365.

Gale, J. (1992) 'When research interviews are more therapeutic than therapy interviews.' *Qualitative Repo 1*(4), 31–38.

Gee, J.P. (1991) 'A linguistic approach to narrative.' *Journal of Narrative and Life History, 1*(1), 15–39.

Gendlin, E. (1978) *Focusing.* New York: Everest House.

Gergen, K.J. (1999) *An Invitation to Social Construction.* London: Sage.

Giddens, A. (1991) *Modernity and Self Identity: Self and Society in Late Modern Age.* Cambridge: Polity Pres

Goffman, E. (1963) *Stigma: Notes on the Management of Spoiled Identity.* Englewood Cliffs, NJ: Prentice Ha

Gold, S.N. (2000) *Not Trauma Alone: Therapy for Child Abuse Survivors in Family and Social Context.* Londo Brunner-Routledge.

Gossop, M., Marsden, J. and Stewart, D. (2002) 'Dual dependence: assessment of dependence upon al and illicit drugs, and the relationship of alcohol dependence among drug misusers to patterns of drinking, illicit drug use and health problems.' *Addiction, 97*(2), 169–178.

Griffiths, R. (1998) *Drug Users Who Were Sexually Abused as Children.* London: Jessica Kingsley Publish

Hanninen, V. and Koski-Jannes, A. (1999) 'Narratives of recovery from addictive behaviour.' *Addictic 94*(12), 1837–1848.

Harber, K.D. and Pennebaker, J.W. (1992) *Overcoming Traumatic Memories.* Hillsdale, NJ: Lawrence E

Harris, P. (2005) *Drug Induced Addiction: Treatment in Perspective.* Lyme Regis, UK: Russell House Pub

Harvey, J.H. and Chavis, A.Z. (2006) 'Stilled but unquiet voices: The loss of a parent.' *Journal of Los Trauma, 11,* 181–199.

Herman, J. (1992) *Trauma and Recovery.* New York: Basic Books.

Herman, J. (1995) 'Crime and memory.' *Bulletin of the American Academy of Psychiatry and the Law, 23,*

Hoffman, J.P. and Su, S.S. (1998) 'Parental substance use disorder, mediating variables and adolesc use: a non-recursive model.' *Addiction, 93*(9), 1351–1364.

Holstein, J. and Gubrium, J. (1999) *The Self We Live By: Narrative Identity in a Postmodern World.* Oxf Oxford University Press.

Itzin, C. (2000) *Home Truths about Child Sexual Abuse.* London: Routledge.

Itzin, C. (2006) *Tackling the Health and Mental Health Effects of Domestic and Sexual Violence and Abus* Department of Health and National Institute for Mental Health, London. London: Home Ofl

Jarvis, T.J., Copeland, J. and Walton, L. (1998) 'Exploring the nature of the relationship between abuse and substance use among women.' *Addiction, 93*(6), 865–875.

Joseph, S., Linley, P.A. and Harris, G.J. (2005) 'Understanding positive change following trauma adversity: structural clarification.' *Journal of Loss and Trauma, 10,* 83–96.

Josselson, R. (ed.) (1996) *Ethics and Process in the Narrative Study of Lives* (Vol. 4). London: Sage.

Josselson, R. and Lieblich, A. (1999) *Making Meaning of Narratives.* London: Sage.

Kaplan, H.B., Martin, S. and Robbins, C. (1984) 'Pathways to adolescent drug use: Self-deroga influence, weakening of social controls, and early substance abuse.' *Journal of Health and Soc 25*(September), 270–289.

Kaplan, H.B., Martin, S. and Robbins, C. (1986) 'Escalation of marijuana use: application of a of deviant behaviour.' *Journal of Health and Social Behaviour, 27,* 44–61.

Kendler, K., Bulik, C., Silberg, J., Hettema, J. *et al.* (2000) 'Childhood sexual abuse and adult p substance use disorders in women: an epidemiological and Cotwin Control Analysis.' *Arc Psychiatry, 57,* 953–959.

King, N. (2000) *Memory, Narrative, Identity: Remembering the Self.* Edinburgh: Edinburgh Univer

Koski-Jannes, A. (2002) 'Social and personal identity projects in the recovery from addictive Addiction Research and Theory, 10*(2), 183–202.

Lampe, A., Solder, E., Ennemoser, A., Schubert, C. *et al.* (2000) 'Chronic pelvic pain and pre' abuse.' *Obstetrics and Gynecology, 96*(6), 929–932.

Plumridge, E. and Chetwynd, J. (1999) 'Identity and the social construction of risk: injecting drug use.' *Sociology of Health and Illness, 21*(3), 329–343.

Polanyi, M. (1974) *Personal Knowledge: Towards a Post-critical Philosophy.* Chicago: Chicago University Press.

Polkinghorne, D.E. (1988) *Narrative Knowing and the Human Sciences.* Albany: State University of New York Press.

Porter, S. (1994) 'Assault experience among drug users.' *Substance Misuse Bulletin, 8*(1), 1–2.

Prime Minister's Strategy Unit (2003) *Interim Analytical Report, Press Release: Many Benefits from Alcohol but some Serious and Worsening Harms.* Accessed on 1/6/2007 at www.cabinetoffice.gov.uk/strategy/news/press_releases/2003/030919.asp.

Quigley, P. (2003) 'Hard cases in hard places: challenges of community addictions work in Dublin.' *Drugs: Education, Prevention and Policy 3,* 211–221.

Rapport, N. and Overing, J. (2000) *Key Concepts for Social and Cultural Anthropology.* London: Routledge.

Ravndal, E., Lauritzen, G., Frank, O., Jansson, I. *et al.* (2001) 'Childhood maltreatment among Norwegian drug users in treatment.' *International Journal of Social Welfare, 10,* 142–147.

Read, J. (1997) 'Child abuse and psychosis: a literature review and implications for professional practice.' *Professional Psychology: Research and Practice, 28*(1), 448–456.

Read, J. (1998) 'Child abuse and severity of disturbance among adult psychiatric inpatients.' *Child Abuse and Neglect, 22*(5), 359–368.

Rennie, D. (1994) 'Human science and counselling psychology: closing the gap between research and practice.' *Counselling Psychology Quarterly, 7*(3), 235–250.

Richardson, L. (2000) *Writing: A Method of Inquiry.* Thousand Oaks, CA: Sage.

Roberts, B. (2002) *Biographical Research.* Buckingham, UK: Open University Press.

Rohsenow, D.J., Corbett, R. and Devine, D. (1988) 'Molested as children: a hidden contribution to substance abuse?' *Journal of Substance Abuse Treatment, 5,* 13–18.

Rothschild, B. (2000) *The Body Remembers: The Psychophysiology of Trauma and Trauma Treatment.* London: W.W. Norton.

Rounsaville, B.J., Weissman, M.M., Wilber, C.H., Kleber, H.D. *et al.* (1982) 'Pathways to opiate addiction: an evaluation of differing antecedents.' *British Journal of Psychiatry, 141,* 437–446.

Prime Minister's Strategy Unit (2003) *Interim Analytical Report, Press Release: Many Benefits from Alcohol but some Serious and Worsening Harms.* Accessed on 1/6/2007 at www.cabinetoffice.gov.uk/strategy/news/press_releases/2003/030919.asp.

Sansone, R.A., Wiederman, M.W. and Sansone, L.A. (2001) 'Adult somatic preoccupation and its relationship to childhood trauma.' *Victims and Violence, 16*(1), 39–47.

Sarbin, T.R. (1986) *The Narrative as a Root Metaphor for Psychology.* New York: Praeger.

Saunders, B. and Allsop, S. (1991) 'Alcohol problems and relapse: can the clinic combat the community?' *Journal of Community and Applied Social Psychology, 1,* 213–221.

Schauben, L.J. and Frazier, P.A. (1995) 'Vicarious trauma: the effects on female counselors of working with sexual violence survivors.' *Psychology of Women Quarterly, 19*(1), 49–64.

Scheering, M.S. and Zeanah, C.H. (2001) 'A relational perspective on PTSD in early childhood.' *Journal of Traumatic Stress, 14*(4), 799–815.

Scott-Hoy, K. (2002) *The Visitor: Juggling Life in the Grip of the Text.* Walnut Creek, CA: AltaMira Press.

Skinner, J. (1998) 'Research as a counselling activity? A discussion of some of the uses of counselling within the context of research on sensitive issues.' *British Journal of Guidance and Counselling, 26*(4), 533–540.

Smith, D., Pearce, L., Pringle, M. and Caplan, R. (1995) 'Adults with a history of child sexual abuse: an evaluation of a pilot therapy service.' *British Medical Journal, 310*(6 May), 1175–1178.

Sorlosi, L. (2004) 'Echoes of Silence: Remembering and Repeating Childhood Trauma.' In A. Lieblich, D.P. McAdams and R. Josselson (eds) *Healing Plots: The Narrative Basis of Psychotherapy.* Washington DC: American Psychological Association.

Stall, R. and Biernacki, P. (1986) 'Spontaneous remission from problematic use of substances: an inductive model derived from a comparative analysis of the alcohol, opiate, tobacco, and food/obesity literatures.' *International Journal of the Addictions, 21,* 1–23.

Stimson, G.V. and Oppenheimer, E. (1982) *Heroin Addiction: Treatment and Control in Britain.* London: Tavistock.

Sulkunen, P. (1992) *The European New Middle Class, Individualism and Tribalism in Mass Society.* Brookfield: Ashgate Publishing Company.

Tedeschi, R.G. and Calhoun, L.G. (1995) *Trauma and Transformation: Growing in the Aftermath of Suffering.* Thousand Oaks, CA: Sage.

Tennen, H. and Affleck, G. (1999) 'Personality and Transformation in the Face of Adversity.' In R.G. Tedeschi, C.L. Park and L.G. Calhoun (eds) *Posttraumatic Growth: Positive Changes in the Aftermath of Crisis.* Mahwah, NJ: Erlbaum.

Terr, L. (1991) 'Childhood traumas: an outline and overview.' *American Journal of Psychiatry, 148*(1), 10–20.

Terr, L.C., Block, D.A., Beat, M.A., Reinhardt, J.A. *et al.* (1999) 'Children's symptoms in the wake of the Challenger: a field study of distant-traumatic effects and an outline of related conditions.' *American Journal of Psychiatry, 156*(10), 1536–1544.

van der Kolk, B.A. (1987) *Psychological Trauma.* Arlington, VA: American Psychiatric Publishing.

van der Kolk, B.A. (1996) *Trauma and Memory.* New York: Guilford Press.

Vygotsky, L.S. (1978) *Mind in Society: The Development of Higher Psychological Functions.* Cambridge, MA: Harvard University Press.

Waitzkin, H. and Magenta, H. (1997) 'The black box in somatisation: unexplained physical symptoms, culture and narratives of trauma.' *Social Sciences and Medicine, 45*(6), 811–825.

Waldorf, D. and Biernacki, P. (1981) 'The natural recovery from recovery from opiate addiction: some preliminary findings.' *Journal of Drug Issues, 11*(1), 61–76.

Walker, E.A., Katon, W.J., Hansom, J., Harrop Griffiths, J. *et al.* (1992) 'Medical and psychiatric symptoms in women with childhood sexual abuse.' *Psychosomatic Medicine, 54*, 658–664.

Wallen, J. (1992) 'A comparison of male and female clients in substance abuse treatment.' *Journal of Substance Abuse Treatment, 9*, 243–248.

White, M. (1992) 'Deconstruction and Therapy.' In D. Epston and M. White (eds) *Experience, Contradiction, Narrative and Imagination: Selected Papers of David Epston and Michael White, 1989–1991.* Adelaide, South Australia: Dulwich Centre Publications.

White, M. (2001) 'Folk psychology and narrative practice.' *Dulwich Centre Journal, 2*, 1–37.

White, M. (2002) 'Addressing personal failure.' *International Journal of Narrative Therapy and Community Work, 3*, 33–75.

White, M. (2004) 'Working with people who are suffering the consequences of multiple trauma: a narrative perspective.' *International Journal of Narrative Therapy and Community Work, 1*, 45–76.

Whitfield, C.L. (1995) *Memory and Abuse: Remembering and Healing the Effects of Trauma.* Deerfield Beach, CA: Health Communications Inc.

Williams, G. (1984) 'The genesis of chronic illness: narrative re-construction.' *Sociology of Health and Illness, 6*(2), 175–200.

Wilson, J. (1998) 'Abuse and misuse: the ultimate hidden population.' *Drug Link, 13*, 10–11.

Wilson, J. (ed.) (2006) *The Posttraumatic Self: Restoring Meaning and Wholeness to Personality.* New York and London: Routledge.

Winnicott, D. (1960) 'Ego Distinction in Terms of True and False Self.' In *The Maturational Processes and the Facilitating Environment.* New York: International Universities Press.

Wosket, V. (1999) *The Therapeutic Use of the Self: Counselling Practice, Research and Supervision.* London: Routledge.

Yehuda, R., Engel, S.M., Brand, S.R., Seckl, J. *et al.* (2005) 'Transgenerational effects of posttraumatic stress disorder in babies of mothers exposed to the World Trade Center attacks during pregnancy.' *Journal of Clinical Endocrinology and Metabolism, 90*(7), 4115–4118.

Zohar, D. and Marshall, I. (2000) *Connecting with our Spiritual Intelligence.* London: Bloomsbury.

Subject Index

Author Index